DELTA FRAGMENTS

DELTA FRAGMENTS

The Recollections
of a
Sharecropper's Son

John Oliver Hodges

THE UNIVERSITY OF TENNESSEE PRESS / KNOXVILLE

Copyright © 2014 by The University of Tennessee Press / Knoxville.
All Rights Reserved.
First Edition.

Photographs are courtesy of the author.

Library of Congress Cataloging-in-Publication Data

Hodges, John Oliver, 1944–
Delta fragments: the recollections of a sharecropper's son / John Oliver Hodges.
—First Edition.
        pages cm
Includes bibliographical references and index.
ISBN-13: 978-1-62190-086-3
ISBN-10: 1-62190-086-X
1. Hodges, John Oliver, 1944—Childhood and youth.
2. African Americans—Mississippi—Delta (Region)—Biography.
3. Delta (Miss.: Region)—Social conditions—20th century.
4. Delta (Miss.: Region)—Biography.
I. Title.

F347.M6H64 2013
976.2'4063092—dc23
[B]
                            2012046687

FOR MY FORMER TEACHERS AND STUDENTS
AND FOR MY SON, DANIEL—
SO THAT HE TOO MAY KNOW

CONTENTS

Acknowledgments   xi
Introduction   xiii

Part I: Learning

The Delta   1
The Wilsons   7
The Hodgeses   15
My Mother   21
My Sister   27
My Stepfather   33
Whittington Plantation   39
Settlement Time   45
One-Room Schoolhouse   51
G Street Boys   55
Schoolmates   61
My Teachers   65
Going to the 'House   71

Part II: Reflecting

Delta Blues   79
Gambling on the River   87
Black Ways and Other Folkways   93

African Gods in Mississippi 101
A Delta Revival 105
The Black Church 119
The Black Preacher 125
The Folk Sermon 131
Is God Good? 139
The Color Line 145
Emmett Till 153
Ruleville Revisited: Reflections Fifty Years After Marius 159
Civil Rights 167
Medgar 175
1963 181
Endesha: A New Walk for Freedom 187
Whites in the Struggle 191
Reunion as Pilgrimage 197
Epilogue: The Delta Then and Now 203

Appendix 1: Table of Black and White Persons in the Delta by Population, Education, and Income 211
Appendix 2: Reports Relating to 1962 Civil Rights Activities in Which Author Was Involved 212
Selected Bibliography 217
Index 223

ILLUSTRATIONS

Following page 107
Map of Mississippi Delta
John Hodges at Age Two
John Hodges at Age Twelve
John Hodges, High School Graduate (1963)
High School Graduating Class, 1963
G Street Boys
Location of Home at 804 Avenue G
Mother with Her Friend Mrs. Emma Brown
Sister Edna and Uncle Fred
Teacher and Friend Solomon "Chief" Outlaw
Cousins Lula, Carlos, and Myrtle, with Their Spouses
Uncle Oliver and His Cousins
Classmates at 2007 Reunion
Classmates at 2011 Reunion
Former Teachers
The Author with Mrs. Ellen Jackson
The Greenes at Reunion Banquet
Cousin Luevina and Her Son Nathaniel

ACKNOWLEDGMENTS

This book has been long in the making. I only trust that the final delivered volume justifies the long gestation period. Numerous individuals have contributed one way or another to whatever success I have achieved here. I offer thanks first of all to members of the Delta community with whom I have shared joys and sorrows, successes and bitter disappointments. My family, friends, and schoolmates from Greenwood know very well that the voice I assume here is at once individual and communal. I have them to thank for much of the substance of the stories I tell as well as for the motivation and encouragement to finally get the work done. My great regret is that many of those who contributed most to this book did not live to see its publication. These include my sister, Edna; my stepfather, Lee Daniel "Bully" Thompson and his brother, Willie B. "Cadillac" Thompson; my first cousin Luevina; my aunts Ellen and Ella Mae; and my cousins Osby and Gladys on my father's side. Those of my family who are still living know just how much they have contributed to this book, especially my wife, Carolyn; my son, Daniel; my nephews and nieces; and my cousins Nathaniel Johnson, Lula De La Cruz, Myrtle Turner, and Carlos Lipsey.

Thanks to my former colleagues in the University of Tennessee Department of Religious Studies, whose kind words of encouragement throughout the years of this project were instrumental in helping me get through. They also read several of the fragments and offered constructive comments in person or in various substantive sessions. I especially wish to acknowledge the support and encouragement of my former department heads: Charlie Reynolds, Gilya Schmidt, and Rosalind Hackett.

My friend Jeffie McNeal has provided encouragement along the way as well as important historical information regarding people and incidents that only he, with his excellent memory, could recall. John W. Pleasant, Robert Hampton, Ollie Carter, Sarah Parker Stanley, Minnie Elliott Whittaker, Alma Greene Henderson, Terry Butler, Rev. and Mrs. Aaron Johnson, Myrene Washington Jones, Carolyn Henderson McNeal, and Perry Lymon, together with their families, have contributed important ideas and insights reflected in this work. Cora Markham Garner and her late husband, Albert, have been dear friends from early childhood on. Albert "Judge" Garner and his entire family have been close friends to me and my family. I have benefitted from their association in church, school, and in the struggle in general. Space does not allow me to mention individually all those who have been a part of this work. Others, black and white, might be embarrassed to have their names presented here. To all of you and to so many others I say, "Thanks!"

Joan Riedl, Anne Galloway, Teresa Bowman, and Teresa Braden Walker have provided either editorial or research assistance. The staffs of the Greenwood Public Library and the Museum of the Mississippi Delta have also assisted me in important ways. Scot Danforth, Kerry Webb, Gene Adair, and others of the University of Tennessee Press have lent their professional talents to improving this volume. Whatever is good here represents in large part the contributions of others. I alone am responsible for any deficiencies.

INTRODUCTION

Over the twenty or so years that I have been at work on this project, I have seen it take several shifts and turns in focus and emphasis until it has evolved into what it is today. Originally, it was meant to be a book of essays on the religion and culture of the Yazoo-Mississippi Delta. The book would help correct certain misconceptions of the Delta and of "my people" that were presented in other works on this region. Furthermore, I wanted it to be of interest to both the general reader and to students and teachers of southern or African American studies. Preparing to write such a book, I obtained all the necessary consent forms required by the University of Tennessee and purchased a tape recorder and camera. With my initial plan in mind, I made numerous trips to the Delta to conduct interviews and search through a maze of newspapers and church and court records.

Yet, I was amazed to notice how often the research pointed me back to various experiences that formed my personal history growing up in Greenwood, Mississippi. It was fully my intention to approach research in this area as any scholar would. I even refused—for the sake of objectivity, I tried to convince myself—the offer to live with relatives while conducting the various interviews I needed or thought I needed for the book. It soon became abundantly clear, however, that while I had gone on to get a PhD at a major research university, what I needed was not so much objectivity as a willingness to explore and understand the relationship between John Oliver, the boy growing up in Greenwood, and Dr. Hodges, the college professor who had returned to examine the past. Even if I was less formal in conducting my interviews, I still needed to be professional in going about my work. But at every turn, I kept noticing that the distance I tried to create between my subjects and me was artificial. After all, these were people who knew me before I could talk or walk. They knew my parents and grandparents, uncles and aunts. They were my friends, relatives, former schoolmates, and playmates, who would, whenever I tried to play professor, gently nudge me back to reality by reminding me of a repressed personal embarrassment with some statement like, "Man, you know, we were some crazy cats back then." Occasionally in the middle of my interviews with relatives and friends, I would find myself interrupting, embellishing, or correcting what I felt to be distortions of the truth, especially when it involved me personally. Thus, they were conversations or discussions rather than strict interviews.

With the realization that my approach would have to change, I soon abandoned my predetermined questions to listen to what *they* really wanted to talk about, which often proved more helpful and interesting than what I had determined was important. Whether discussing religion, race, politics, sex, white folks—no matter the topic—my respondents would often resort to telling some story to make or clarify a point. What I have done here, then, is to use stories or episodes from my own life to illustrate aspects of culture in the area known as the Yazoo-Mississippi Delta. Though the work would now be more autobiographical than I had planned, I still didn't want to give up on my original idea for a book that would be informative, interesting, and useful in the academic community. That is, I needed to find a way of writing about my own personal history and that of the entire Delta community as well. The reader must determine how well I have done. I can honestly say, however, that I have some personal experience or story that links me to all the events, beliefs, and traditions I discuss in this volume.

I feel a further note is needed to explain the purpose, approach, and methodology I use here. I refer to these vignettes or stories as "fragments" for several reasons. First, while I have attempted to be as sincere and truthful as possible, I realize that I am presenting only one side of issues that are complex and multifarious. The stories are meant, therefore, to create some dialogue, the kind I often had with my students as we attempted to discuss the knotty matters of race in this country and the sort of dialogue I wish I *could* have had with whites during the days of my youth. It is my belief and hope that southerners, black and white, are now willing to undertake such a dialogue, which would have been impossible a generation or so ago.

They are also fragments because I really don't know the complete story, even that of my own personal history. But most African Americans find it especially difficult to trace their roots back over several centuries. In most cases blacks themselves did not keep records, except, perhaps, in family Bibles. So much has come down by word of mouth, through oral tradition, through stories.

In my own family, furthermore, and I suppose in a number of others as well, the older folks simply did not want to talk about matters most personal to them—not so much to be secretive but to protect curious youngsters from very painful knowledge that might prove psychologically or even physically dangerous should anyone attempt to redress the wrongs of the past. Margaret Bolsterli, in her book *Born in the Delta* (the Arkansas Delta, not the Mississippi Delta), was able to trace her family history back to the early 1800s. I haven't been able to go back so far. But in my investigations, I have uncovered a great deal—that is, bits of information here and there—which, while revealing much about my past, also at times seem to cloud it in greater mystery. Now that I had come of age, would the folks (not many were still alive) finally reveal those secrets to me? After so many years, many of the events were still too painful or too embarrassing to recall. It was much easier for them to discuss matters involving someone else than to recall strictly personal incidents. These, then, are also the stories of an entire community's pains, sufferings, and joys. It is, of course, not surprising that other individuals, depending on their own relationship to the subject figures, would give quite different accounts of the same situations. Taken as a whole, then, these fragments are my best effort to lay bare the soul and emotions of a community coming to self-understanding, even as I take that journey along with them.

These fragments are intended for several audiences. I have long wanted to assemble a series of stories or episodes that would give a sense of the difficult but rich and fulfilling lives that blacks of my generation experienced in the Delta. We witnessed the slow metamorphosis of the Old South into the New South. Those of us who worked on plantations saw tractors replace mules and mechanical cotton pickers replace human hands. We remember Emmett Till and the fear that gripped the black community as our parents feared that we, too, might challenge the taboo of touching a white woman. We were involved in voter-registration efforts to win back the franchise and saw Medgar Evers and many others lose their lives in the struggle. The long hot summers of 1963 and 1964 were played out on the Delta landscape with personages as varied as Bob Moses, Dick Gregory, and Police Chief Curtis Lary. Since other public buildings were off-limits to us, our churches became not only houses of prayer but also schoolhouses, wedding chapels, banquet halls, and mass-meeting venues for our civil rights movement.

But it was not all about struggle—not at all. There were dances to the sounds of B. B. King, Fats Domino, and Bobby Blue Bland. We enjoyed our fish sandwiches in the Buckeye on Saturday nights as we shot craps and played cards and got home just in time to catch a couple hours of sleep before going to Sunday service at Good Hope Missionary Baptist or Turner's Chapel AME Church. We did our courting on Saturdays at the Walthall and Dixie theaters and at church on Sunday, where we hoped to meet a God-fearing mate, or, later in the afternoon, at the baseball game between Race Track and Pink Service Station (outlying communities in the Greenwood area), where any man strong enough to make a crop might be suitable. These are the stories, then, that I present to help those of my generation and their children and grandchildren recall moments of struggle, sadness, and joy that will give them a sense of pride in their ability to endure.

I also want these reflections to be of value to students and scholars of the South and of African American history and culture. I believe that my own experiences embrace a number of issues of concern to the academic community. I have used several of these stories in my own classes in African American religion and American studies to illustrate particular points. I believe that the best way to understand a concept is to view it within the context of a story. But I hope I have not attempted to stretch or overreach, just for the sake of making a point. One of my distinct joys as a teacher was to have students wrestle with issues and questions that have no single, clear-cut answers. Several of the fragments will touch on subjects that will provide opportunities for open and honest discussion.

The present work has some similarities to other well-known autobiographical accounts of life in the Mississippi Delta. Two such accounts were written by whites of an earlier generation, David Cohn's *Where I Was Born and Raised* and William Alexander Percy's *Lanterns on the Levee: Recollections of a Planter's Son*. Among other topics, these works discuss issues of religion and race relations from the perspective of the white southerner of a few generations ago. My work offers not only a different perspective on these issues but a more recent one as well. But so do the works by two other black authors of my generation, Clifton Taulbert's *Once Upon a Time When We Were Colored* and Endesha Holland's *From the Mississippi Delta*. And I have benefited greatly from their recollections on their experiences growing up in the Delta towns of Glen Allan and Greenwood respectively. Since Holland and I were schoolmates in Greenwood, we certainly shared a number of experiences, though we moved in different circles.

Her book details the pilgrimage of a young woman's rise from life as a prostitute to become an important figure in the local civil rights movement, to earn a PhD from the University of Minnesota, and finally, to become a professor at a major research university. It is a marvelous story of triumph that I chronicle and celebrate in one of these fragments. But while we grew up in the same place, knew many of the same people, and ended up as college professors, it is clear that our stories are very different, as are our ways of narrating them.

My work tends to be less confessional and more analytical and provocative. Indeed, it will appear at times that I wish "to pick a fight" to get dialogue and discussion started. Therefore, I have attempted to tell my personal history in such a way that many of the experiences may be used as the subjects of classroom lectures or discussions. This is not an easy task, and I don't know how well I have succeeded. But even if I haven't been completely successful, I hope the work points in some way to my interest in what some have called the scholarship of teaching. This intention of engaging the academic community has, in large part, determined my methodology.

I have divided the fragments into two parts. Part I, "Learning," is more autobiographical and looks forward to my career as a college professor, an awareness that became more apparent to me during the process of autobiographical reflection. The fragments in this section are arranged in a chronological manner so as to reflect my coming of age. Part II, "Reflecting," while continuing to treat my personal experiences, also attempts to examine those experiences in a more critical and reflective way. Part II is designed especially to promote discussion on a range of controversial and sensitive issues arising from my personal experiences in the Mississippi Delta.

The fragments making up this volume range in length from around a thousand to just over two thousand words each. These are bite-size morsels that can be ingested and digested in a single sitting. They are meant both to provide discrete portraits and to dovetail with others to form a larger mosaic. The reader is encouraged to view the incomplete and undeveloped nature of the fragments not as a stylistic flaw but as an opportunity to provide one's own perspective and to draw his or her own conclusions. I have included a bibliography to assist in further research and reflection. The bibliography should also be supplemented by texts and materials the reader has found helpful but with which I may be unfamiliar. As I suggested above, I wish to be provocative without being insistent or definitive. After all, the goal is to open the door for discussion, not to close it.

PART I
LEARNING

THE DELTA

> Every few years [the Mississippi River] rises like a monster from its bed and pushes over its banks to vex and sweeten the land it has made. For our soil, very dark brown, creamy and sweet-smelling, without substrata of rock or shale, was built up slowly, century after century.
>
> **William Alexander Percy,** *Lanterns on the Levee*

The place I call home is a land of profound contradictions and paradoxes, beginning with the history of its founding and extending to the people who have settled there. Located on the eastern edge of the Yazoo-Mississippi Delta, Greenwood, the major town and county seat of Leflore County,[1] is truly representative of the culture and way of life of the entire region. Considering several facts and questions may help explain why I consider this whole area to be so baffling, interesting, and contradictory. How is it that an area long ravaged by floods and a population plagued with swamp fever should nevertheless have produced such rich soil and such hearty people with the vision and cleverness to tease it into an endless blanket of snowy white cotton? Why would the citizens of this region name a town and county for an Indian of French and Choctaw descent who was loyal not to the Confederacy but to the opposing side? Indeed, most baffling to me was not that Greenwood LeFlore would lend his name to the city and county—many other cities and counties in the state are named for Native Americans—but that he, to his dying day, remained faithful to the Union.

There are other questions, even more personal, that have puzzled me. Why is it that those most responsible for the wealth of the region have ended up at the very bottom of the economic ladder? Moreover, how can we explain that, until fairly recently, a community constituting over 75 percent of the population had little or no political representation? And, finally, how can I proclaim that a region that has often made it difficult for me, as for so many other black boys and girls, to achieve my potential should also have given me the motivation and determination to make something of my life?

The Delta, wrote David L. Cohn, "begins in the lobby of the Peabody Hotel in Memphis and ends on Catfish Row in Vicksburg."[2] Specifically, it is a fertile strip of flatland in the northwestern part of the state, stretching along the Mississippi River from just below Memphis to just above Vicksburg and extending inward to beyond Greenwood. Somewhat deltoid in shape, the Delta measures about 160 miles north to south and 60 miles at the widest east-west point. Ten counties lie completely within the Delta and several others lie partially within its confines.[3] Any observer will immediately note that the area appears to be flat—"as flat as a pancake," more than one commentator has noted. But historian James Cobb points out that the surface is actually a bit uneven as a "result of centuries of flooding and sedimentation by the Mississippi and its tributaries." He continues, "When confined to its normal channel, the Mississippi dumped its rich load of silt in its true delta at its mouth."[4] The result was a rich alluvial soil "endlessly, deep, dark, and sweet"—just the type of soil needed to grow an abundance of cotton. The Delta would become the capital of the cotton kingdom. This was aided in no small measure by the presence of black laborers, who were holdovers from slavery.

William Alexander Percy, an aristocrat of the first order, described the "basic fiber" of the Delta (and, by extension, the whole South) as woven from three dissimilar strands: the slave holders and their descendants, poor whites, and Negroes. He regarded poor whites with particular antipathy. Whatever notable contributions they may have made to the culture of the South, Percy wrote, one could "admire them, trust them, love them—never."[5] They were, in Percy's hierarchy, "intellectually and spiritually inferior to the Negro, whom they hate." In Percy's view of things, it was this group that was most responsible for mob violence against blacks; his main point was that "the Delta was not settled by these people; its pioneers were slave-owners and slaves."[6]

Even if we set aside for now the fact that Percy was no friend of blacks in this region, we must wonder where he would place the American Indian, the first true pioneer in the Delta. I heard my mother mention on a number of occasions that there were Indians in our family. This will not come as startling news for anyone living in the South—or the nation, for that matter. I don't know what I made of this; it was just a fact that, in itself, was not that extraordinary. But as I grew older, I became more and more interested in this aspect of my family heritage, given the way Native Americans and blacks have been treated in this country. As I understand it, my great-grandfather was an Indian of some distinction, probably a Choctaw who was married to a woman named Hattie. I was told he had a great temper. When I learned that Greenwood and the county in which it's situated were named for an Indian of Choctaw-French ancestry, Greenwood LeFlore (LeFleur, in the original French), I became even more interested in this aspect of my heritage. Furthermore, Noxubee County, the site of the 1830 treaty of Dancing Rabbit Creek, was the birthplace of my mother and her parents.[7]

LeFlore was a wealthy individual who owned a large number of slaves. I knew of several black families who went by the name of LeFlore. Some had features that blacks in the South long associated with American Indians: high cheek bones, a honey complexion, and "good hair." There was a good chance that these families were either direct descendants of Greenwood LeFlore or of slaves from his plantation. I don't suspect that I am personally a descendant of LeFlore, but, as my parents assured me, I am a descendant of the Choctaw nation.

According to Frank E. Smith, a onetime Mississippi congressman who chronicled his native region in his book *The Yazoo River*, Greenwood LeFlore was born on June 3, 1800.[8] He was a compelling and enigmatic figure who took the lead role in getting the Choctaws to surrender their land in 1830 at Dancing Rabbit Creek. Opinions of LeFlore range from accusations that he was a traitor to celebrations of him as a hero. As a Union loyalist who was also a slaveholder, he was obviously a complex man. Was he, for example, a traitor to his people or a realist who attempted to salvage what he could for them? As Smith wrote, "Greenwood LeFlore realized from the beginning that the fate of the Choctaws appeared to be that of falling before the advancing white man, and his solution was to learn the ways of life of the white man. Any improvements in the Choctaws, however, could not thwart the primary aim of the white settlers—to take control of all the rich Indian lands."[9]

LeFlore realized that the Choctaws were not in a strong bargaining position. President Andrew Jackson had already urged Congress to reject a previous treaty that would have given too much to the Choctaws. The September 1830 meeting at Dancing Rabbit Creek was not so much a meeting between equal parties as an effort on the government's part to reach a diplomatic settlement. When the Choctaws rejected an earlier draft of the 1830 treaty, the government negotiators led by John Coffee and Secretary of War John Eaton quickly called the Choctaws' obvious bluff. As Coffee and Eaton packed up their gear and prepared to leave, the Choctaws implored the commissioners to continue negotiations, with the tacit assurance that any reasonable offer would be accepted.

The treaty called for the Choctaws to surrender all their land east of the Mississippi. The removal was to take effect in three stages from 1831 to 1833. In exchange for their land, the Choctaw Nation was to receive a pledge of "perpetual peace and friendship" with the United States as well as the promise to convey "a tract of country west of the Mississippi River, in fee simple to them and their descendants." Although there were considerable grumblings and dissatisfaction among the Choctaws over the terms of the treaty, the government's success was virtually assured by its willingness to dole out certain gifts of land and money to the various Choctaw chiefs. Greenwood LeFlore, who "led the arguments against the folly of fighting and who proposed the compromise that the United States and the Choctaw Nation finally accepted," secured for himself the best of these parcels. LeFlore claimed a large portion of land in Carroll County and became one of the area's largest landowners and most prominent citizens. He was elected in the 1840s to the state legislature.[10] The city that became Greenwood was originally part of Carroll County.

The story of Greenwood's establishment adds to the complexity of its honoree, Greenwood LeFlore, who upon his death in 1865 held the rank of colonel in the United States Army. According to Smith, LeFlore became upset with a man named John Williams, who owned a cotton warehouse on his settlement, known as Williams Landing. When LeFlore discovered that a large shipment of cotton he had sent to Williams's warehouse was in fact stored outside on the muddy riverbank, even though Williams billed LeFlore at the rate for storage within the warehouse, LeFlore vowed to ruin Williams and subsequently purchased a large tract of land nearby that he called Pointe LeFlore. Williams Landing fared poorly in competing with LeFlore. Smith writes:

> Fighting back was a hard matter, but the Williams Landing people finally found the solution through Titus Howard [another major

landowner in Carroll County]. They would officially incorporate a town with the Mississippi legislature. Howard ceded half of the lots in the townsite to the town government, in return for a promise from the town to maintain a road to the hills. The town was to be named Greenwood, in honor of LeFlore, and it was incorporated in 1844.[11]

At the height of his career, Greenwood LeFlore was a powerful and wealthy man. He owned fifteen thousand acres of the richest land in Mississippi, unchartered sections of Texas, and over a thousand slaves. He also financed a number of commercial enterprises.[12] In 1854 he had a lavish home called Malmaison built, and there he entertained his friends irrespective of political allegiance. But near the end of his life, LeFlore was estranged from both his fellow Choctaws, who felt he had betrayed them, and from white Mississippians, who could not forgive him for being an unyielding Union loyalist. At the end, wrote Smith, "he had himself wrapped in the flag of the Union that had become sacred to him, and, looking out over the broad fields he had cleared from virgin forests, the stern old Choctaw consigned his soul to the God he had taught his tribesmen and slaves to respect."[13]

Leflore was, indeed, a compelling character, a man whose life and career leave us with as many questions as answers. One wonders about his real motivations for signing the treaty of Dancing Rabbit Creek. Was he a pawn of the U.S. government or a shrewd negotiator who wanted to get the most for his people?[14]

The questions themselves again point to the contradictions that one can see everywhere in the Delta. It is a place of great beauty and perhaps even greater squalor. At one time the Delta was among the richest areas in the country, only to be later considered one of the poorest. There is probably no place where the disparity between the rich and poor is so great. It is amazing, furthermore, that a place with such high illiteracy should also be the home of some of the greatest writers in the world. In the various essays that follow—social, political, religious—I will search for some meaning and coherence in these contradictions through the life experiences of this one native son.

NOTES

1. When referring to the county, "Leflore" is usually spelled with the *f* lower-cased, even though it is upper-cased in the name Greenwood LeFlore.

2. This often-quoted phrase appeared first in Cohn's book, *God Shakes Creation*, which he published around 1935. His more famous *Where I Was Born and Raised* appeared in

1948. This was essentially a revision of the earlier work in which Cohn attempted to account for changes in culture and attitudes over that time.

3. The ten counties lying completely or largely within the Delta are Bolivar, Coahoma, Humphreys, Isaquena, Leflore, Quitman, Sharkey, Sunflower, Tunica, and Washington. Since a large portion of Tallahatchie County lies within the Delta, it is often considered in discussions about this region.

4. James C. Cobb, *The Most Southern Place on Earth: The Mississippi Delta and the Roots of Regional Identity* (New York: Oxford Univ. Press, 1992), 4.

5. William Alexander Percy, *Lanterns on the Levee: Recollections of a Planter's Son* (1941; repr., Baton Rouge: Louisiana State Univ. Press, 1967), 19–20.

6. Ibid., 20.

7. The site of the treaty was between the two prongs of Dancing Rabbit Creek, located in Noxubee County. See Arthur H. DeRoiser Jr., *The Removal of the Choctaw Indians* (Knoxville: Univ. of Tennessee Press, 1989), 120.

8. Frank E. Smith, *The Yazoo River* (1954; repr., Jackson: Univ. Press of Mississippi, 1988), 52.

9. Ibid., 54.

10. Ibid., 55.

11. Ibid., 57–58.

12. Ibid., 58.

13. Ibid., 61.

14. My view, considering the value of the land that was ceded to the United States, not only in the Delta but throughout the country, is that Native Americans have never been properly compensated.

THE WILSONS

> Aunt Sue has a head full of stories.
> Aunt Sue has a heart full of stories.
> Summer nights on the front porch
> Aunt Sue cuddles a brown-faced child to her bosom
> And tells him stories.
>
> **Langston Hughes, "Aunt Sue's Stories"**

I never knew my maternal grandfather, Eli Wilson, but those who did said that I resembled him not only in appearance but also in aptitude. According to my cousin Luevina Lymon, he was a stout, dark-complexioned man. "That boy," some friends of the family said of me, "is the spitting image of Eli." I always appreciated what seemed to me to be a compliment, so much so that I, quite unofficially, added Elias as a second middle name. My grandfather was considered a "professor," a title one could have with only a ninth-grade education. When Luevina told me this, I was surprised and ready to question how he became a professor, she said, "Yes, a professor."

"Like me," I wondered aloud.

"Yes, a professor, like you!"

Actually, Eli only taught in grade school, though no doubt he was called on to teach students at multiple levels, since typically students were placed in the same church room and seated according to their particular grades. I do know that some of the girls were older, because, as I was told, he once got into trouble for making unwelcome advances toward one or more of them. In any case, teaching school was only a side job, for he and his students could only be in school during those few months when their labor wasn't required for the cotton fields.

My grandfather's brother, Uncle Thorn, was said to be every bit as smart as Eli. He probably also taught school, though I don't know that for certain. My mother told me he could write with his toes, and another of my uncles said Thorn could tell by the sound of a freight train just how much weight it was carrying. Well, I'm not sure about all that, but this is what I was told.

My grandfather grew up in Noxubee County, where he met and married my grandmother, Alice. They had a large family of thirteen children, although several died early on. In fact, only five of his children were alive when I was born: Scott, Fred, Arybelle (whom we called Abelle), Obe, and my mother, Samantha. Since I spent my very early years with the Wilsons,[1] I got to know them fairly well. This includes my grandmother, Alice, who outlived her husband and a number of their children.

The circumstances of my grandfather's death were never completely clear to me. It's a matter that has continued to vex me, though there seems to be more reliable evidence to support one of the two versions I heard. According to one story, Eli was poisoned by a jealous plantation overseer, who knew that my grandfather would be able to keep account of expenses and therefore have a good sense of what was owed to him at settlement time each year—that day in December when sharecroppers were paid (or, more often, not paid) for the fruits of their labors during the previous months. Eli thus posed a direct threat to the white man's authority. This story is quite in keeping with the deep prejudices and racial hatreds of the South of that era, and I accepted my grandfather's martyrdom with a sense of pride. A number of years later, however, I learned a different version of how my grandfather died. According to this story, Eli had been carrying on an affair with a woman who lived not far from his home. On his last visit to her house, he died of a heart attack.[2]

My grandfather *was* known to be something of a womanizer. And my grandmother warned him that something would happen if he continued to see that "hussy," who, she said, was no good for him, besides being ten or twelve years his junior. She warned him not because of her own pride, though she was known to be a very beautiful woman of fair skin with "good hair." Rather, her plea to Eli was for his own good. My grandfather, of course, didn't appreciate that kind of talk, which provoked him to violence. Some even suggested that on several occasions, he hit his wife, causing her to miscarry at least once.

My grandfather passed his penchant for gambling and womanizing down to John, his oldest son, who lived a fast and hard life. John's first daughter, Rosa, died in infancy, and he himself died in 1942 at the age of forty-six or forty-seven. He spent most of his time away from his family, gambling and hustling with his brother Obe. Often, they ended up fighting each other, and their mother had to serve as peacemaker. John's youngest child remembers her father as being highly irresponsible. He, like his father, had a nasty temper and admonished his wife, Della, about wearing pants or talking to other men. Often his jealousy led to rage and violence. He was, in every respect, a chip off the old block.

As I mentioned, I spent much of my early years with my grandmother and aunt and uncles. My uncle Fred, the youngest of the children, lived his life in the twilight; he neither married nor even had a serious romance so far as I could tell. Retarded, he never attended school and couldn't read or write, although he did have a lot of common sense. His brother, Scott, took charge of Fred's life early on, as he did for that of my aunt Abelle, who was crippled from birth. Fred and Abelle were wonderful human beings, but no one thought to protest that they never received the care that is now considered standard. They seemed not to complain much either. Well, at least Fred didn't; Abelle, on occasion, let Scott know where to get off. Fred, though, simply did whatever Scott told him, which consisted largely of performing household chores, running to the store on errands, and getting water from the well when needed. Fred did a lot of the work around the house. He was something like a mule for my uncle, who drove him very hard. Fred paid dearly for not being able to make decisions for himself. For Scott's part, he did assume the job that the other brothers and my mother would not: taking care of his disabled brother and sister.

Scott himself was a barber. How he learned to cut hair, I don't know. I remember that he charged a quarter for a haircut, even my own. It upset my mother that her own brother charged his nephew to cut his hair. But Scott was a businessman. The only people who were known to slide by without paying were some women he was seeing or attempting to see. In those cases, he was known to give a trim on the house. I remember that he set up his makeshift barbershop in the shed of the plantation commissary on Saturdays. There he cut the hair of as many sharecroppers as time allowed. The men were anxious to have their hair cut before going to town that night and to church the next day. At a quarter a head, he did fairly well. This income supplemented what he made from tending the pecan orchards, although the pay there was largely in kind—that is, he received all the pecans he wanted. But all this was his side hustle; he made a crop like the rest of the hands and depended on Fred and Abelle—we pronounced it A-bell—to help him with the chopping and picking. Uncle Scott was quite a character. Short in build, with a bald head, he wore fine clothes. Fred kept his shoes shined, and Abelle, even from her knees, washed and ironed his clothes.

Scott was known to be a ladies' man. He fathered several children by at least two different women. He believed that he came by this honestly. He was, after all, a Wilson, and his father and several brothers were known to be philanderers. My mother called them whoremongers. He was also one of the head deacons in the church and the superintendent of the Sunday school. As far as I know, no one thought to question the morality of his life. He simply was doing the best he could by his family and himself. For all the hard work he did, didn't he deserve some pleasure?

I always gravitated toward Fred and Abelle, largely, I suppose, because I was left in their charge when my mother went off to take care of her business. Perhaps it was also because they were similarly dependent on others. I often accompanied Fred to the store and to the well. Fred had to walk what seemed like a mile each way, but he did this without protest. Abelle often played games with me. One of them was with pecans. She placed several nuts in her closed fist, and I had to guess how many were there. If I got the number right, I won all the pecans she held. If I guessed incorrectly, I had to give her the difference between what she actually held and the number of the incorrect guess. Then it was my turn. "Old gray mare," I'd say to get the game going. "I'll ride her," she'd reply. "How many times?" I'd ask. She then gave me her best estimate of the number of nuts in my closed hand. Since my small hands couldn't hold many pecans, I had to devise a way of pretending that I held more or fewer than I actually did by occasionally letting the nuts protrude through my fingers. This was one of the ways we passed many hours. It was also a way of learning simple arithmetic. As I think of my aunt and the pitiable state in which she lived her entire life, especially those last years after she was placed in a nursing home, I wonder if I was justified in denying her plea to come to Chicago to live with my family when I was studying there. She assured me that her federal check was a good one, which, in her thinking, would compensate me for the trouble of providing housing. I knew that her staying would involve much more time and energy than I could afford as a graduate student whose wife was also in graduate school. Though I feel I made the right decision, I do wonder if I made it for the right reason.

Another of my uncles, Obe, was so mean to his wife, Susanna, and so unrepentant about it, that once, during a church revival, she made him sit with the candidates for baptism—children at least a third his age—before she would take him back. She did take him back, at least for a while. At his funeral, the pastor remarked that he wasn't so sure about Obe's chances in the afterlife. Most pastors were able to find a way of reassuring family members and the congregation that the deceased had settled things with his maker, who would certainly be waiting for any of them when they arrived at the pearly gates. For those who came up just a bit short, a good minister could preach him into the kingdom. But Obe's fate was a task beyond even this preacher, who had helped open the gates for many a backslider. Where did Obe get his mean streak? Perhaps it came from Eli, his father, from whom he and his brother Andrew had run away to escape his abuse. Rather than make those older boys return to the hills of Noxubee County, Eli brought his wife and younger children to Leflore County, where the entire family would settle down.

On one of many visits back to Greenwood, I had an opportunity to talk to a woman named Melissa Blanchard, who lived with my uncle Obe for a while. She confirmed the views of so many others, including my mother, that Obe indeed was a mean one. But Melissa would have none of his meanness—at least, that is, without fighting back. She reminded anyone who doubted her toughness that Obe died with only one ear, because she had bitten off the other one. What could it have been like to live with someone like Obe, who was known to draw a pistol if he didn't like the way you went about business?

My sister had warned Melissa about Obe's meanness, that he wouldn't treat her any better than he had treated Susanna or any of the other women in his life. In fact, he didn't treat his family much better than he did his lovers. His sisters and nieces regarded him with a mixture of loathing and dread, and they hated their own reluctance to confront him directly. But Melissa was different. She could match his meanness as well as his productivity in the fields. She didn't particularly care for his gambling; she only tolerated it. But on that fateful night of the ear-biting incident, she refused Obe when he came asking for more money to get back into a card game. Naturally, he was ready to fight. "I declare," she told me. "I won't let a man beat me." She said this while reaching for a can of Miller

Lite, which she always seemed to have at her ready. My question about why she had bitten off my uncle's ear seemed to rekindle a kind of fierce anger in her, and I had to reassure myself that she wasn't angry at me or at all men.

This is not exactly the story my cousin Luevina tells of the matter. According to her, Obe was ready to kill Melissa with an axe when another man, Johnny Garner, happened to come by and pleaded with him not to do something he would regret for the rest of his life.

For some reason, I was always attracted to the outlaws, those who lived on the edge and didn't play it safe. There was certainly something real and earthy about Obe. He made few pretensions of being good or moral. He was simply himself. And I suppose I liked that. I knew that he could be evil and hateful. But I never experienced any of this in his dealings with me. He always seemed to like me and appreciate my intelligence. He always asked me a question to which he was sure I knew the answer because I had been asked it before so many times. "Boy, is a tomato a vegetable or fruit?" he'd ask. "Fruit," I'd say. "Ninety percent fruit," he'd concur. And thus again he had undeniable proof that his nephew was the smartest kid in those parts. I suppose I never wanted to let him down. I always tried to meet his high expectations of me. For years after he had retired from being a straw boss[3] in the cotton fields, he was able to give his life to his real passion, playing checkers and cards. He played checkers for fun but cards for money. He was one of the very best checkers players around. And I became a fair player by watching him. At poker, to hear him tell it, he was even better. His success at gambling was based partly on skill and partly on his ability to cheat. He was an expert dealer, something of a card mechanic. This just may explain how he lost his finger—not, as he said, in the closing door of a train in Cleveland, Ohio.

My mother never wanted me to spend much time at Uncle Obe's home for fear of his being a bad influence on me. She couldn't know that I enjoyed my visits with Obe as much or more than attending Sunday school each week, which I felt required to do. It was exciting to be at Obe's place, where drunks and fallen women routinely stopped by. I loved to hear their stories of mischief. In later years, Obe lost both his legs because of diabetes, from which he had suffered for some time and which was, for too long, left untreated. Unable to get around, he seemed to become meaner than ever, taking pleasure in reminding folks that he owned a pistol and didn't mind using it if he had to protect himself.

Whenever I mentioned my affection for Obe to anyone in my family, I always heard about some incident that was meant to prove he wasn't the person I thought he was. His stepdaughter even told me that he once attempted to court her, making her lose any respect she ever had for him. She well knew that I couldn't condone such behavior, even if it came from one of the Wilsons, a family whose men all felt there was something in their genes that made them whoremongers and womanizers. It was the same excuse my uncle Scott, the barber, used to explain why, as tightfisted as he was, he felt obligated to give certain women and their boys free necklines and trims. But Junior (Nathaniel), my cousin, and I wondered about our uncle Fred, who probably died without ever having been sexually intimate with any woman. How could this be, even if he was slow? Wasn't he as much a Wilson as Obe, or Scott, or John, or their father, Eli?

Notes

1. My mother returned from California to assist in the care of my grandmother. So, I spent much of the time before starting to school with my grandmother and my aunt and uncles.

2. There seems to be some question about whether he died there on the spot or whether he died later after receiving treatment. In any case, the visit turned out to be deadly.

3. A straw boss was one of the workers who helped supervise a small group of other workers in addition to doing his own job.

THE HODGESES

> I've learned that people will forget what you said, people will forget what you did, but people will never forget how you made them feel.
>
> **Maya Angelou**

Unlike my sister, Edna, I had no knowledge of my father, Tommie James "T.J." Hodges, when I was growing up. I was only about three when my mother left Richmond, California, where we lived, to return to Greenwood to help take care of my grandmother. The separation would prove permanent, though that wasn't my parents' intention at the time.

Thus, at the age of nineteen, when I arrived at the Greyhound bus station in Portland, Oregon, where my father was then living, I had no real idea of the man who would meet me there. My mom had done her best to describe him to me, but this was based on her memory of sixteen years prior. I think she mentioned something about bowed legs, which may explain my own slightly bowed legs. But I needed more than just her description. When I finally got to Portland, I saw a man looking expectantly at the bus, and as we both started walking toward each other, I wondered what all the concern and worry had been about.

Arriving at his home, I was quite taken aback when he offered me an alcoholic beverage instead of food. I had been riding that bus for over three days, and I was hungry, dirty, and sleepy—and not even of legal drinking age yet. If this was how things would be, I was in for a long summer indeed. Apparently, Jessie, my father's new partner, was a borderline alcoholic, which probably accounted for the presence of liquor bottles throughout the house. Although, technically, Jessie and my father never got married—he hadn't divorced my mother, you see—they lived together as man and wife and paraded around as such. My mother always seemed to take some satisfaction that she was Samantha *Hodges*, T.J.'s true wife and the mother of his children. That she had moved on and was living with my stepfather struck her as a trivial detail.

My father never got to know his own parents. Born in Greenwood, he was around four when his parents and several other close relatives died in the great influenza outbreak in 1918.[1] He and his brothers, Oliver and Rayfield, along with their cousin Stone Griffin, went to live with his aunt Jessie and uncle Willie Chandler and their boy, Arthur, who was called Big Son. Jesse and Willie lived near Yazoo City, Mississippi, where they owned land, cattle, and horses. They gave the boys what was, for southern blacks at that time, a life of relative luxury. The boys, including my father, took the name Chandler, which Cousin Stone kept after my father and uncles later changed their names back to Hodges, the surname of their parents. Their father's Christian name was Oliver. Oliver Junior (or Hodges as he was called) was two years older than my father. Rayfield was the youngest, but sadly, he would die long before his time—the victim of an accident in which a car fell on him while he was working underneath it. He was only in his twenties.

My uncle Oliver, my father (who by then had married my mother in Greenwood), and Stone all went to California around 1943 to take jobs in the Kaiser shipyards in the San Francisco Bay area. Big Son stayed behind to see after his parents' farm. He wasn't a good custodian, however, and allowed whites to dupe him out of the property. They told him that his parents owed them money, and they frightened him into signing over the deed. He was given a suitcase and told he could leave with his life. I don't know whether his parents owed anything or not, but if they did, the sum probably didn't come near the value of the property that was taken.

My father vowed he would never return to Greenwood because of the way he had been treated there. California offered advantages—namely better wages and fewer racial tensions—that were not to be had in Mississippi. When he left, my mother, who was pretty far along in her pregnancy with me, stayed behind with my sister, Edna, who had been born in 1936. Oliver's wife, my aunt

Ellen, was also pregnant with my cousin Lula, and like my mother, she wanted to have her baby in Greenwood before making the long train ride to the West Coast to join her husband. Thus, Lula and I were only infants when our respective parents finally reunited in Richmond, California, by June 1944.

It was about two years later when my uncle Scott contacted my mother to tell her he needed help taking care of the family. I've already described the situation with Abelle and Fred, but now my grandmother had taken ill. Scott claimed that he had more on his hands than he could manage. Heeding his urgent call, my mother packed up my sister and me and headed back to Greenwood. As I indicated, my parents never got back together, though they evidently planned to do so.

I mentioned that my father took the last name "Chandler" for a while. In fact, that was his name when he and my mother were married in 1934, and that was the name under which Edna was born. But by the time I came along in 1944, T.J. had changed his name back to Hodges (as did Uncle Oliver). So I was born John Hodges, while my sister was known as Edna Chandler until she later changed her name to Hodges as well.

But even though I was a Hodges, I knew precious little, as I've noted, about the man who had given me the name. It wasn't until that summer of 1963, in faraway Portland, Oregon, that I got to know T. J. Hodges and his companion, Jessie, who treated me like a country hick unused to being around anything nice. I can't say that she was mean to me, but I could sense that she wasn't completely happy about my being there either. I needed to find a job, since my father had already indicated that he didn't have any funds to contribute to my upcoming college education. I searched high and low and was only able to come up with a job selling encyclopedias. Well, I wasn't really selling the encyclopedias but rather the yearbook that accompanied the set and kept it updated. Since I wasn't convinced of the real value of the product, I made few sales. I do remember being assigned to some area away from the city where there were few if any blacks. The young children delighted in telling their parents about the chocolate man walking the streets in the area. I was told on more than one occasion after I made my presentation that they weren't so much interested in the product as they were in hearing the pitch that this young, strange, brown man might deliver.

I left Portland without any more money toward my education than I had before arriving. The money spent on my support that summer might well have been better used to help with my expenses at Morehouse College, where I was to enter the freshman class in the fall. But at least the trip accomplished two things: I met my father, and I was out of the tense hot air of the Delta. The former pleased me, and the latter, my mother.

It had been decided that right after leaving Portland, I was to head down the coast to California to spend a couple of weeks in Richmond with Uncle Oliver and his family. Two of his children, Lula and Osby, were close to me in age. There were other folks in Richmond who knew me as a baby there, including Aunt Ellen's mother, Clara Wilson, the midwife who had delivered me.[2] It was quite a pleasure to be in Richmond and to see all the folks called Hodges. My cousin, Osby, was a pianist and was already at his young age playing at churches and directing choirs. I had been playing the piano as well but with nothing like the success of my cousin.

Aunt Ellen and Uncle Oliver made sure that I was able to visit places like the zoo and nearby Berkeley, as well as to get over to Oakland and see Aunt Ellen's mother and sister Ella, whom family members referred to as Aunt Nig. I remember that Aunt Ellen always commented on how smart she thought I was, which made me adore her even more. Unlike at my father's house, no one inside Aunt Ellen's house dared to drink. She and her children were Seventh Day Adventists who took their religion seriously, though I don't remember them imposing their beliefs on me. After services on Saturday, the family gathered back at Aunt Ellen's for a delicious meal, all prepared without pork.

Uncle Oliver seemed to enjoy his role as head of this clan. I indicated earlier that he was named for his father. He in turn named his first-born son Oliver, and so did his son after him. Thus, there is an Oliver Hodges IV, with presumably more to follow. So proud was I to see myself as part of a family tradition that I insisted on being referred to—in California, at least—not just as "John" but as "John Oliver." And my son, Daniel, bears the same middle name.[3]

Later in life, I gained an even greater appreciation of Uncle Oliver and Aunt Ellen (or "Kid," as Uncle Oliver always referred to her). They both made sure that they kept in touch with my sister and me, especially after our mother's death in 1971. Aunt Ellen called us almost every Saturday evening, and Uncle Oliver made it a point to visit his sister and my family in Chicago and other friends and family in Mississippi. He even made an effort to attend my wedding in Chicago in 1972, although he was unable to find the specific location. We had no idea that he would be coming from California. He always liked to show up unannounced with his tape recorder in hand, ready to record the words of any unsuspecting souls. He seemed like a kid at play with a new toy, deriving a lot of pleasure from these innocent pranks.

Thus, a summer I thought would be devoted in large part to making money to help pay for college expenses was spent instead getting to know a part of my family, and thus a part of me, that I didn't know—a knowledge that has made a huge difference in my life.[4] My mother seemed pleased when I returned home safely, for I had never spent such a long period away from her. As for college funds, she seemed assured that somehow God would make a way. All we needed to do was to keep praying.

Notes

1. The great influenza epidemic of 1918 claimed more lives than did World War I. Estimates of the number of victims vary widely, from 20 million to well over 50 million. It was termed the "Spanish flu" because Spain was the first country to officially recognize it. The first reported cases came from Camp Funston, an army base in Fort Riley, Kansas. For some reason, the strain seemed especially virulent among those between the ages of twenty and thirty-five. My grandparents, who perished in the outbreak, were within that age group. One of the most readable books on the subject is Stephanie True Peters, *Epidemic: The 1918 Influenza Pandemic* (Tarrytown, NY: Benchmark Books, 2005).

2. Clara was no relation to the Wilsons who make up my mother's side of the family.

3. Aunt Ellen's father was named Daniel, though my son was named for my stepfather, Lee Daniel (Bully) Thompson. This is a bit of serendipity that I welcome.

4. After I entered graduate school at the University of Chicago, I got to meet another member of the Hodges family: my father's sister, Ethel Mae, whom we all called "Sweet."

MY MOTHER

So boy, don't you turn back.
Don't you set down on the steps
'Cause you finds it's kinder hard.
Don't you fall now—
For I'se still goin', honey,
I'se still climbin',
And life for me ain't been no crystal stair.

Langston Hughes, "Mother to Son"

My mother was called Sister, Menthe, Mantha—everything, it seemed, except her real name of Samantha. I always thought that was a shame since she had such a beautiful name. My mother and I were close, and I loved her dearly, despite the near-death whippings she gave me. For a long period following her death in 1971, I seemed to lack the will to go on.

Those familiar with Saint Augustine's deep affection for his mother, Monica, will understand the bond and love between my mother, Samantha, and me. She wanted so much for me to grow into a responsible and successful man and imparted the wisdom and dispensed the punishments she believed were necessary to insure the desired outcome. Augustine referred to his mother as Saint Monica, but anyone who knew my mother would quickly recognize the inappropriateness of such a label. She was a decent woman who could be your best friend or worst enemy. My sister, Edna, said our mother had a bad temper and that she used to carry an ice pick around in her bosom. She used the ice pick on at least one occasion—when she stabbed my stepfather after he threatened her with a shotgun.

    Edna also recalled that before I was born, Mama pulled a gun on a woman who lived next door to them on Fulton Street in Greenwood. This woman apparently had the gall to name her child after my father. Whether or not the child was my father's, the act angered my mother, who saw it as meddling. The woman called my father over all the time to ask him to do little things around her house, all of this despite the fact that she was also married. On another occasion, Edna said, Mama threatened some women she believed were laughing at her. As my mother passed by, the women laughed loudly and said in a voice that Mama was sure to hear, "I'm tickled pink." Mama responded, "You're going to be tickled red after I ram my foot up your ass." So, no, Samantha was no Saint Monica. Of course, neither am I a Saint Augustine. She was, however, a God-fearing Christian, cheerful, and completely devoted to her baby boy. While Monica was chiefly concerned with Augustine's spiritual health and development, my mother seemed to be concerned about every facet of my life. She was perhaps overly protective. There was a litany of do's and don'ts that accompanied me at every stage of my development. As a child, I couldn't go to the swimming hole the black kids used, and as a result I never learned to swim. I wasn't allowed to go out for the football team as many of my schoolmates were. When I studied in France, my mother warned me about drinking wine, though I believe she was finally persuaded by my point that all French people drank wine at dinner. When I went to graduate school in Chicago, I was warned about driving on the Dan Ryan Expressway, which she had heard was extremely dangerous. "But, Mama, you can't get anywhere in Chicago without getting on the Dan Ryan," I countered.

    She was equally as concerned with my health. Whenever I had the slightest malady, my mother made sure I saw the doctor. I remember such occasions with great fondness because afterwards she always got me something nice like a Popsicle or some ice cream. She absolutely would not take any chances with my health. One Saturday night when we were all gathered in town, I drank a soda without noticing that the lip of the bottle was slightly cracked. Whether I had swallowed a piece of glass or not, my mother wouldn't take any chances. She rushed me to the doctor's office, which was open on Saturday nights to treat cuts and bruises and stabbings as well as minor injuries. Another time, my mother thought I had swallowed a fish bone; again, she made sure I received medical attention, which this time consisted of making me eat almost a whole loaf of light bread.

My mother was born in 1912, though she often said that 1919 was the year of her birth. Perhaps she wanted to make the age difference between her and my stepfather—she was ten years his senior—seem more respectable. She was born in the hills of northeastern Mississippi but moved to the Delta fairly early on. She and my father were married on December 31, 1934. They had three children: Edna; Tommie James Jr., who died early on; and me. The move to California, as I mentioned earlier, came shortly after I was born in 1944, only to be followed by my parents' permanent separation, when Samantha returned to Greenwood with Edna and me to help Uncle Scott take care of their ailing mother.

Although she had never finished high school, I have early memories of my mother assisting me with my arithmetic and reading. She often tried her hand at writing poems called "Dunbars," so labeled because they were modeled after the work of the vernacular poet Paul Laurence Dunbar. I don't recall if the poems were any good, but her desire to write *something* was impressive. One interesting memory I have is of competing with her to see who could get dressed the fastest to go to town. The race would start after we had each taken a bath in the shiny galvanized tub that was used for washing clothes and bobbing for apples as well as for baths.

I always considered my mother to be a hard worker, a fact my sister confirmed, adding that she always did whatever necessary for the family to survive. I never asked my sister exactly what she meant by that. I only know that my mother always had another job besides that of sharecropper. We simply couldn't have survived otherwise.

The family for whom my mother worked as a maid always called her Sarah, although Samantha sounded nothing like that. My mother, for her part, had to refer to the white woman using the title of Miss or Mrs. Laurent. What is perhaps most appalling is that the woman's son, who was about my age, also called my mother Sarah. While southern white children were normally taught to be polite to their elders, this in no way applied to blacks. And adding insult to injury was this: as soon as the boy became a "young man," around the age of twelve, my mother was expected to call him Mister or Master Vicki. I don't know if she ever did so, but she was expected to nonetheless.[1]

My mother often took me with her to her job. When the white folks had eaten their meals and departed the house, she would sit me down to corn flakes and Pet milk. Occasionally, I got to eat bacon and eggs, but this was rare. I suppose it was easy for the white folks to keep track of the eggs and bacon, but not so easy when it came to corn flakes. I was allowed to play with Vicki Jo when his white friends were not present. But when they came over, I had to go off by myself. I couldn't accompany them as they went off to their ball games. I don't recall making much ado about this at the time, but it must have left deep scars and feelings of inadequacy and self-doubt. I like to think that it at least had some effect on Vicki Jo as well.

My mother also sold vegetables to the whites in the city so that we could have some spending change for clothes and the church collection plate and to keep up payments on life insurance and burial policies. It now occurs to me that without the vegetable sales, we would have had absolutely nothing. My mother—the fastest sheller of peas I ever knew—sold the peas by the pint and quart: twenty-five cents per pint and fifty cents a quart, I believe. We had our regular customers who purchased the peas, corn (five cents an ear), butter beans, and potatoes. As we had no means of transportation, we walked from house to house. Later, when I got a bicycle, that became my means of transportation.

There is no doubt that if my mother were alive today, she could face charges of child abuse. Anyone who knew my mother would remember her as a kind, jovial individual who was slow to anger but definitely could be pushed in that direction. The notion of child abuse, which is now so prevalent an issue, simply didn't exist then. I can't consider my mother an abuser, however—not because she always said before the whippings that "this is going to hurt me more than you," but because I knew that she did love me. Those whippings were designed to save me from more disastrous consequences in the white world, which I'll explain in a moment.

Almost every black child, and many whites as well, will tell you of times when they were told to fetch a switch. If they brought one too small, they simply had to get a larger one. Then the whippings began. I remember one day I determined to steel myself and not cry no matter how hard the beating. "Ah! Ah!" my mother said. "So you're not going to cry, okay, okay." And then the beatings began afresh. Another strategy—screaming at the top of my lungs—was even less effective. "Stop it, I say, stop it," she would tell me. "Somebody'll think I'm killing you." And when I reminded her that that was precisely what she was doing, the plea fell on deaf ears.

Though I can't recall all the details, I remember that one of my worst whippings came after some friends and I ate their father's dinner. My mother and stepfather had left me at my friends' home while the adults all went to church. The father hadn't had time to eat his supper. We got hungry and so decided to help ourselves to his meal. I, of course, thought of it only as food, not really knowing that it was already spoken for. My friends assured me that it was all right to eat it. And so we did. The poor unsuspecting father had probably worked up quite an appetite singing and praying at the prayer meeting, but happy to know that he had greens, cornbread, and ham hocks waiting for him at home. I didn't understand the startled look on his face when he looked into the covered dish atop the wood stove and found only the green pot liquor where his dinner was supposed to be. Then there were the questions, the finger pointing, the "it-couldn't-be my-fault-since-I-didn't-know-better." I was whipped, I think, within an inch of my life. It's an incident I'll never forget.

It was perhaps because of such beatings, as terrible and frightening as they were, that I was able to escape the fate of the lynching victims Mack Charles Parker and Emmett Till. I know for sure that the same was true for many of my friends. When Richard Wright spoke of the whippings he received as a youth in his autobiographical writings *Black Boy* and "The Ethics of Living Jim Crow," I believe the same principle was at work. Recall the first episode in "Ethics" in which Wright told of the punishment he received for fighting with white boys. Beaten and bloodied from the cinders hurled at him and his friends, he went to his mother for solace and understanding, only to receive another beating on top of the one administered by the white kids. "You were lucky that they didn't kill you," she told him. In her mind, the beating she gave him might save his life one day. Had he been fighting other black boys, he'd have gotten a very different message, that of the necessity of standing up for himself by fighting back. It was the parent's responsibility to instill within the child that he wasn't fighting on equal terms. Although we don't generally use the same tactics in correcting our children today, most of us understand and even appreciate the correction we received as children. Furthermore, it just seemed to me that those children who didn't get the punishment we had received turned out bad or came to a bad end. In the Emmett Till case, Mose Wright, Emmett's great uncle, offered to whip the

Chicago-bred boy after he had offended white Mississippi racists. Wright was ready to use the only weapon he had to try to save Emmett's life. Emmett never realized the danger he was in.

At some point, parents realize that you're getting too old for whippings, though I think my mother was a bit late in realizing this. For a couple of my friends, Jeffie and John McNeal, that time came in a humorous way. Their mother was preparing to whip them for not doing their chores, but John simply lifted her up with her heels off the ground and swung her gently around as if in a loving waltz. She laughed and said to the boys, "You better get those dishes washed." Parents didn't give up on corporal punishment easily. When they did, you would almost rather be whipped than left in God's hands when you did something wrong. That was an uncertain fate, indeed, that made you think of hell and damnation. At least with a whipping you had a sense that the matter was settled.

My mother died on April 3, 1971, at the age of fifty-nine. I regret that I was not at her side when she passed, nor was my sister able to reach me. I had taken a weekend away from my studies to visit a friend, and I made certain that I couldn't be reached. Her death came quickly and unexpectedly and perhaps unnecessarily.[2] At the time of her death, I was unmarried and hadn't yet completed my doctorate. Some of her friends told her about the significance of the degree and that it was from a prestigious school. She wanted me to know that she approved of what I was doing when she told me that "the PhD is a man." She would also approve of the young woman I married and would be especially proud of her grandson, Daniel.

NOTES

1. In *I Know Why the Caged Bird Sings,* Maya Angelou recalls an incident in which white girls disrespect her grandmother by calling her by her first name.

2. I long suspected that my mother was not receiving proper health care from her physician, who, it was widely known, drank heavily.

MY SISTER

> When you learn, teach.
> When you get, give.
> As for me,
> I shall not be moved.
>
> **Maya Angelou, "Our Grandmothers"**

The house we lived in was not unlike that of the other sharecroppers in our area. In fact, the color of the houses identified them as belonging to the same planter. It was a green, three-room, frame shotgun structure with a tin roof. There were front and back porches. We had no running water and, of course, no indoor bathroom facilities. The toilet, or outhouse as we called it, was about twenty feet in back of the house at the edge of our watermelon patch. I mention this because the melons there always seemed to be bigger. There was a wood stove in the kitchen and a fireplace in the middle room. The front room was heated by a coal stove. My sister and I shared a bed in the front room, which I appreciated, as the nights often got very cold and the heat from her body made those winter nights more tolerable. She was also responsible for getting the fire going in the morning and was the first to hit the cold wooden floor. At times like those it was good to have a big sister. Although life on the plantation was tough, I never remember feeling deprived. Generally, everyone else was in the same shape, and people made do with what they had. It was only when I accompanied my mother to her job as a maid that I became aware that we were poor.

In fact, there were moments of great joy that we spent in that house. I remember the sound of the rain dancing on the tin roof, and the smell of sweet potatoes baking in the ashes of the fireplace. Here, my sister and I spent hours thinking up the names of movie stars. We'd name the most famous ones first, saving the tougher ones for the time when we were stalled, when the pickings became slim. (I don't remember thinking of black movie stars at the time. There were so few, and their roles made us question whether they qualified as stars or not.) The one who failed to produce a name lost the contest. To vary the game, one of us would choose women and the other men. Whoever got to choose the male stars had it easier, so we would switch up to make the game fairer.

We used to read the newspapers our stepfather plastered on the walls. I remember that I particularly liked to read the sports pages. We got the old newspapers from the white folks for whom my mother worked. My stepfather would make a stiff paste out of Argo starch and brush it on strips of newspaper. The newspapers were excellent reading material but did very little to keep out the cold during the winter months.

Edna enjoyed going to the movies, reading, and talking to her friends. She especially liked to read *True Confessions* and *True Story* magazines. She remembers that the only thing she ever stole was one of those magazines. For someone my age, going to the movies was about the only recreation we had in Greenwood. Some of the older kids could go out on dates, which often meant going to the movies or to Hotel Plaza on Sunday nights. I heard some of the older boys who had cars talking about taking girls out by some levee or pumping station and making them walk back if they decided not to put out.

I don't think that my sister enjoyed anything like a courtship as one might describe it today. You met someone at church and maybe spent some time together walking back and forth to church or school—which often was either in the church or located next to it. But since she married at such a young age she seemed to get shortchanged even in that minimal form of dating. I remember the Saturday in December when my sister got married in the Leflore County Court House. She was fifteen at the time but told the judge that she was sixteen, even though her birthday was still more than two months away. Her husband-to-be, John Eddie Keys, was only nineteen. His family seemed happier about the marriage than ours, for Mrs. Keys planted a big snuff-filled kiss on my sister's cheeks. I was perhaps most saddened by the wedding, for I was losing not only a sister but also a close friend, despite the eight-year difference in our ages. She had been the one who graciously warmed the bed for me on cold winter nights and fanned me in the heat of summer. She was the one who took me to the movies with her girlfriends, who made much of me as their "boyfriend." So, I wasn't very happy to see her leave our home.

But what were the options open to a young black plantation girl of fifteen? They seemed as limited as the plantation itself. Even now, I occasionally wonder whether she had been encouraged to go to school as I had been. Those who knew both my sister and me believed that she had as much natural ability as I had and possibly more. But here the difference in our ages might have made a huge difference in our educational pursuits. When she went to school, split sessions were the order of the day for those on the plantation. Sharecroppers' children could go to school only at those times when they weren't needed in the cotton field. When I came along a few years later, this was beginning to change. And as I'll discuss in the next fragment, my stepfather intervened on my behalf.

Edna absolutely hated going to the field. But when you were ten or older, you were simply expected to do field work. There could be no exceptions, of course, except in a very few cases, including my own. But if she hated the fields, she absolutely detested going to school in split sessions. She passed her classes, but the arrangement wasn't at all to her liking.[1] So she just stopped going to school and got married—an act that seemed to doom her to a life in sharecropping despite any native intelligence she may have had. She was thus stuck early on with a husband who was only nineteen and actually appeared younger than that in terms of maturity. He worked at the cotton gin, one of the better jobs on the plantation. I remember having to take him his lunch of greens and cornbread as he worked in the heat amid the lint and seed. He seemed happy to get the food, although I know that it couldn't have been that good. My sister had not yet developed into the fine cook she later became.

Her husband had a mean streak. I recall a time when I struck him over the head with a bottle because he was attacking my sister. I hit him with all the energy a seven-year-old could muster. I believe that the blow did slow him down a bit, if it didn't completely stop him. John Eddie never seemed to be accomplished in much of anything he did. He tried to play baseball with the guys but wasn't a good hitter or fielder. When he gambled, everyone wanted to join in because they knew their chances of winning improved markedly with him in the game.

Little over a year into the marriage, my sister became pregnant with her first son, John Junior, and after that several others came in fairly rapid succession. Thus stuck in the marriage, she could do very little to extricate herself from the situation. John Eddie was neither a good husband nor father. My sister told me that he was often violent, that he once threatened her with an axe, and that he didn't give her money. When they went to town on Saturdays, she often stayed in the car with the children while John Eddie paraded around arm in arm with his girlfriend, flaunting his infidelity in front of my sister. Very early on, Edna realized that marriage was no way out of her predicament. In fact, it only made matters much worse. When she went to St. Louis with John Eddie, he became even more abusive. Having taken all she could stand, she finally left him and returned to Greenwood. She never got a divorce from her husband but simply went her own way while he went his.

I was actually able to bond once again with my sister after she moved back to Greenwood. We continued our close friendship, and I assisted her financially whenever I could. This might have been the very best move she made for her own career. Her last job was probably the best one she ever had. She was a nurse's assistant with a noted physician and surgeon in Greenwood and had an excellent working relationship with both the doctor and the nurses, becoming especially close to one of them. I know she enjoyed telling all the folks in the office about her baby brother who was teaching at the University of Tennessee. And I was happy to get the praise. My mother didn't live to see me get married, finish my degree, and get to know her daughter-in-law and grandson. But my sister did live long enough to share these precious moments with me. As she reminded me, she now had become both my sister and mother, and I think she meant it. Whenever we visited her, she made sure that she had plenty of apple juice, which was my son's favorite drink.

In 1997, I took Edna to Richmond, California, to visit Aunt Ellen Hodges and Mae Chandler and our cousins on our father's side. It was a marvelous adventure for two reasons. It was my sister's first and only flight on an airplane, and it was the first time she had been back to the Bay area since she was a child. I was happy to make both of those things happen for my beloved sister.

After a period of ill health, my sister died in June 2001 at the age of sixty-five from complications brought on by emphysema. She began smoking at an early age and continued until she began to suffer from the illness that took the lives of both our uncle and father. She outlived both her mother and natural father but died, it seems to me, much too soon.

NOTE

1. Dr. Aaron Henry, the civil rights leader from Clarksdale, once protested to his parents about why he, unlike white children, had to go to school in split sessions. His mother assured him that since he was smarter, the white kids needed the extra time. See Charles Payne, *I've Got the Light of Freedom: The Organizing Tradition and the Mississippi Freedom Struggle* (Berkeley: Univ. of California Press, 1995), 17.

MY STEPFATHER

> [E]nlightenment was viewed as the greatest single opportunity to escape the indignities that whites were heaping upon Blacks. Children were sent to school when it was a great inconvenience to their parents. Parents made untold sacrifices to secure the learning of their children that they had been denied.
>
> **John Hope Franklin,** *From Slavery to Freedom*

> Let my son go to school; I'll go to the field.
>
> **Lee Daniel Thompson, my stepfather**

My stepfather was always difficult for me to understand. Here was a man who seemed to have very little ambition. He wanted, I suppose, to provide for me and my mother and sister. But he seemed not to want very much for himself. The only thing I ever saw him drive was a pair of mules pulling a sled loaded with stuffed cotton sacks or a barrel of water he had gotten from the commissary well. I remember this because I enjoyed riding atop the sacks, balancing myself so that I wouldn't fall off. When he hauled water, I enjoyed the occasional splash from the barrel onto my face. I don't know if he ever learned to drive an automobile. It wouldn't have mattered in any case, since he had no vehicle to drive. I was always puzzled by his nickname, Bully, when his parents had given him such a pretty name: Lee Daniel. Also, given his character, his nickname seemed odd and out of place.

Lee Daniel was the oldest of six children born to Willie Green Thompson. Mr. Thompson's first wife, Ida Ross, was the mother of Lee Daniel and three others. When she died around 1933, Mr. Green, as we called him, married Ruth White. Mr. Green and Miss Ruth had two children, Pearlene and Katie. They raised their children on Moore's Lake in the small plantation town of Schlater. All the children seemed to turn out fine except for A.G., the middle son, who always found himself in trouble and running afoul of the law.

Unlike A.G., Bully was a decent and honest man. Known to be a good worker, he often admonished me by saying that laziness will kill you. I don't remember being very moved by this, since I believed that the kind of hard work he did would more than do me in. Bully had gone to school around Shellmound on Bledsau plantation. According to his younger brother, Shellmound in those days was a rough place in which to grow up. As long as the murder of a white man wasn't involved, the plantation owner could reassure his best hands that "if you stay out of the grave, I'll keep you out of jail." Despite Bully's upbringing and the period he spent in the army, he always appeared quiet and unassuming—that is, when he wasn't drinking. When he drank, he became a completely different human being—assertive, boisterous, and even abusive to my mother.

There were many nights when my mother had to wait up for my stepfather, only to learn the next day that he had been taken to jail. We would find terrible bruises on his body where "Smitty," the deputy sheriff, had beaten him. Often he brought his anger home and took out his frustrations on my mother. If they argued, I simply stood aside, hoping they would soon stop. But if, as was frequently the case, he attempted to strike my mother, I tried to take her part, and on one occasion I struck him in the head with an ashtray. So, while he was generally a quiet, reserved, perhaps even timid fellow who tried to avoid confrontation at all costs, he could be a bear of a man when he drank—which was every weekend.

But all that aside, my memories of him remain favorable. He certainly should receive credit for a large part of any academic success I've achieved. It was he, after all, who insisted to the foreman of the plantation where we lived that I should be allowed to go to school rather than to the fields, the fate of so many other black boys who reached the age of seven or eight.

Whites in the Delta thought it not in their interests for blacks to receive an education. I don't believe truancy laws applied to the children of black sharecroppers. But Bully assured the foreman that he could produce even more work to compensate for my absence from the fields. After all, how much work could a child of seven or eight produce? I was likely to have been more of a hindrance than any real help.

As I noted in my recollections of my sister, the school system conspired with planters by offering split sessions for the children of sharecroppers. In most rural communities, children were allowed to go to school only when there was no work to be done in the fields. One learned very early on that cotton was king, and education, especially for blacks, was of secondary or tertiary importance. Planters were of the general opinion that education for blacks ran counter to their interests. They needed blacks to work in the cotton fields, and an education wouldn't help blacks make cotton.

My stepfather came to get me whenever I was caught at school during a rainstorm. For a year or so, before buses were provided, I walked to school from the plantation. I remember being there several times when a big rainstorm hit. My stepfather, on those occasions, walked to the school himself wearing boots and rain gear to get me. As he didn't have his own means of transportation, we had to walk back home in the rain, taking shelter here and there and picking those moments of lesser intensity to make a mad dash for the next convenient place of shelter. Those were acts of genuine care and consideration on my stepfather's part, and I recall them with great fondness.

He often told me that he wished he and my mother had gotten "those papers," by which he meant that they were never legally married. She had never divorced her first husband, my father. My stepfather, as I learned just a few years before his death, was ten years younger than my mother. Apparently, he and she met shortly after he was honorably discharged from the army and after she came back to Greenwood from California. He outlived my mother by twenty-nine years, though a number of those later years found him incapacitated and living in a nursing home. That was where he died in September 2000 at the age of seventy-eight. I read the following letter at his funeral as a kind of memorial to him:

> Dear Bull—
>
> I come not to glamorize your life; you wouldn't want that. It was a life that knew pain and sorrow, joy and pride. There were moments of personal weakness. You had to face many obstacles in

your life and you faced them the best way you could. A man does not have to be perfect to be good. One thing for sure, you were no hypocrite. I liked that most of all.

During my early childhood, you were the only father I knew. And a boy needs a man, if for no other reason than to let him know how hard it is to be a man. So on this day that you are laid to rest, I want you to know I have not forgotten.

I remember the times you took me for a ride on your broad shoulders—you seemed to enjoy the trips as much as I did.

I remember watching you plough, and plant, chop and pick, insisting to Mr. Kerr that you would go to the field but that I should go to school. I thank you for that wonderful act of personal sacrifice—which has made all the difference.

I remember the baseball games on Sunday afternoons between Whittington and Race Track and Pink Service Station. Sometimes you played first base, but more often you were the catcher. Though you had neither overwhelming speed nor power, you were my Josh Gibson, my Roy Campanella. They could never intone: "Cream, cream, the sun is going down." The pitcher would know by these words to throw his cut-off drop.

I remember the times you walked to school in driving rain, so that you could walk me back safely to our shotgun house on Lawyer Whittington's Plantation.

I recall the many newspapers you got from the white folks' house which you used to plaster the bare wooden walls. Little did you know that those walls would help improve my reading skills.

I remember the greens and neck bones, cornbread and buttermilk—and the smell of fried chicken on Sunday mornings.

I know you remember that red Murray bicycle you and mom bought me for Christmas—which was a great joy for me; but served as your sole means of transportation.

But I also remember the disappointment you faced at the end of each year at settlement time—when you were told once again that you had come out in the hole.

I remember the personal insults you faced, the police brutality, and your own special way of trying to cope. In those moments,

I realized just how tough your life had been. Sometimes, it's hard to be a black man.

I remember my trips to Golden Age [the nursing home]—and the rides we took back over the land that you once worked. I wanted you to be proud that I had not forgotten.

When I saw you for the last time in mid-August, you had become so weak. Those strong shoulders that once held me had now drooped. Those feet and legs that once took you from Whittington to the Buckeye to Carrollton Avenue and back again could not take you from your own bed. I knew that you were tired and weary and wanted rest and peace. I hope that you have found that peace. I will miss you, and I will never forget the personal sacrifices you and my mother made to make sure that my life would not be as tough as yours.

Love,

Your boy, John Oliver

WHITTINGTON PLANTATION

> What the planter class wanted was an abundant supply of cheap, docile, hungry, and subordinate laborers, the only productive workforce conceivable to them. Recognizing that former slaves possessed neither land nor money for rent or supplies, planters exploited their poverty to exact black labor and to control black lives.
>
> Leon F. Litwack, Trouble in Mind

Several of the major planters in the Delta also had careers in regional and national politics. There were, for example, U.S. Senators Leroy Percy of Washington County and James O. Eastland of Sunflower County and Representative William M. Whittington of Leflore. As chairs and members of powerful committees, these men wielded power and influence in Washington that redounded to the benefit of planters, including themselves, in the southern cotton economy. As a child, I grew up on Congressman's Bill Whittington's plantation, which was run chiefly by his son Aven Whittington.[1]

These larger plantations were nearly self-sustaining. We had carpenters, blacksmiths, barbers, midwives, grave diggers, and preachers. We generally had to go to town to see a doctor, but there were one or two individuals known to do root work.[2] They could recommend remedies that could heal maladies ranging all the way from a headache to a feeble mind to a broken heart. Moonshine, beer, and wine could be made right on the plantation, which had all the desired ingredients: corn, barley, plums, and peaches. Cards, dice, checkers, and even marbles were always there for fun or wagering. You could buy food, coffee, tobacco, kerosene, and work clothes at the commissary. You paid extra, of course, for the convenience of having supplies so readily available and the ability to charge all purchases against this year's or next year's crop. There was no library, of course. But who has ever heard of a library on a plantation?

Lawyer Wittington placed his sons, Aven and Billy, in charge of his places in Greenwood and Schlater. Aven put his Princeton degree in economics to good use, serving as the manager and bookkeeper for several places. We lived in the place just outside Greenwood.[3] In fact, we lived near the front of the plantation, which was just a short walk from the city limits. While we had very little, I don't remember being hungry. Some land was allotted for a generous garden spot where we grew all manner of vegetables. We could have vegetables and cornbread any time, even if we didn't always have meat. But we often had neck bones, ham hocks, or pork skins in our greens. My stepfather had his cornbread and buttermilk after his greens and skins. Any greens that were left over could be had for breakfast the next morning. We didn't have pigs or chickens as did many of the other croppers, but my stepfather was more than willing to help out killing hogs when the weather turned cooler in late November and December. For his assistance, he received a piece of meat to bring home. He also hunted rabbits and quail to supplement our food supply.

Living on the plantation, it now occurs to me, was a full-time occupation. I don't mean we were in the fields all the time. But when we weren't in the fields, we were busy doing something. Life on Whittington was often inconvenient but seldom boring. Every minute of our lives seemed to be regulated, even down to the time dedicated to fun. That was Saturday night, a time when it was all right to let your hair down. It was a kind of reward for those who, throughout the week, had taken care of the fields, washed and ironed clothes, fed the pigs and chickens, milked the cows, and tended to the orchards and gardens. But Saturday noon, one could hear a big sigh from the back of the plantation, where Charlie Parker and Stonewall Garner lived, all the way to the front, where Reverend Keys and his family held forth. Living near the front, we could actually walk to town, as we did so often when we sold our vegetables. Those who lived anywhere from the back to the middle of the plantation had to wait for a truck that went to the city. This truck was often packed by the time it reached our house. But we either took it, or walked, or rode along with those few who were fortunate enough to have their own means of transportation. Somehow, we all got to town, where we met fellow sharecroppers from such nearby communities as Money, Sidon, Shellmound, Schlater, and Race Track. They would all be there. Businesses looked forward to the event perhaps even more than we did. As I was a youngster, I either went to the Walthall Theater to see a double feature or chased girls around Mr. Hodges's store. (This Hodges, a white man, was no relation to me.) The three or so hours spent in this way gave my mother and stepfather time to do whatever they wanted to do. Generally, what they did wasn't done together. In fact, my mother and stepfather often returned home alone. Sometimes, he didn't get home at all; those were the times, we supposed, that he had spent the night in jail and needed someone to pay the ten dollars to bail him out, just in time for him to get to the fields early Monday morning.

Once, while I was supposed to be at the movies, I decided to join some older boys who pocketed the thirty-five or forty cents they received for the show and peanuts and popcorn. With this money, we roamed the streets, watching the grownups eating fish, drinking beer, dancing, laughing, swearing, smooching, playing the pinball machines, and shooting craps. Downtown Greenwood in those days was very busy and exciting compared to the way it is today. Everything seemed to be packed into the few hours left before the truck fetched us to return home by 1:00 or 2:00 AM. so that we could get ready for Sunday school the next day. For me, skipping church was not an option. Many of the men and older boys, though, stayed away to gamble, drink, and play baseball.

After Sunday school on those Sundays when we weren't meeting for regular church services, a number of us boys from the plantation gathered behind the commissary to play football. Sometimes we played among ourselves but more often against kids from G.P.[4] or Baptist Town or some other nearby area. This wasn't touch football, which we thought was for sissies; to us, tackle football was a game for real men, even if most of us were under eighteen. In fact, our ages ranged from about twelve to twenty. And yes, this was real football like that played by Jim Brown or Bart Starr or Johnny Unitas, only without pads or any protection at all. When you factor in differences in ability, fierceness, weight, and age, it's surprising how few really serious accidents we sustained. I was a notable casualty. I was thirteen at the time. I ran the ball around the end, where a boy we called Cat Tail was standing guard. He hit me so hard that I thought I'd never get up. Cat Tail was unremorseful—he was actually jubilant and proud—and looked down on me, asking for all to hear: "Do ya want some mo'?" He would be satisfied with nothing short of my unequivocal surrender. I muttered something, intentionally unintelligible, hoping that someone would intervene and hold me back as I rushed to get up. That didn't happen, but I was told to sit out for a play or two. This was about the next best thing to happen to allow me to save face. I went home and then to get X-rays. I had broken my collarbone. It would be a while before I could play football again.

I've indicated that on Sundays the older boys and men often played baseball. Although I was too young to play, I often watched my stepfather play. I remember the spirited rivalries between the teams from Greenwood, Race Track, Tchula, the Buckeye, Charles Whittington, Itta Bena, Sidon, and Pink Service Station (Shellmound). To make the games more interesting, the players each put up a dollar and ten cents, the dollars going to the victorious team and the dimes to the umpire. The umpire usually stood behind the pitcher if he had no one to help him. Here, he could see the entire field and was responsible for calling balls and strikes as well as all the bases. It was a daunting task. And he earned every bit of the two dollars or so he received for calling the game. Those were some interesting characters. I fell in love with the catchers who communicated with the pitchers in what seemed to be a sermonic tone. It was simply not enough to catch the ball. One had to call the game correctly. My stepfather was a catcher, probably because he was considered too slow to play any other position, with the exception of first base, which he did from time to time. Quiet though he was in actual life, at the games he was quite vocal, intoning, "Cream, Cream, the sun is going down." The pitcher then wound up and hurled the ball with great velocity and seeming accuracy, but when it reached the batter, it altered its course and dropped straight down. This was what the old guys called the drop, better known these days as a slider. The batter swung and came up with nothing but air. Was that the pitch he was calling for? The crowd of women and children screamed, and my stepfather felt a sense of great accomplishment. And this was only strike one!

I was around ten or eleven years old when I started to play baseball. I played catcher, but I don't remember having a choice in the matter. I'm sure it wasn't because my stepfather played that position. This was some years later after we had moved to town. I wasn't very good. I remember missing about as many pitches as I caught. The umpire, Solomon Dickerson, who stood right behind me, always urged me to try to catch the ball, if not for the team's sake, then certainly for his own, as he was sure to get hit by my missed balls whenever our team played.

The problem was aggravated because the pitcher, whom we called "Blackout," could throw really hard, earning his nickname. And each time he threw, I thought I would pass out. "Son," Mr. Dickerson would say, "you simply going to have to catch some of these balls."

NOTES

1. William Whittington was born on May 4, 1878, in Franklin County, Mississippi. He received his law degree from Ole Miss in Oxford in 1899 and was admitted to the bar that same year. In 1904, he took his law practice to Greenwood, where he also began pursuing a career as a planter, mainly of cotton. After serving several terms in local and state politics, he was elected to Congress in 1925 and served there until 1951. His brother Charles Whittington was also a planter, as were his sons, Charles Aven and Bill Junior. Both sons were graduates of Princeton University.

2. I refer to those who practiced conjuring and hoodoo. I discuss these practices more fully in the piece "African Gods in Mississippi."

3. This place was sold some years later, and the commissary was moved to another plantation. Hotels and other businesses are now located along the Hightway 82 bypass, where the plantation was once located.

4. G.P. is a place so named because its northern boundary was formed by the Georgia Pacific railway that once ran through Greenwood. In local lore, the name was sometimes said to stand for something else: "good people" or "good pussy." The latter, naturally, infuriated the young women from that section of town.

SETTLEMENT TIME

> Nought from nought is nought
> Five's a figger
> All for the white man;
> None for the nigger.
>
> **Southern folk rhyme**

Though most families knew the outcome, settlement day was filled with excitement and expectation. It was always held just a few days before Christmas. Whether or not one cleared anything could spell the difference between a joyous holiday season and a disappointing one. But even if our family didn't clear anything, which was most often the case, we were generally allowed, even encouraged, to borrow on the next year's crop.

On settlement day, the sharecroppers stood in line, beginning around ten in the morning. Some tried to arrive early, hoping to be done by a decent hour. Croppers from all the farms owned by the planter met at the head commissary, generally on the same day, but this depended entirely on the size of the plantation. It often took until well after midnight before the last account was settled. Thus, the farmhands sat for hours, standing occasionally to ease the weariness in their limbs. Boredom wore on the older men, while the younger ones told jokes about sexual exploits of a few nights before, being careful not to offend a father or brother within earshot. This fraternity of young and old simply waited. Somehow they realized that they were all in this thing together. But this didn't keep some of the more imaginative and suspicious among them from wondering how one cropper could come out in the black when he produced significantly less than some of the others. This led to a few unkind rumors about how the cropper's wife or daughter was engaging in activities unrelated to farming. These were just rumors, mind you, with no facts to back them up. In the meantime, the sharecroppers just waited to be told what they already knew: "It was not a very good year for cotton or prices, and you had a number of doctor bills." How many bills and just how much indebtedness there was only the bookkeeper knew, and his recollection wasn't subject to question by a farmhand. The medical bills, weekly rations of molasses and salt pork, Vienna sausage, potted meat, the rent on the two- or three-room shotgun house, and the "furnish" offered to some of the sharecroppers (those with big families who produced large quantities of cotton) all had to be deducted. Each year, it was the same thing. We always seemed to come out in the hole, no matter how hard we worked.

A few days before one particular Christmas, when I was about three years old, my stepfather went to settlement. This year there was genuine hope that things would be better. My mother, stepfather, and sister had worked especially hard. I had been taken to the doctor a time or two for my tonsils and adenoids but nothing really major, so there was reason to hope that this year would be different. Waiting to see how you came out was always charged with great expectancy, despite the many disappointments of the past. So, just as my stepfather waited at the commissary, we waited at home. It was the same all over the plantation. We all stayed up waiting, and even if we fell asleep on the floor, we'd soon awaken to see if our fathers had returned with any good news at all. When my stepfather did return, he was angrier than he'd ever been. Unable to vent his frustrations toward the bookkeeper or the owner, he came home and vented them toward his family. He now knew that there was nothing he could have done to turn the books in his favor. He simply took the twenty-five dollars the planter/owner loaned him and gave it to my mother and sister. The owner wanted it to be known that he was no Scrooge. He understood the meaning of Christmas, so he was quite prepared to lend my stepfather a few dollars against the next year's crop so that I could have a visit from Santa Claus and my sister might perhaps get an outfit. Although I was quite young, I remember this episode very well. At least, I remember the beautiful blue and white jumper suit my sister purchased for me. Later on, I learned the details of how it was acquired. I don't believe that my stepfather kept any of the money for himself. With her portion, my sister bought me the wonderful blue outfit, which I could now wear to the Walthall Theater on Saturday afternoon and to church on Sunday. I don't feel that I was ever able to repay that act of generosity and love, though I've tried.

Borrowing against next year's crop was a way of perpetuating a vicious cycle of indebtedness. At settlement time, a stack of money lay on the table, and some of the hands were asked what they wanted to borrow. This open offer, of course, was extended only to those who were considered reliable and had made money for the owner in the past. Others were offered something closer to twenty or twenty-five dollars. There was at least one case in which a sharecropper fled the plantation, and presumably his debt, which he thought was unfair and too large a sum to repay in any case. With his fire going and smoke coming out his chimney to give the impression he was still at home, he lit out one night for one of the large urban centers, most likely Detroit, St. Louis, or Chicago. This is the way many black sharecroppers avoided being held in peonage by the system.

William Alexander Percy, among others, attempted to justify the system by claiming for it a general benevolence. Percy's grandfather, for whom he was named and to whom he referred as "Fafar," was responsible for reestablishing white supremacy in his part of the Delta. During Reconstruction, blacks had been elected to such offices as sheriff and justice of the peace, and it was Fafar Percy who successfully disfranchised them—an act that required vote buying, the stuffing of ballot boxes, chicanery, and intimidation. Percy felt that his grandfather's actions were justified, because in his mind blacks were unfit to hold public office.

After emancipation, Fafar had made a contract with the newly freed blacks to provide them with food and shelter for their manual labor. According to his grandson, it was an arrangement initiated by the blacks themselves after they discovered that while slaves were not allowed to go hungry, freedmen could go hungry and often did. The contract was explained thus:

> I have land which you need, and you have muscle which I need; let's put what we've got in the same pot and call it ours. I'll give you all the land you can work, a house to live in, a garden plot and room to raise chickens, hogs, and cows if you can come by them, and all the wood you want to cut for fuel. I'll direct and oversee you. I'll get you a doctor when you are sick. Until the crop comes in I'll try to keep you

> from going hungry or naked in so far as I am able. I'll pay the taxes and I'll furnish the mules and plows and whatever else is necessary to make a crop, this is what I promise to do. When the crop is picked, half of it will be mine and half of it yours.[1]

This seems to be a fair explanation of how the sharecropping system ideally should have worked. Percy's effort to defend the system notwithstanding, it often proved grossly unfair to black sharecroppers.

My stepfather was proof of this. He was, like many other blacks on this plantation, well mannered in his dealings with whites. But one day something got into him, and he asked to see the books so as to determine for himself what his fair share should be. This was taken as an act of great insolence: no one should dare to question the bookkeeper's fairness in dealing with black tenants.

In her research in the early 1930s in Indianola, Mississippi, anthropologist Hortense Powdermaker reached a conclusion much like my stepfather's about the realities of sharecropping: "Unless the landlord or manager presents a statement of purchases from the plantation store and receipts from the cotton, the tenant rarely asks for it. If he is illiterate, it would not do him much good. He may know how to read and figure, and still not be shrewd enough to want a statement. He may want it and know indeed it would be impossible to get, or simply be afraid to ask for it." She further contended:

> One reason for preferring Negro to white labor on plantations is the inability of the Negro to make or enforce demands for a just statement, or for any statement at all. He may hope for protection, justice, honesty, from his landlord, but he cannot demand them. There is no force to back up a demand, neither the law, the vote, nor public opinion. Even a request voiced too insistently, may lead to trouble. The landlord may become offended or angry, in which case there are ways open to him for retaliation and for forcing submission.[2]

Even William Alexander Percy himself admitted that the system allowed for dishonesty to reign, for as he noted:

> The Negro is no more on an equality with the white man in plantation matters than in any other dealings between the two. The white

planter may charge an exorbitant rate of interest, he may allow the share-cropper less than the market price received for his cotton, he may cheat him in a thousand different ways, and the Negro's redress is merely theoretical.[3]

Terry Butler Sr., one of the more productive sharecroppers on Whittington Plantation, learned this lesson very early on, though he had no such luck in passing it on to his son, Terry Junior. While the younger man preferred to see the figures, the old man always told the owner that since the amount wouldn't change, he would just accept the figure on the bottom line. He did this not so much to acknowledge the bookkeeper's honesty but to save time and accept the inevitable.

Notes

1. William Alexander Percy, *Lanterns On the Levee: Recollections of a Planter's Son* (1941; repr., Baton Rouge: Louisiana State Univ. Press, 1973), 276.

2. Hortense Powdermaker, *After Freedom: A Cultural Study in the Deep South* (1939; repr., New York: Russell & Russell, 1968), 86.

3. Percy, *Lanterns on the Levee*, 284.

ONE-ROOM SCHOOLHOUSE

> The function of education is to teach one to think intensively and to think critically. Intelligence plus character—that is the goal of true education.
>
> **Martin Luther King Jr., "The Purpose of Education"**

Unlike some of my classmates, who were eighteen when they graduated from high school, I was nineteen when I got my diploma in 1963. This was true not only for me but for several others who spent their first years attending plantation schools. In those days, as I've mentioned, school was held only during those times when blacks weren't needed in the fields. This situation began to change as I moved into the second and third grades. But I spent my first years in Little Primer, Big Primer, and the first grade going from one school to the next. And as far as I can recollect, those schools weren't open year round. I recall trying to convince my mother that I had spent enough time in first grade and should be in second grade, but having no report card to indicate a promotion, I was stuck. And that's why I was older than many of my classmates when things finally did change and I started attending school regularly.

As far back as I can remember, I always wanted to go to school. Perhaps this resulted from fear of what would happen if I didn't go. My mother and stepfather both instilled in me the importance of getting an education so that I wouldn't have to pick and chop cotton or do some other menial task all my life. Of my first year or so spent attending a rural plantation school, I only remember the long cold walk in the winter and our stopping at Craig's store to buy pencils and cinnamon rolls. By the time I got to the one-room school house, the bigger boys were already there and had made the fire in the pot-bellied stove.

The next year I moved to another one-room schoolhouse in the Buckeye. This building was located next to our church, Good Hope. The large room housed all grades from first to twelfth. The children in the upper grades often assisted Miss Ollie B. Sims, our teacher, with the younger children. They checked our spelling and arithmetic. One teacher couldn't possibly attend to so many different levels in a single day, but she did the best she could along with her assistant, Miss Price. A stout, handsome woman of dark complexion, Miss Sims was completely dedicated to teaching. She knew that, given our situation, she had to do much more than teach facts. She had to motivate us and instill within us a sense of dignity and pride. When words failed to reach us, she didn't mind using the strap or a switch to get our attention.

Since we had no cafeteria in which to receive meals, hot or cold, we had to bring our lunches to school. On some occasions, Miss Sims permitted one or two of the older, more responsible boys to go to Mr. Dantone's store around 11:30 to get us Baby Ruth candy bars, Double Colas, Stage Plank cookies, and Moon Pies, which would fuel our bodies through the afternoon.

There were no indoor plumbing facilities of any type. We had to use the twin outhouses, generally understood to be one for males and one for females. These were the same outhouses the church used on Sundays and Wednesday evenings. We had to ask for permission to leave the room. If we stayed too long, we were sure to get a good switching from Miss Sims when we got back.

As with most children our age, we looked forward to recess. It was a gay time. The younger boys and girls popped the whip and played ring around the roses or jacks, while the bigger children were involved with more serious pursuits such as spinning the bottle and playing house. We could hear one of the boys in another small circle cry out, "I'm in the well."

"How deep?" someone asked.

"Ten feet," came the reply.

"What's it gon' t' take to get you out?"

"A sweet kiss," he said.

"From who?"

Most of kids wanted a kiss from Lucy Dell, a fair-skinned girl from up the road. I don't remember any of the darker-skinned girls getting asked for kisses. When the name of the desired one was given, the episode concluded and another lad entered the circle to begin the game all over again.

I attended McLaurin Street School in Greenwood for second grade and was in Mrs. Collier's room. She was a dark beauty, and I fantasized about her being my wife. In the third grade, I again had Miss Sims, who had by now made her way to the city schools. I particularly remember this as a most important year. Teaching only one grade, Miss Sims could be much more effective than she had been at the one-room Buckeye school. I remember learning a great deal of material, but mostly I recall the spelling bees we had at least once a week. Often it was the boys against the girls, and usually it came down to Emma Clay and me, dueling to the finish.

Before the county provided buses for those of us living on the plantations and in the Buckeye, we had to get to school the best way we could. For most of the year we could walk the two or three miles to school, but during the colder months it was most unpleasant to walk. There was a gentleman who owned a truck and provided transportation for the children at a cost of three or four dollars per week, depending on whether one sat in the cab or not. This truck was often crowded and very unpleasant for anyone sitting in the back during the winter months. But it was the only transportation we had, since the cost of a taxi was prohibitive. But even this mode of transportation didn't help my own situation a great deal. The plantation foreman didn't allow the truck to pick up on the plantation. This was the same gentleman who insisted, when I reached the age of seven or eight, that I should help out with the field work. This situation, along with a number of others, fed my desire to obtain as much schooling as possible. For this reason, I find it difficult to understand why some younger blacks play hooky from school. While my strivings to get an education were not nearly as difficult as those Frederick Douglass and other slaves faced, it was certainly much more difficult than it should have been. Vestiges of the codes prohibiting anyone to teach blacks to read and write were still found in the plantation system. But efforts to prevent me from getting an education only encouraged me all the more.

During the days when I had to walk to school from Whittington, I had to contend with the bulldogs the white children tried to sic on us. We were in a tough situation, as we couldn't hit the dogs nor did we want to get bitten. Many of us had to go far out of our way getting to and from school.

Our situation improved tremendously when school buses were approved for transporting us to and from school. I had only a short walk to the highway from our house. From where I lived, I could watch the bus as it went to the Buckeye to pick up passengers. I would have sufficient time to make it to the highway to catch the bus on its return. Because we were bused to school, some of the city kids liked to refer to us as bus people. I never minded this at all, for I knew that my being able to go to school under any circumstances was sufficient motivation to keep me at the head of the class.

G STREET BOYS

> I insist that the object of all true education is not to make men carpenters, it is to make carpenters men.
>
> W. E. B. Du Bois, "The Talented Tenth"

Believing we could do better in town than on the plantation, my family moved to 804 Avenue G in Greenwood around 1957, when I was about thirteen. About that same time or a little later, two other families with teenage boys moved to homes on Avenue G, the McNeals and the Elliotts. It was a matter of providence that we should all end up there at the same time, and we began a friendship that continues to this day. At that time, we didn't make much of this happenstance. We just played together and generally enjoyed each other's company. We especially liked to race down Avenue G and to play basketball behind Stone Street School. Jeffie McNeal and I often studied together as we were both at the same grade level and were enrolled together in several classes. Jeffie had a good mind with a special gift for recalling details and historical facts. Although the Elliotts—Roy, Joe, and Frank—were a bit ahead of us, their younger sister, Minnie, to whom I was especially attracted, was at our grade level, and like Jeffie, Minnie was a good student.

    We all lived in rather small houses, although we probably didn't realize just how small they were at the time. Typically, they were shotgun houses of three rooms: front room, middle room, and kitchen, with a very small bathroom. The houses were built on the same pattern as those on the plantation we had just left. At first, our house had only one room and a kitchen, which was not considered too crowded since there were just three of us there at the time. Edna had married by then and lived in St. Louis. My mother and stepfather slept in the front room, and I had a small bed in the kitchen. Our house was annexed to Mrs. Ethel Edwards's store in something like an L-shape, such that the one room stood alongside the store but farther back from the street, while the kitchen curled right behind the store. When her husband built another small room at the front of the house, we thought that we were living in luxury.

Perhaps we were, compared with other, much larger families who had to live in houses about the same size as ours. For example, Jeffie and his two brothers, John and Charlie, all lived in such a place. His mother slept in the front room and the three boys slept in the middle room, with Jeffie and John sharing a bed and Charlie sleeping alone on a cot in the same room. At one point, the Elliotts had as many as nine people living in their three-room house. Needless to say, almost no one had a bed to himself, but this was generally the case throughout our community. In fact, it was rare indeed to see a house without a bed in the front room or one with a bed that wasn't shared. But through it all, none of us on Avenue G considered ourselves to be poor. We had clothes to wear and food to eat. I didn't particularly care for my stepfather standing in line with the poor folks to pick up the cheese, canned beef, and powdered milk that the government provided to the indigent. It was only later, after living in houses with living rooms and dens that had no beds in them, that my friends and I came to realize that we had been poor and occupied substandard housing.

The boys in the G Street gang had at least one other thing in common. Our parents had all recently been sharecroppers, though on different plantations. The Elliotts worked on a plantation in Duck Hill, and the McNeals lived on Charles Whittington's place, while my family lived on Charles's brother's place. Since there were few jobs to be had in the city, we continued to go to the field when we weren't in school. Having left the plantation, we weren't sharecroppers at this point but hired hands who were paid at the end of each day. We were roused at 3:30 AM so as to be ready to catch the truck for the field, which came by around 4:00. As our parents usually accompanied us, we were generally awakened in time to catch the truck. Most of the time we went to the field in a truck driven by "Miss Nancy"—that was the only name we knew her by—who lived down the street from us on Avenue G. In those rare situations when we weren't ready for the truck when it came by the 82 Grill to pick us up, we knew that we could always catch it at the Chinese store a few blocks away at the corner of Percy and Roosevelt. It always stopped there so that the hands could buy bologna, Vienna sausages, potted meat, sardines, and the crackers or light bread they used to make sandwiches. The only concern was that there wouldn't be space for everyone. As Miss Nancy was paid fifty cents per field hand, it was to her advantage to get as many folks onto the truck as she could. This overcrowding, of course, worked only to her advantage and not to ours.

Of the many times we boarded this truck to pick or chop cotton, there was one time in particular that Jeffie, John, and I recall with some hilarity. When the three of us boarded the cotton truck that morning, we had no reason to think it would be different from any other morning when we went to the fields. We had our brown bags containing the makings for our lunches. As we took our places, the small pickup truck had already begun to fill up, so we had to weave our way carefully through the women, men, and children who had already claimed the best seats. When we arrived at Charles Whittington's place, we saw that the cotton that day was especially bad. Knowing there would be little to harvest, I quickly realized that I wouldn't do well that day. Jeffie and especially John, both of them much better pickers than I was, were not interested either. So we decided to partake in a favorite pastime: we ran track on the levee in full view of the older folks who were determined to make the best of a bad situation. We had no such commitment. So, after we tired ourselves out, we simply walked off and hitched a ride back to Greenwood.

I was never much good at picking cotton, even after I got older. I couldn't understand how I could work alongside my mother and she always ended up with almost twice the amount of cotton I had. One day I made a conscious effort to keep up with her, no matter what. I was certainly working as hard, even harder than she was. I decided to choose two rows just as she did and keep up with her, but first I had to determine that her rows weren't better than my own. I found two good rows beside hers. My effort to match her energy and keep up with her was tough going. When she filled her first sack around 9:30, my own sack seemed too puny to take to the scales. But I did anyway, finding she had still outpicked me. What was going on? It made no sense to me. (Someone later suggested that I probably left some cotton on the stalks.)

Whether chopping or picking, tending the cotton fields from dawn to dusk is hard, demeaning work. *Chopping* cotton, I should note, refers to weeding and thinning the plants with a hoe to ensure a more bountiful yield. *Picking* cotton, of course, refers to harvesting the plant. For chopping, everyone was paid the same per day, whether the sum was two, three (as it most often was), or four dollars, depending on the generosity of the plantation owner. The most I ever made in any one day for chopping cotton was four dollars, and I only reached that level for a short period near the end of my days in the field. If we were asked to help the owner out on another of his plantations or to help a fellow sharecropper on the same plantation get caught up, we were paid much less, something like two dollars a day. It was a ridiculously low amount, even for those days. But it was the way we were able to help out at home and have money for school clothes.

My friends and I often quizzed one another on history or political science to make the long days of chopping cotton go faster. Jeffie, I remember, with his excellent recall and great enthusiasm, was our leader, and he asked us many questions about the First or Second World War, or about various presidential candidates and their running mates. I suppose my own forte was recalling various quotations from noted authors and citing biblical passages and expounding on their meaning. My favorite subject was word origins. Various others lent their own special knowledge to our intellectual pursuits. In this way, we managed to make sure that the "ignorant stick," as we termed the hoe, wasn't a tool that kept us in darkness but became instead an instrument of intellectual empowerment. We made sure that "ignorant" referred to the tool we were using and not to ourselves. As much as possible, given the situation, I actually looked forward to going to the field with the G Street gang, with John and Jeffie and Minnie and her brothers: Teen (Roy) and Frank and Joe. But when it was time to report to school, we were more than ready to return.

We were too busy to play any games while picking cotton, for which our take-home pay depended on the amount we harvested, usually about three bucks per 100 pounds. For this labor I never made much money. While some of my friends could boast of picking close to 300 or 400 pounds, I had a very good day whenever I could pick over 150 pounds.

Two of my classmates, Charles Griffin and Michael Lindsey, who didn't have to go to the field, decided that staying home was not much fun either. After pressuring their parents to let them go to the field, they both had memorable experiences. Michael misunderstood what chopping cotton really meant and proceeded to *chop up* the cotton until he was told what he was supposed to do. Charles reported having a similar experience and that he actually passed out from the hot labor and had to complete the day by changing places with the water boy. In any case, Charles's mother soon discovered that the lunch of chicken and sodas and fruits and cakes cost more than he stood to earn. This, coupled with the torrid heat, spelled the end of his field days.

Recently, Mary Alice Buckner, another classmate, told me of an experience similar to that of Charles and Michael. She had pressed her father to let her go to the fields with him, but he would rather have paid her to stay home than to follow him there. "Sallie," he begged his wife, "keep Mary Alice at home with you." Since her father owned the bus that transported the field hands, Mary Alice was allowed to carry the water bucket. Considered an easy job, it still demanded that one haul around a heavy, water-filled bucket in the hot summer sun and then endure the complaints of workers who were cross because the water didn't arrive fast enough or because the dipper was soiled with someone else's snuff or tobacco juice. (Those who twisted and turned the dipper to find that one clean spot by the handle soon realized the futility of the task.) Carrying water was a thankless job, in other words, and, truth be told, there were few if any meaningful activities for youth in Greenwood, especially if you were black.

On Saturday evenings, the G Street Boys often met at Mrs. Ellen Jackson's house on Percy Street. She had one of the few televisions in the neighborhood and a house large enough to accommodate us all. We realized that it was cheaper and safer to watch TV and stay away from downtown. Furthermore, it was much more fun, and our parents liked the idea of having us nearby. Although I never heard Mrs. Jackson or her husband complain about our being there, it must have been quite an imposition on her family. But we never felt unwelcome. We were fairly quiet and well behaved, but to have five or six youngsters going in and out of one's house throughout the day and night was intrusive, to say the least. We watched such shows as *Gunsmoke, Have Gun Will Travel,* and *The Rifleman.* Our favorite pastime was checkers. Since we played so often, we got to be pretty fair players. Of our group, there were two boys, Joe Elliott and his brother Franklin (or Yank, as we called him), who came closest to challenging the best players in town, including my uncle Obe and "Prof" Threadgill, the high school principal.

We all graduated from high school but then went our separate ways. The brothers Elliott all served with distinction in the army. Frank and Roy made careers of their military service. Frank served twenty-seven years and rose to the rank of first sergeant. Roy served thirty years, rising to the rank of command sergeant major. Their brother, Joe, retired after serving for ten years and later joined the Greenwood Fire Department, becoming the first African American in the town's history to rise to the position of assistant fire chief. A street near one of the firehouses was named in his honor in 2009.

The McNeal brothers also joined the army. John retired after serving twenty-four years and rising to the rank of sergeant first class. He now lives in Tacoma, Washington. His brother, Jeffie, attended Tuskegee Institute, where he graduated in June 1968 and was commissioned a second lieutenant. He rose to the rank of captain in three years and now lives in Dallas with his wife, Nora. They both are proud of their daughter, Nneka, who earned an undergraduate degree in chemistry from the University of Pennsylvania in 1996; she later finished medical school and a surgical residency in obstetrics and gynecology. She is now a practicing physician in a major city.

Friendships begun in the 1950s and strengthened and challenged by many turbulent events of the era, including the civil rights movement and the Vietnam War, have nevertheless continued over the years.

SCHOOLMATES

> The man who shoots and burns and drowns us is surely our enemy, but so is he who cripples our children for life with inferior public education.
>
> **Roy Wilkins, NAACP Convention speech, 1969**

> There was never a time in my youth, no matter how dark and discouraging the days might be, when one resolve did not continually remain with me, and that was a determination to secure an education at any cost.
>
> **Booker T. Washington, *Up from Slavery***

While I felt a special connection with the boys on Avenue G, I had many close friends who lived throughout the city. One of my closest friends was Albert Garner, whose name appears prominently in several of these fragments. We attended the same church and worked alongside each other in the civil rights movement. Indeed, I was at his home so often that his mother treated me like one of her own children. Albert was bright and exhibited leadership skills that landed him such positions as superintendent of the Sunday school, senior class president, and student government judge. Judge Garner, as we called him, took his job seriously. He was responsible for sentencing any student found guilty of such charges as loitering in the hall without a pass or chewing gum in class. He had such a reputation for fairness that he once sentenced his own girlfriend, Cora Markham, to mop the hall after she was found guilty of some minor violation. He explained to her that he couldn't show any favoritism and that his job required that he be fair to all students, which seemed to her at first as unnecessary and cruel. Later she saw it as a mark of integrity in the man who would become her husband.

The students in our school system who later went on to outstanding careers are too numerous to name here. But it's clear that the lack of equipment and a poor physical plant didn't keep some students from excelling at the very highest levels. Actors Morgan Freeman and Tonea Stewart and playwright Endesha Ida Mae Holland have earned praise for their contributions to stage and screen. Willye B. White, the celebrated Olympian, grew up only a couple of blocks from me and sometimes returned to Broad Street High School to offer her knowledge and encouragement to those of us on the track team. I mention these individuals not so much to boast about what Greenwood produced but to offer them as inspiration and role models to a younger generation too easily distracted by the lure of a quick buck and material excess.

I certainly had role models not only among the faculty but among the student body as well. Among the older students, there were a number of outstanding scholars who competed with one another in the classroom just as others did on the athletic field. Individuals such as Wisdom F. Coleman, Louis McCaskill, Mary Threadgill, Mary Lou Taylor, Annie Garner, Pauline Pearson, Leo Buchannan, and many more removed any stigma from being smart. My favorite in this regard was Fred L. McDowell, who was three years ahead of me in school. I admired Fred because he was as meticulous in diction as he was in dress. Because of his high seriousness, he appeared older than he actually was. His role model seemed to be his government teacher, James Robinson, who had a knack for eloquence and fine dress.

Although I lacked the focus and discipline that Fred exhibited, I shared with him a love for language and *le mot juste* that led both of us into teaching. We both thought that missing class was an unpardonable sin, punishable by a lowered grade. We simply expected students to attend class regularly. It never made sense to either of us that students would pay for something they didn't want to receive. Fred was serious when he told his students that he expected them to be in class unless they were dead or dying. Fred, who seemed to be sick his entire life, probably made this pronouncement as he was suffering acutely from his final illness. Earning his PhD, he embarked on a college teaching career, only to die at the age of thirty-seven. We will never know what contributions he might have made had he not died at such an early age.

Unlike Fred, my friend Joe Lee Lofton had no great inclinations toward the scholarly or intellectual life. Yet, he did achieve some academic success, earning both undergraduate and master's degrees. Joe was a resourceful individual, and when he wanted something, he went for it, no matter the cost. He could even be a bit foolhardy on occasion, as on the night he chased some white boys down an alley and into a building where he ended up hiding from the police while in plain view of two white prostitutes. There is no doubt that Joe Lofton could hustle with the best of them. He got his gasoline from Jake McGhee, the school bus driver, who after filling up his bus, allowed Joe to siphon off some of it. Joe went to extremes to get the siphon started, sometimes swallowing a bit of gas as he primed the line.

On another occasion, Joe needed a bumper for his 1953 Pontiac and learned of a similar car at the junkyard with a bumper he could use—that is, if he could get the thing off. On the night he decided to go after the bumper, he found a few things standing in his way, including a big dog and a fence. Joe managed to avoid the dog, crawled under the fence, and crept slowly to the car. There was the shiny bumper, but Joe saw that he couldn't pry it loose because of all the rust that had collected on the old car over the years. Ever resourceful, Joe went back for some oil to apply to the rusted parts. When this didn't yield results, he tried again—and again—on subsequent nights. Each time he crawled on his belly so as not to be spotted. On his last attempt, he discovered that the bumper had been sold that very day. Apparently, thanks to all the oil Joe had applied, the junk dealer was able get the bumper off. The dealer probably thought it was serendipity, but in fact it was Joe Lofton.

Being a friend of Joe Lofton had its advantages. Joe was one of the few classmates who had a car and a steady job. He also had a shoe-shine business that kept him busy. He was always generous and kind towards Jeffie and me. He hired Jeffie to shine shoes and employed us every so often to help clean the department store where he worked. He did his best to teach me to drive, though his best effort only landed me in a ditch. There was a young lady I wished to impress, and as I drove past her home, I had my eyes on her window instead of the road. I'm glad she wasn't looking, because I certainly didn't want her to see me in the ditch.

This was not my only experience of a driving mishap or of trying to gain the attention and affection of young ladies. I enlisted my friend Robert Hampton to help me get my driver's license the very day of the high school prom. With my permit, I could drive Hamp's car as long as he was with me. I was doing all right, I suppose, until I swung too wide making a right turn and ended up hitting a car parked along the street. Hamp to this day will not let me forget that, while I settled the matter with the owner of the car I hit, I still haven't paid for the damage to his car.

With no car of my own, I depended heavily on Joe Lee to get around, and he often took me along with him when he went for gas at Jake McGhee's house. While Joe filled up his tank, I spent the time talking to Jake's sister, Anne. Later on, as I became more involved in the civil rights movement, I spent most of my time in the company of Dorothy "Cookie" Greene, whose entire family was involved in the Greenwood movement. It was a good thing she didn't insist on being driven the short distance to the Walthall Theater or to the café in the Hotel Plaza. I was never quite the Romeo that a certain classmate was. That fellow, proud of his sexual prowess, told my friend Charles Griffin, in more direct and earthy language, that while Charles might *talk* to a lot of girls, he didn't do a lot of scoring. But for Charles, me, and a number of others, building friendships was a more important goal.

MY TEACHERS

> Many a child called dull would advance rapidly under a patient, wise, and skillful teacher, and the teacher should be as conscientious in the endeavor to improve himself as he is to improve the child.
>
> **Frances Coppin,** *Reminiscences of School Life*

> While most girls run away from home to marry, I ran away from home to teach.
>
> **Mary Church Terrell,** *A Colored Woman in the White World*

As I mentioned earlier, I always liked school, perhaps because I feared the alternative. My mother assured me that if I stayed in school, the heaviest thing I would pick up would be a pencil. That was a good bargain for someone who had spent his childhood on a southern plantation. Not only would I go to school, but I would try my best never to stop going to school.

Fortunately, as someone who enjoyed going to school, I have throughout my life been blessed with great teachers, men and women, black and white, American and foreign-born. Some were nationally and internationally known and had achieved honors and awards commensurate with their status. I am pleased to note several of those scholars here, though a complete list is impossible. At Morehouse, I was privileged to study under Stephen Henderson, Delores Stephens, and Jeanette Hume, who taught English, and E. A. Jones, who taught French. Vincent Harding and C. Eric Lincoln taught me in seminars during the summer terms. I studied under Madame Susanne Hughes, Al Raboteau, and Michael Cook in classes in Nantes, Princeton, and Yale, respectively. At Atlanta University, Richard Barksdale directed my master's thesis and Richard Long, Charles Duncan, and Barbara Higgins ushered me through the English Department. At the University of Chicago, Charles Long, George Kent, Anthony C. Yu, Giles Gunn, and Jonathan Z. Smith taught classes in literature, religion, and comparative religion, which helped prepare me for work with the eminent scholar Nathan A. Scott Jr., who had studied under Paul Tillich and others. A tough taskmaster, Professor Scott insisted on only the best from his students. It was he who shepherded me through many revisions of my doctoral thesis.

All these individuals and many more I could name played a significant role in my education. But none have had quite the impact on my life and career as those who taught me during my formative years in Greenwood. They knew their students and understood them better than the students understood themselves. In some cases, they had been around long enough to have taught our parents and older siblings. We might have thought we were hiding things from them, but to them our lives were an open book. They had our number. As appropriate, they begged, cajoled, teased, and punished us, but most of all they encouraged and loved us. Thus, what we learned from them was much more than what came from textbooks. That our textbooks and lab equipment were often worn and outdated mattered only slightly as they were able to supplement these resources with their own ingenuity, imagination, and life experiences. From them I learned lessons about life and to trust my instincts, which proved valuable later on in college and graduate school.

Several of my teachers, such as Miss Ollie B. Sims, whom I've already talked about, and Miss A. O. Martin, achieved legendary status because of their longevity in the school system and because they had taught generations of students. In several cases, they had taught our parents, aunts, uncles, and many of our other teachers.

Miss Martin preached that cleanliness was next to godliness. She frequently left her classroom to wash her hands and mouth (yes, her mouth!) especially if someone had the nerve to say something silly or, God forbid, use foul language in her presence. She often called her students black, which coming from anyone else, was reason for a fight. But from her it referred not to our skin but to our hearts. She was very eccentric, to say the least, and most of us thought she was a bit "touched," but there is little doubt she was especially effective in teaching grammar, the multiplication tables, and all else that fifth graders were supposed to know.

Like most of my schoolmates, I didn't fully appreciate the work that our teachers put in and the numerous sacrifices they made on our behalf. Mrs. Olivia Perry, for example, taught English and French, coached the debating team, wrote speeches, and played the piano for a local Baptist church two Sundays each month. When I studied in France, I sent her a postcard thanking her for helping prepare me for my work there. She was kind enough to place the card on her bulletin board for all to learn about the good things that had happened to one of her former students.

Coaches such as William Ware, Minnie Barfield, and George Twyner taught classes in their subject fields and often outside their areas of expertise, ran homerooms, and served as head coaches in one sport and assistant coaches in several others. A typical day for them might begin at seven in the morning and not end until well after seven in the evening. The schedules of many other teachers were equally onerous. Consider, for example, Leola Williams, who directed the senior class play, coached the dramatics club and verse speaking choir, wrote speeches for competition, served as senior class sponsor, and read drafts of her colleagues' papers and theses.

Then there was Thomas "Quote" Barnes, who taught government by having us conduct our student government elections in the manner that presidential elections are held under the current two-party system. Our two parties were the Blue and the White. The process resembled U.S. presidential politics in every way, including, speeches, debates, and conventions. I was the candidate of the Blue Party, while Tommy Hoskins was the White Party's candidate. So serious were the rivalries that I came very near to blows with Bill Perry, the advisor of the White Party. Our advisor was Solomon N. "Chief" Outlaw, who always rallied us with his call, "Remember the Blue." Thus we learned about government by being involved in it.

Of all my teachers, I felt closest to Chief Outlaw. He was a gifted instructor who made learning a pleasant experience or, rather, as pleasant as history could be made for teenagers. In his way, he made the personages we were studying come alive. He was especially gifted at phrase making, which often helped us remember an important idea. "No work, no eat," he often reminded us as he explained an important aspect of the Protestant ethic. He had this knack for bringing out the point of the lesson with some appropriate aphorism. For those who insisted on not learning despite being given every opportunity, Chief Outlaw would say, "You can lead a horse to the well, but you can't make him drink." And what young woman failed to get his message when the Chief said, "If a mule kicks you once, it's the mule's fault, mean mule? But if that same mule kicks you again, it's your fault. You like the way that mule kicks." The sharpest and most piercing arrow in his quiver was reserved for those who seemed completely beyond redemption: "You're a good fuck thrown away." The Chief, in fact, had so many such sayings that one could compile a small compendium of his most famous utterances. He was, in all other respects, a deeply religious man who was completely dedicated to his students. I had great affection for the man, and he seemed to have had a similar affection for me. I don't know of any students who, looking back, would disagree with my assessment of him. When he left the classroom for the principal's office (where he was an able administrator), there was a great void that has gone unfilled perhaps even to this day. I was deeply honored when he asked me to speak on the occasion of his retirement from the Greenwood school system.

Mrs. Leola Williams, however, was the instructor who had the greatest intellectual impact on my life and career. She taught me English and Latin and wrote the speeches I delivered for oratorical contests. She directed the short plays we performed in statewide drama competitions, which brought our school major honors. I often teamed with Tommie Harris, Gary Harper, Willie Buckner, and others to bring back such awards as best actor, best actress, and best play. I simply don't remember a time when Broad Street High didn't bring home at least one or more of the major awards. She was simply that good and a force to be reckoned with in language arts circles throughout the state and the South. She could count Morgan Freeman, Tonea Stewart (Tommie Harris), Fred Spruell, Alice Leonard, and many others among her charges. She demanded clear diction and enunciation of those who worked closely with her. I remember the one time I tried to deliver a speech with a southern drawl, so prominent among southern congressmen from Mississippi. She would tolerate no such affectation and roundly criticized me for what she considered a mistake and poor judgment on my part. I never did that again.

My interests in oratory and the theatrical arts were fed by my love for language. Mrs. Williams's classes in Latin fueled the fire within me for the magic of words. By learning Latin prefixes and suffixes, I could often decipher the meaning of words, especially the longer and more complex ones. In certain instances, I tried to use the roots together with various prefixes and suffixes to create what I thought were new words, only to find that they, or close variants, already existed. While some of my classmates spent their study periods socializing or doing homework, I usually spent that time perusing the dictionary in search of interesting and curious words. My fellow students didn't consider me strange for this, for there were many others who wanted to excel in math, history, or science. Our teachers supplemented such pursuits by giving of their time to sponsor math and other clubs after school.

Thus, when I consider the wonderful teachers I had growing up in Greenwood, it's difficult to look upon myself as academically underprivileged in any real sense. We certainly didn't have the facilities that were found at Greenwood High, but I can't believe that that school had more dedicated and caring teachers than those at Broad Street. It is perhaps always the case that a generation will see all succeeding ones as lacking in some regard. Many of us knew that after integration came, things would be different, hopefully better but maybe worse. I happen to believe that all the changes were not for the better. Would black students be nominated for and receive the academic and social awards and honors they had received at Broad Street? Perhaps even more important, would students be afforded the individual and special attention that often spelled the difference between success and failure?

On the positive side, perhaps there would be a better physical plant and more facilities. Teachers would not be so overworked and could enjoy classes with fewer students. And most of all, perhaps equal pay would be available for black and white teachers, which was a most vexing problem during my youth. It seemed to me that, if anything, blacks should be paid more because they had to work much harder. They not only had to teach, but they often were called upon, because of their education, to organize and head various civic and social programs. And if you happened to be an English teacher, you could expect to be asked to help write letters and proposals. Solomon Outlaw not only taught us history but was often called upon to help fill out IRS tax forms. The shop teacher was asked to help remodel houses in the community. I wonder now how they were able to do all that without the aid of computers.

As I contemplate the present state of affairs, I realize that this whole era is long gone. I don't think that the present generation of teachers lacks the training that the older ones had, but I do question the dedication. Yet perhaps an even greater problem is that teachers today, because of various laws regarding privacy and restrictions on punishment, are not permitted to be as actively involved in the lives of their students as they once were.

Nothing I've said regarding the strength and dedication of my teachers should imply that I think they were perfect and not prone to error like anyone else. Being human, of course, meant that they weren't without their shortcomings. I've heard, for example, that some of the younger male teachers competed with their students for the affection and attention of certain female students in high school. This might well have happened in a few cases, although I am aware of just one. It's perhaps not so surprising since our instructors were often only a few years older than we were. Generally, however, the teachers comported themselves with the dignity and grace that they demanded of us. In most cases they became our role models for decorum and standards of etiquette and good taste. This shouldn't be taken to mean that they were in any way soft. For those students who were determined to be rude and disruptive, they more than found their match in our math teacher Frances Robertson and our chemistry teacher "Fess" Hayes. Indeed, those who took Mr. Hayes's class will recall his reminder to any disruptive student that "the old man ran the class, and the student only ran his shoes over." Mrs. Robertson, meanwhile, had no equal in verbal sparring with her students, but only with those who insisted on acting out. This wasn't for me, for I had, as many others did, a great respect for and fear of Mrs. Robertson, who seemed to like me as well.

In general, I think our teachers deserve great credit for helping prepare us for the next stages in our lives. For some, it meant finding jobs or joining the military, but for a fairly large number of us, it would be attending college. That was the route that several of my closest friends and I chose. And Mrs. Lorrine Miller, the school guidance counselor, spent a great deal of time getting our records in order and sending along letters to support our applications.

GOING TO THE 'HOUSE

> It must be borne in mind that the tragedy of life does not lie in not reaching your goal. The tragedy of life lies in having no goal to reach.
>
> **Benjamin E. Mays, "What Man Lives By"**

I knew fairly early on that I would be going to college. Both my mother and stepfather, in their own ways, made great sacrifices on my behalf. My teachers and members of my church also expected it of me. I also knew that if I wanted to get the law degree that I thought at the time was essential to help my people, a college education was absolutely indispensable. I just didn't know where I would go. It's not that I had unlimited choices. I knew, for example, that I wouldn't attend a white school in Mississippi or even in the South for that matter. Blacks were only just beginning to desegregate those schools in the early 1960s. And all those who did—Harvey Gant in South Carolina, Vivian Malone and James Hood in Alabama, Charlayne Hunter and Hamilton Holmes in Georgia, Theotis Robinson in Tennessee, James Meredith in Mississippi—paid a very heavy price. My mother simply couldn't stand to see her son go through that kind of humiliation and danger. So my choices were actually limited to predominantly black colleges and to the white colleges in the North that might take a chance on southern blacks. Although my grades and motivation were good, I don't think that my test scores were high enough to land me in one of the premier colleges in the United

States with the financial aid I needed. The one school that expressed some interest in me was Amherst. Some civil rights workers I knew were willing to write recommendations to help me get in. I don't remember ever applying to Amherst. More likely choices for able blacks were Tougaloo, Howard, Tuskegee, Knoxville College, and Morehouse.

Many of the top students in my class attended Tougaloo, about one hundred miles south of Greenwood. The school had a good reputation in both academics and civil rights activism. Knoxville seemed to be a natural pipeline, since both the Broad Street High School principal and Leola Williams had graduated from there. Our school colors, garnet and blue, were the same as Knoxville's. I never knew whether this was by chance or design. A number of promising students attended Knoxville College. I also had two very good friends who went to Tuskegee, Jeffie McNeal and Claudette Phifer, but Thomas Barnes and, I suppose, several others decided I should attend Morehouse College. Mr. Barnes had done graduate work at Atlanta University and was apparently quite impressed with Morehouse, which was just next door. A student from Morehouse, Amos Brown, now senior pastor of the Third Baptist Church of San Francisco, paid me a brief visit. It was he who took charge of my application. My choice was also helped along by Dollie Scott, our class salutatorian, who had decided to attend Spelman College just across the street. Her uncle, Enoch Florence, had gone to Morehouse and enjoyed a degree of status as a Morehouse alumnus.

Morehouse had the reputation for producing more black doctors, lawyers, ministers, and college presidents than any school in the nation. Later, it could boast of its share of state and national political leaders.[1] It was known for producing a certain type or brand: "The Morehouse Man." He was proud, confident, and a leader among his people. Certainly, I wanted to be among this group of individuals.

Founded in 1867 by three individuals, including a former slave, in the basement of Springfield Baptist Church in Augusta, Georgia, Morehouse was originally known as the Augusta Institute. Like several other schools founded for the education of newly freed slaves, the school's first president, Joseph T. Robert, was a white man, as were Samuel Graves and George Sale, who followed him. John Hope was the school's first black president, although in appearance he, too, seemed white. While Hope and his predecessors had made notable achievements at this, the only historically black four-year college for men in the country, it was not until the presidency of Benjamin Elijah Mays (1940–67) that the school earned its reputation as a leading liberal arts college in the South and in the nation. The school boasted a long list of notable alumni, headed by Martin Luther King Jr.

Being accepted at Morehouse was only part of the task. I had to find some way to finance my education, and we had no money at all. I remember the joy of opening that fat envelope from Morehouse. The fatter the envelope, I was told, the better one's chance of receiving good news. I was accepted with a full-tuition scholarship. This was indeed good news, but even with this, I still didn't have enough money to pay for room and board, health insurance, and other incidental fees. Several family members and individuals in the community helped raise enough money for me to get to campus and have some spending change. When it came time for me to leave, tears welled up in my eyes. I remembered all those who had committed whatever funds they had and their love toward me. I remember sweet Samantha, my mother, as she stood watching her baby go away from home. It's a scene I'll never forget as I caught the Trailways bus for Atlanta.

When I arrived at Morehouse, I had very little, but I determined early on that I wasn't going to leave without my degree. The kind administrators and teachers at Morehouse did all they could to make sure that once there, financial considerations would not stand in the way of my receiving an education. The one person who was most instrumental in my receiving a college education was the late Julius Lockett, the college bursar; many a Morehouse man has been indebted to him for his creative and imaginative ways of making sure that every student serious about his studies and willing to work received the necessary financial aid to get through. At the end of my first year, I received one of the school's major scholarships. It had been awarded to someone else, but that person lost it because he hadn't met the minimum GPA requirement to keep it. This was certainly a godsend for me. This meant that I now had the financial resources to get my college education. With that worry behind me, I seemed to lose some of the hunger and fear that had motivated me during my freshman year, and I didn't make the Honor Roll the first semester of my sophomore year. Dr. Brailsford Brazeal, the academic dean, promptly chided me for a seeming lack of discipline and integrity. I soon righted the ship and kept on course for the rest of my time at Morehouse.

I was helped in this regard by the compulsory attendance at Tuesday morning chapel in Sale Hall. While any compulsory activity tends to make students rebellious, I don't think you can find a single alumnus who now regrets having had to attend chapel for that hour, when President Mays addressed us. We were told that there was no excuse for us not to succeed. He reminded us that each moment of our lives was precious and not to be wasted in idleness, for we had just so long to accomplish our goals. To underscore this, he pointed out that the poets John Keats and Percy B. Shelley died in their twenties but were still able, in their short lives, to create bodies of verse that would inspire generations. He taught us to be proud black men and that we were the equal of anyone. As a young man, Benjamin Mays once shocked his grandmother by saying that if he believed God had created him inferior, he would never pray again.

How could we not listen to Dr. Mays, whose parents were slaves and who was born in 1894 during one of the most repressive periods in our nation's history? None of us in that room could claim to have gone through what he had endured and survived. Yet he had been a Phi Beta Kappa graduate of Bates College, earned a PhD from the University of Chicago, and received over fifty honorary degrees. He had lent his name, even then, to more scholarships, lectures, and schools than almost any other black man in the United States with the exceptions of Booker T. Washington and Martin Luther King Jr. As he spoke to us, it was not about his accomplishments. He was much too humble for that. Having no son of his own, he told us of the values he would have wanted in a son. We felt, in a very real way, that we were his sons. He made us feel privileged and proud to be at Morehouse, and he seemed to have a certain way of intoning the school's name that conveyed both a sense of uniqueness and responsibility.

As with most other individuals, my college years marked my transition from adolescence to adulthood. It was filled with a number of wonderful memories. I met people at Morehouse and Spelman, both students and faculty members, who became lifelong friends. Amos Brown, whom I mentioned earlier as having had a hand in my attending Morehouse, was a homeboy from Jackson. During my freshman year, he was a resident assistant in the dormitory where I lived, and I was his roommate. One incident in particular I remember vividly. Some of the guys at Morehouse had made arrangements with a group of Spelman women who agreed to throw their panties from their dorm windows at an appointed time to the screaming men who waited expectantly below. As much as I wanted to participate in the "panty raid," I listened to Amos's wise counsel. Any untoward behavior on my part, he reminded me, could jeopardize my scholarship. I can't remember what punishment, if any, the students who did participate received, but Amos was correct in warning me that it wasn't worth taking the chance. Later, during my junior year, when I became a resident assistant in one of the freshman dormitories, I was able to give younger students the same kind of advice Amos had given me. And, of course, I had opportunities to meet the young ladies at Spelman under more conventional circumstances than those of a panty raid.

One of my best friends among my classmates was Roswell F. Jackson Jr. He and his family befriended me early on and invited me to their home in Atlanta on several occasions. Active in campus affairs, Roswell was the president of our junior class and I was vice president. The next year Roswell became president of the student government. His father and fellow Morehouse alum, Roswell Jackson Sr., taught religion and physical science at the college and was pastor of Mount Calvary Baptist Church. He was every bit the active and engaged man that Dr. Mays urged us all to become. Back then, teachers could smoke in the classroom, and for some, including Reverend Jackson, the lighted cigarette in hand was about as common as a piece of chalk. I was a student in one of his world religions classes. Little did I know then that I would end up teaching a course in the same subject and using a later edition of the Huston Smith textbook we had used in his class.

Certainly, the single most significant achievement during my time at Morehouse was being awarded a Merrill Overseas Studies and Travel Scholarship that enabled me to broaden my vision beyond the South and the United States in general. While in Nantes, France, I acquired fluency in another language, which I achieved by completely immersing myself in the culture. I not only stayed with a French family but also went to restaurants, cafés, and movies. I traveled, went on dates, and acted in plays, in addition to sitting for and passing exams denoting levels of proficiency in French.

But there were also tough periods and times of challenge. I was at Morehouse when John F. Kennedy was assassinated in November 1963 and when Martin Luther King was murdered in April 1968. I was in Stephen Henderson's freshman composition class when news came of Kennedy's death. I was sitting in the college snack bar when the news came of King's death. Both events were shattering for our school, especially King's assassination.

The most ticklish and potentially explosive situation occurred, I believe, during my sophomore year when Dr. Jeanette Hume, who taught English and humanities, suggested that I had committed plagiarism. Now, she didn't come right out and say this. She simply didn't believe that I was capable of writing the paper I had turned in. She admitted that she had no proof of plagiarism but believed that the paper showed such improvement over the first one I had submitted that it couldn't have been from the same hand. I made my case, but to no avail, and even asked Dr. Henderson as chair to intervene. He only suggested that I had shown tremendous progress in my writing but otherwise didn't want to dictate how a colleague should handle the matter. Without proof, Dr. Hume didn't feel that she could make me rewrite the paper, but she didn't grade the paper either. She only said that if it was my work, I should be proud. This didn't make me any happier, but I decided not to press the matter further. She may not have changed her mind about the paper despite my selection later on as a Merrill Scholar and my acceptance at a summer program at Yale University, her alma mater. Perhaps she shouldn't have doubted her ability as an instructor after she met with me about that first paper. Once she told me what I needed to do, I simply dedicated myself to learning how to put into practice what she was suggesting.

Dr. Hume, in fact, was a gifted teacher who cared greatly for her students. I know I'm not alone in stating that she was one of the college's most dedicated instructors. I will always remember her kindness during my summer at Yale, when she took Benjamin Ward, Michael Lomax, and me out to dinner at one of New Haven's finest restaurants. For her to include me in any activities with those two luminaries was proof enough that she held me in great esteem.

In general, my attendance at Morehouse afforded me many opportunities that I wouldn't have had if I had gone elsewhere. When it came time for my own son, Daniel, to go to college, I naturally wanted him to follow in the tradition of so many other sons of Morehouse alums and attend my alma mater. With offers in hand from several outstanding colleges and universities (including Morehouse), Daniel finally settled on Northwestern University in Evanston, Illinois. Forty years earlier, I had fewer choices open to me. While Morehouse was the best choice for me, Northwestern turned out to be a great choice for him, especially in his field of computer engineering. He was one of the top graduates in his class and made a number of lifelong friends at the university. I believe he would have been successful no matter where he went. And just as fervently, I still feel that there is a place for the historically black university in our time.

NOTE

1. Herman Cain, a candidate for the 2012 Republican Party nomination for president, was a classmate of mine at Morehouse.

PART II
REFLECTING

DELTA BLUES

> If you ever been mistreated,
> You got to know what I'm talking about.
> Worked five long years for one woman,
> And she had the nerve to kick me out.
>
> **Muddy Waters, "Five Long Years"**

According to a woman I knew as Miss Emma, one of my mother's closest friends, my uncle Obe was the meanest man she had ever seen; she asked for water but he gave her gasoline. That line, of course, comes from the Muddy Waters[1] song "Meanest Woman," which he recorded in June 1960:

> I asked for water she brought me gasoline, oh
> The meanest woman boy I most ever seen
> I asked her for water and she come runnin' with gasoline.

Miss Emma flipped the script to express her own feelings of hurt and pain. She, like Muddy before her, was expressing the most classic theme in the blues: a relationship gone bad between a man and his woman. Again, Muddy Waters expresses this type of rocky relationship in his song "Mean Mistreater":

> She's a mean mistreater,
> And the woman she don't mean me no good
> Well you know I don't blame you baby,
> I'd be the same way if I could.

In the following lines from "My Fault," recorded by Waters in 1961, the singer takes full responsibility for the broken relationship:

> It's my own fault, I don't blame you
> For treating me the way you do
> When you was deep in love with me,
> At that time, little girl,
> I didn't love you.

It seems to me that the blues always deal with relationships, if not between a man and a woman, then between a man and his boss or overseer, or between himself and his own existential circumstances.

Growing up during the 1950s and 1960s in the Mississippi Delta, I got to see the pain of thwarted relationships in my own family between my mother and stepfather and between my sister and her husband. There was also the pain of trying to get the plantation owner to pay a fair wage for services rendered. So, around mid-afternoon on Saturdays, my parents and sister, along with a number of others, crowded into a truck bound for Mr. Hodges's store on Henry Street. From there, it was a fairly easy walk to Johnson Street and Carrollton Avenue, where most of the juke joints were located, or to some of the good-time houses scattered along Main and McLaurin streets. These businesses were prepared to offer, for a reasonable price, whatever sedative was necessary to soothe an aching heart, but nothing seemed to do the job as well as the blues. Too young myself to have the blues, I experienced them vicariously through others. After skipping the second movie of the double feature at the Walthall Theater, I would amble across the street to get a closer look at the frenzy. Except for the presence of liquor and profanity, you might mistake the scene for one that took place the next day at Good Hope Missionary Baptist Church as the Reverend W. H. Kingston neared the end of his sermon. It was not church, but the people seemed to be just as refreshed and revitalized and, yes, determined to get through another day.

The fried fish, the liquor, and the blues, the staple of Saturday nights in Greenwood, were repeated throughout various venues in the Delta. There must not have been much of an age restriction then, for I couldn't have been more than eleven or twelve. There was no real worry or concern as long as I was back at Mr. Hodges's store in time to catch the truck heading back to the Whittington plantation around midnight. While liquor was off limits, I had a healthy dose of the blues and fried buffalo fish, washing them down with a Double Cola. In some joints and houses, the music went from nine o'clock Saturday night to early Sunday morning, finishing just in time for those willing to make it to Sunday school.

When we moved to Greenwood, we lived right across the street from the 82 Grill. Now older, I could venture as much as I wanted into these places. Although it had a juke box and smoke and fried fish, the 82 Grill was not really a juke joint. For one thing, there was little room for dancing. Just a few blocks over, however, was a place that qualified as a juke joint in every sense. Occasionally, I ventured over there to dance with some older women. I really couldn't dance as well as Jeffie McNeal and Joe Lee Lofton. But I could slow drag well enough to get by. I waited for a slow record and would ask a woman who was kind enough to dance with anyone who asked. I placed my head on her breast, and we did a slow grind to the music of John Lee Hooker. I learned that the blues was not only a sedative; it could actually help you make out.

The lyrics were filled with various codes. Several years earlier, they didn't make much sense to me: "Nobody can bake a sweet jelly roll like mine." The sexual innuendo was rampant in this music: "Jelly, jelly, jelly, all the time!" Was this what the big boys meant when they called out to a woman with an ample backside? "It must be jelly, 'cause jam don't shake like that." Or, this: "My pencil won't write." The key was being able to break the code. Earlier, I had asked my stepfather what these words meant; he only dismissed me as a mannish boy.

It was not until my freshman year at Morehouse, however, that I gained a real appreciation for what I'd been hearing all those years in the Delta. The 1960s marked an important revival of interest in the blues. Those artists who once played an entire weekend for two or three dollars, a bottle of whiskey, and the company of a willing woman were now being discovered and their music was being electrified. One could see gigs performed now in towns outside the Delta and often outside the state. So, when Prof. Stephen Henderson found out that he had a student in his class from the Mississippi Delta, he immediately approached me about getting some recordings of these artists for his own collection. He believed, as did Langston Hughes and Sterling Brown before him, that the music held significance as great literature. In his book *Understanding the New Black Poetry*, he pays tribute to this art form.

Langston Hughes, in his book *Fine Clothes to the Jew*, offers us a definition of this form: "The Blues, unlike the Spirituals, have a strict poetic pattern: one long line repeated and a third to rhyme with the first two. Sometimes the second line is slightly changed and sometimes, but very seldom, it is omitted. The mood of the Blues is almost always despondency, but when they are sung people laugh."[2] Hughes's definition could be expanded, but it does suggest a major aspect of this genre. Singing gives the individual the ability to cope with his or her circumstances. The very singing of the blues is a way of acknowledging the "isness" of one's situation. The hope is not so much to overcome that situation but to share it with someone who understands and is willing to listen. The blues thus have a communal effect, and the blues singer can say with some assurance: "If you ever been mistreated, you know what I'm talking about."

While scholars are not in complete agreement about the origins of the blues, most have indicated that the Mississippi Delta is the likeliest birthplace.[3] B. B. King[4] has gone so far as to indicate a specific plantation, the old Dockery farm near Cleveland. For it is only on such plantations that we find the major ingredients that make up the stuff of the blues: plantation life, low wages, huge disparities between the haves and the have-nots. The region also had a large state penitentiary, Parchman, which was perhaps more like a big farm than a correctional facility. It was a brutal place that was, by some accounts, worse than slavery. Some of the greatest artists did stints there: Son House, Bukka White, and others.

We have only to consider the many artists who were either born in the region or spent a large period of time there. Indeed, the Mississippi Delta has made the greatest contribution to this uniquely American art form. Each year, in various cities in the Delta, there are blues festivals that celebrate the music's rich history in the region as well as introduce the world to the next generation of artists determined to keep the tradition alive.

Of all the artists from this region, we immediately recognize the work of B. B. King, John Lee Hooker, and Muddy Waters. But there were also David "Honeyboy" Edwards and Son House, among many others. In fact, the bluesman who has proven to be the most influential spent only a short time on the stage: Robert Leroy Johnson, who was himself influenced by House and Charley

Patton. As a youngster, Robert followed the two older artists around and played whenever he got the opportunity. After a year's absence, Johnson reappeared, and to the amazement of both Patton and House, his musical skills had improved dramatically from just the year before.

Johnson was born in Hazelhurst, Mississippi, in 1911 but spent a great deal of his short and enigmatic life in Greenwood, where he died and is buried.[5] The myth is that he sold his soul to the devil for the gift of playing the guitar. Honeyboy Edwards first met Johnson in Greenwood in 1937. At that time, Johnson was playing in a number of country towns throughout the Delta, places like Leland and Indianola, as well as Greenwood. Robert Johnson, according to Honeyboy, had his own style: while others like Rube Lacy and Tommy Johnson had that "bookity-book Delta style, Johnson had a classic Blues style, with mostly a lot of minor chords. He had a lot of seventh chords in his Blues and it sounded better than just playing straight. And that took with the people, because he had a different sound."[6]

A man of mild temperament, Johnson had just two vices: he loved whiskey and was crazy about his women. Those two things proved to be his downfall. By Honeyboy's account, a beautiful married woman visited Johnson every Monday at a rooming house in Baptist Town, where he was staying, and spent the entire day with him. When the cuckolded husband got word of his wife's indiscretions, he had one of his lady friends poison Johnson's whiskey. Falling ill almost immediately, Johnson hung on for a few days, but in the end "he was crawling around like a dog, and howling."[7] He was just twenty-seven years old when he died. As with many incidents associated with Johnson, the actual specifics of his death haven't been clarified. If, indeed, he was poisoned, as most commentators argue, what poison was used? Those claiming it was strychnine would have to reconcile their claim with the fact that, as Honeyboy Edwards pointed out, this poison causes almost instant death. Johnson couldn't have survived for just over three days. Some accounts indicate that a woman stabbed him to death. Then, there is the famous Faustian myth of his selling his soul to the devil. Had he bargained away his life at the crossroads?

While there are those who downplay the crossroads legend, there seems to be little doubt that Johnson's guitar playing improved dramatically and within a very short span of time. During Johnson's brief life, his talents went generally unappreciated and unpaid. Only since his death have there been efforts to pay tribute to his talent and influence. He was inducted into three major halls of fame: the Blues Hall of Fame in 1980, the Rock and Roll Hall of Fame in 1986 (Kudos owing more, perhaps, to Johnson's influence on artists like Eric Clapton and Bob Dylan than to any real achievement in the rock and roll genre, which hadn't yet emerged when Johnson was alive), and the Mississippi Musicians Hall of Fame in 2000. He was also posthumously awarded a Grammy Lifetime Achievement Award in 2006. By the time of his death at age twenty-seven, Johnson had, in just two short years, produced a body of work that would have a greater impact than that of any of his contemporaries, including Bukka White and Blind Willie McTell. Bob Dylan, who was among the first to publicly perform one of his songs, "Rambling On My Mind," had this to say about his music: "From the first note, the vibrations from the loudspeaker made my hair stand up. . . . Robert Johnson started singing, he seemed like a guy who could have sprung from the head of Zeus in full armor. I immediately differentiated between him and anyone else I had ever heard."[8] But, as I noted, such praise would come only long after his death.

Unlike Robert Johnson, some blues artists have received and are now receiving a bit of their just due—better contracts, better royalties, and acknowledgment of the blues' influence by such rock and roll artists as Elvis Presley, Keith Richards, Bonnie Raitt, Jack White and the White Stripes, and numerous others. John Lee Hooker actually lived long enough to enjoy fame and commercial success. Born somewhere near the Mississippi Delta town of Clarksdale in 1917, Hooker made a number of appearances on late night shows near the end of his life. His appearances with rock stars such as Clapton, Raitt, Richards, Stevie Ray Vaughan, and Carlos Santana boosted their careers as well as his own.[9] But had Hooker moved too far beyond his Delta roots? Had he become so electrified that he had, by the time of his death, moved beyond that classic Delta blues style? Some suggest that indeed he had.

There is no doubt, however, that Hooker, Johnson, Waters, and all the other great bluesmen paid their dues. For them, it was just about the music. Fame and commercial success, when and if they came, were extra. Honeyboy Edwards spoke for this group when he closed his autobiography, *The World Don't Owe Me Nothing*, with the old line popularized by several bluesmen: "I've had my fun, / If I don't get well no more."

Notes

1. Muddy Waters (1913–1983) was born McKinley Morganfield in Rolling Fork, Mississippi.

2. Langston Hughes, *Fine Clothes to the Jew* (New York: Alfred A. Knopf, 1927), 13.

3. For a fuller discussion of the origins of the blues and its tradition, see Robert Santelli, "A Century of the Blues," in *Martin Scorsese Presents the Blues: A Musical Journey*, ed. Peter Guralnick, Robert Santelli, Holly George-Warren, and Christopher John Farley (New York: Amistad, 2003), 12–59.

4. B. B. King (1925–) was born Riley B. King in Berclair, Mississippi. I understand that "B.B." stands for "Blues Boy."

5. There are, in fact, three sites in and around Greenwood that are claimed to be the final resting place of Robert Johnson.

6. David Honeyboy Edwards, *The World Don't Owe Me Nothing* (Chicago: Chicago Review Press, 1997), 102.

7. Ibid., 104.

8. Quoted in Tom Graves, *Crossroads: The Life and Afterlife of Blues Legend Robert Johnson* (Spokane, WA: Demers Books, 2008), 75.

9. Several essays in *Martin Scorsese Presents the Blues*, ed. Guralnick et al., provide important information on traditional blues artists and their influences on later rock and blues artists.

GAMBLING ON THE RIVER

> I'm a gamblin' man
> Gamblin' ... all night long
> Well, I'm a gambling man
> Gamble ... all night long
> Yeah, I'm gonna gamble this time, baby
> Bring my good gal home.
>
> **David Edwards, "Gamblin' Man"**

The Delta bluesman David "Honeyboy" Edwards not only gambled all night long; he also gambled from town to town. Edwards was only one member of a breed for whom this type of hustling often meant a willingness to go anywhere the action appeared most promising. Malcolm X observed that, when it comes to gambling, you're either the fox or the rabbit, the hunter or the hunted. To find rabbits and leave town before they realized their gullibility was an occupation that required a readiness to travel at a moment's notice. My uncles John and Obe, who probably crossed tracks with Honeyboy, were known for being away from their families. Luevina, John's youngest daughter, recalls that she saw very little of her father and that he was not only absent but irresponsible toward his family as well. And as for Obe, I've already recounted how Melissa Blanchard told me of a fight that began with Obe's asking for money to get back into a card game and resulted in her biting off a good part of his ear.

When we lived on the plantation, I used to watch the older boys and men gamble much of their meager salaries away in dice games and tossing coins to the line. On Saturday nights, in particular, the guys took whatever money they could scrape up and headed to the Buckeye or the back of some juke joint on Carrollton Avenue or Johnson Street. After the house took its cut and the sharps had their way with them, there was little money left for food and other necessities. Perry Lymon, husband to my cousin Luevina and a plantation foreman, told me that the gambling problem on one plantation got so bad that the owner built a shed on his property so that his hands could gamble among themselves rather than take their "furnish" to town to lose it to some city slickers. In problem cases, the bookkeeper wouldn't settle at the end of the year with the husband alone. His wife had to be there if any funds, no matter how small, were dispensed.

Although I confess to enjoying a bit of gambling myself later in life, I was too young for it at that time, and indeed I had no interest in it because I had heard of and seen its evil effects on others. My brother-in-law, for instance, was known to be unlucky, which is to say he was considered a sucker. He often lost much of his pay before he got home to my sister. However, I did like to hear Uncle Obe and Jonas Garner talk about their gambling exploits. Their stories fired my imagination. Obe, at least before he lost his finger, was such a good poker mechanic that he would purposely give his stooge a hand he deemed too good to toss, only to beat him with a slightly better hand. But no one had better try the same trick on Obe, lest he pull out his pistol. That, at least, was what he said, and I believed him. Yet I did wonder about the truth of some other gamblers' stories. How could they gamble and always come out ahead? Clearly, they had never gambled with Obe.

While in high school, I sometimes stopped by the pool room to see some of the boys shoot pool. They would put a dollar or two on the game to make it interesting. I often listened to the colorful language of these players when an opponent was called on to make a tough shot, or when they called to the rack man before attempting their own of similar difficulty: "Rack man, walk slow," "Eight ball, two in the corner." And another unlucky sucker went to the woodpile. When we lived on Percy Street, I used to watch several old geezers, Todd McDowell, David Jackson, and Bill Lewis, gather across the street at Shamrock's store for their little late afternoon delight of Seven-Up: "Gift, High, Low, Jack, and the Game and gone from two."

Gambling in Mississippi has a long and interesting history, going back to its first inhabitants, the Choctaws, Chickasaws, and other Native Americans.

Historian Deanne Nuwer of the University of Southern Mississippi points to early accounts indicating that these groups were fond of wagering on stick ball or *ishtaboli*, a sport similar to today's lacrosse. Gambling practices continued after Europeans and Africans established themselves in Mississippi. They often wagered on cards, checkers, and billiards. Gambling continued in the form of horse racing among the Spanish. So, by the time Mississippi became a state on December 10, 1817, gambling was a well-established activity. It continued along the Mississippi River during the early 1800s, where it was found in many of the small towns that had established clubs to attract dollars from wealthy passengers aboard the riverboats. The Civil War may have dampened the spirit of gambling somewhat but didn't completely extinguish it. And during World War II and afterward, gambling seemed to increase rather than decrease. More recently, in the late 1980s, Biloxi has allowed ships to use its ports to take passengers to international waters in the Gulf of Mexico, where they can gamble legally. Declared the poorest state in the union by the 1980 census, Mississippi continued to look for ways to increase its revenues. "In 1989," writes Nuwer, "Mississippi became the first state to permit cruises to conduct gambling in state waters when the ships were on their way to or from international waters."[1] Thus, gambling, legal or illegal, has always been present in the state.

Yet, I was surprised when gambling was legalized in Mississippi. While gambling had always flourished there, it generally was not openly sanctioned and sponsored by the state. Given Mississippi's place in the center of the Bible Belt, I thought that it would be the last place to approve legalized gambling, but with the passage of House Bill 2 on June 29, 1990, establishing the Mississippi Gaming Control Act, legalized dockside gambling was approved by the state. The act requires that casinos be permanently docked in the water along the Mississippi River and Mississippi Gulf Coast. While restaurants, hotels, and meeting and entertainment facilities may sit on land, the casinos themselves must actually sit on water. After passage of the bill, each county was given an opportunity to determine whether casinos were to be allowed in its jurisdiction. While counties along the coast refused to allow the casinos in, Biloxi itself voted to approve gambling within the city. At the time, Biloxi was experiencing serious financial difficulties as was Tunica to the north. So, it's not surprising, then, that these two areas were the first to approve legalized gambling. Isle of Capri in Biloxi became the first casino to open in the state. Splash, owned by local investors, opened its doors in Tunica on October 15, 1992, and closed in May 1995.

In general, revenues in the state had slowed to the point that legislators turned to legalized gambling as a way of increasing state revenues without increasing sales or income taxes. In just a few years of operation, the casinos in the state brought in huge profits, making Mississippi third only to Las Vegas and Atlantic City in terms of gambling revenues received. In terms of area, it was second only to Las Vegas.

But increased revenues would not come without risks that could be seen as threats to the health and well-being of the state's citizens. There was, of course, the pervasive moral question of the state sponsoring an activity that encouraged its citizens to lose their way in pursuit of quick riches, thus contributing to the epidemic of compulsive gambling. There was also the question of increased crime and corruption, especially organized crime. If the state needed to make the case for increasing its coffers, and it did, it also needed a strong and active gaming commission to monitor the industry.

No doubt the area that has benefitted most from the casinos is Tunica, located in the northern portion of the Mississippi Delta, about twenty-five miles south of Memphis. This is the city Jesse Jackson visited in 1985 to find an open sewer that locals had termed "Sugar Ditch Alley." Tunica County at the time was the poorest in the United States. After Jackson's visit, the television news show *Sixty Minutes* did an investigative report on what Jackson called America's Ethiopia. Within just a few years, the casinos contributed millions of dollars to the state treasury and provided jobs for most of Tunica County's citizens. Today, if you were to ask individuals who remember Tunica before and after the casinos, you'll generally receive a thumbs-up sign regarding changes in this small town. Few, if any citizens, including ministers, want to go back to life before the casinos.

While the casinos have been a positive force in some ways, they haven't solved all the problems in the area. Schools haven't shown an appreciable improvement relative to the funds received. Furthermore, while the percentage of those below the poverty level has improved greatly in terms of the county's standing relative to its position in 1990 and in relation to other Delta counties, it is still at 25.7 percent, as compared with 21.2 percent for the state and 13.8 percent for the nation. A partial explanation lies in the fact that the area was so depressed prior to 1992 that it will take a much longer period and resources beyond what can be provided by the casinos before any appreciable improvement can be realized.

The problem of compulsive gambling poses a threat here just as it does in other areas with casinos—a problem nurtured by the presence of billboards picturing individuals who have hit it big at one or another of the casinos. But as those close to me know, it would be disingenuous of me to rail here against casino gambling—or any other form of gambling, for that matter. I truly enjoy the recreational aspects of "gaming"—a euphemism meant to make the activity seem more acceptable—and have done my share since my days in college. I'm also known to be tight with money. Over the years, I've lost much more time than money at the gaming tables, which can be a problem in itself. For this reason, I've striven to be disciplined and to view gambling as a form of recreation rather than as an investment opportunity. I always set aside an amount equal to what I would ordinarily spend on each day of any other vacation. When I consider the reduced rates for hotel rooms and the comps that are often provided for food and other amenities, I've found that what I spend on a casino vacation compares quite favorably to what I spend at other vacation venues. I've also found it wise to cut back on the amount of alcohol I drink and to budget the time I spend at the tables.

With all that said, I acknowledge that casino gambling can be especially hypnotic and addictive and that not everyone has the necessary discipline to remain in control. It's for this reason that the state's Gaming Commission must be constantly aware of patrons who show signs of compulsive gambling.

Note

1. For information on the history of gambling in Mississippi, I'm indebted to Deanne S. Nuwer's article "Gambling in Mississippi: Its Early History," in *Misssissippi History Now*, an online publication of the Mississippi Historical Society. See http://mshistorynow.mdah.state.ms.us/articles/80/gambling-in-mississippi-its-early-history.

BLACK WAYS AND OTHER FOLKWAYS

> Some envious outsider made the suggestion that no one was eligible for membership who was not white enough to show blue veins. The suggestion was readily adopted by those who were not of the favored few, and since that time the society, though possessing a longer and more pretentious name, had been known far and wide as the "Blue Vein Society," and its members as the "Blue Veins."
>
> **Charles Chesnutt, "The Wife of His Youth"**

As a black child growing up in the Mississippi Delta, I was surrounded by many attitudes, sayings, and customs that seemed to mark my community as special. Anyone seeking to understand this community can ill afford to ignore the rich reservoir of what we might call the folk or vernacular tradition. It consists of the music (gospel, spirituals, the blues, work songs, jazz), folk sermons, folktales, rhymes, and rap that spring from the African American tradition and, in turn, help define it. A few of these have been mentioned in this volume. We should add to this list certain attitudes on skin color and hair, the verbal repartee called signifying and the dozens, as well as the whole catalogue of expressions best summed up by Zora Neale Hurston's category "A Colored Way of Saying." Although Hurston did much of her research in her native state of Florida, some of the expressions she identifies would be recognizable in the Mississippi Delta.

She noted, for example, the tendency among blacks to use the double descriptive as in "tooth dentist," "sitting chair," and "chop-axe."

That many other writers on the South, black and white, have commented on one or more of these expressions suggests that something significant and revelatory about the culture is being indicated. But what precisely? That is, do certain aspects of the vernacular point to a culture's weaknesses or its strengths? Should they be seen as evidence of pride or self-hatred? What are the origins of the various attitudes and expressions? To what extent are they independent of or a mere reaction to the dominant white culture? I don't consider myself an expert in any field that can provide answers to these questions. Nor am I completely convinced that I've properly phrased the questions themselves. But here, as I've done on so many occasions with my students, I hurl a few stones at my audience and then run and duck behind my desk.

SKIN COLOR

During my youth, I was often warned against drinking coffee, not because of the caffeine but because coffee, my mother said, would make me black. Certainly she knew that there was no biological basis for such a belief. Whites drank coffee all the time, and they continued to be white. She probably knew that coffee was not good for me and wanted to use the one fear I had to regulate my behavior, the fear of becoming even blacker than I was. During my youth, there were two things that could start a fight: talking about someone's mama and calling someone black. I don't think that it was pride in being black or a love for Africa that led some to refer to a classmate as an ABC (African Black Child). The saying one hears even today used to be pronounced without fear of contradiction: "If you're white, you're all right; if you're brown, stick around; but if you're black, get back!" Little wonder, then, that some would say, "I don't want nothing black but a Cadillac." Or, again, "I don't haul no coal."

We considered the fairer-complexioned girls more beautiful and asked them out, while the darker girls were often ignored or scorned. The darker children were not left completely defenseless, however, if they could repeat with some degree of assurance: "The blacker the berry, the sweeter the juice." The problem of *colorism*, as it is now called, has persisted throughout the history of blacks in this country. Some suggest its origins go back to slavery, when fair-skinned blacks were favored over those of a darker complexion. Those who were fairer, especially women, often worked inside the quarters, leaving their darker sisters to labor outside. During slave auctions, those of fairer complexion brought higher sums.

In his autobiography, Malcolm X discusses the problem of self-hatred in his own family, which he associates with skin color. He noticed how his father seemed to favor the lighter children and his mother the darker ones:

> Nearly all my whippings came from my mother. I've thought a lot about why. I actually believe that as anti-white as my father was, he was subconsciously so afflicted with the white man's brainwashing of Negroes that he inclined to favor the light ones, and I was the lightest child.[1]

Malcolm moves quickly to draw the moral:

> Most Negro parents in those days would almost instinctively treat any lighter children better than they did the darker ones. It came directly from the slavery tradition that the "mulatto," because he was visibly nearer to white, was therefore better.[2]

Malcolm here examines some deep psychological motives and brings to the fore what many blacks might rather keep buried in the subconscious. Using his own past experience as a barometer, he attempts to alert blacks of the subtle ways in which America's institutions attempt to brainwash them. He himself admits that his image of Africa at that time "was of naked savages, cannibals, monkeys and tigers and steaming jungles."[3] Later on, in several of his speeches, he insisted on the importance of Africa to black Americans by reminding them that it's impossible to love a tree and hate its roots.

This expression of self-hatred is most noticeable in women as suggested by such works as Toni Morrison's *The Bluest Eye,* Maya Angelou's *I Know Why the Caged Bird Sings,* and Wallace Thurman's *The Blacker the Berry.* In all three works, the female protagonists—Pecola Breedlove, Marguerite Johnson, and Emma Lou Morgan, respectively—see themselves condemned by their color and suffer the low self-esteem that such feelings bring. Thurman's Emma Lou Morgan expresses the desperation and frustration of this group and of so many other women with dark skin during the 1920s. As she grew older, Emma Lou "began to feel that her luscious black complexion was somewhat of a liability, and that her marked color variation from the other people in her environment was a decided curse."[4] It was not so much that she minded having some colored skin or even being black, "but she did mind being too black." This seemed to be an unnecessary injustice and she couldn't "comprehend the cruelty of the natal attenders who had allowed her to be dipped, as it were, in indigo ink when there were so many more pleasing colors on nature's palette."[5]

Emma Lou's problem might well have been avoided had her mother married someone fairer in complexion than her father. I, along with others of my generation, was warned about the pitfalls of marrying someone of a darker hue. The person may be admirable in all other respects, but skin tone may determine who is a suitable or unsuitable mate. Although you may love the person, you always had to think about the children. If Emma Lou's mother had been more careful, she could have spared her daughter a great deal of pain and grief. Now, despite every effort, she was saddled with a life-long sentence "of moaning and grieving over the color of her skin. Everything possible had been done to alleviate the unhappy condition, every suggested agent had been employed, but her skin, despite bleachings, scourgings, and powderings, had remained black—fast black—as nature had planned and effected."[6]

It is not only a matter, however, of one's perception of oneself; those so victimized claim that skin color has been used to deny them employment or to exclude them from certain sororities and colleges. Marcus Garvey claimed in his autobiography, *Philosophy and Opinions,* that his dark complexion was a major reason for the discrimination and problems he suffered throughout his life.[7]

Good Hair

When my friends and I were growing up, we had clear notions of what was considered good and bad hair. Many of the bigger boys conked their hair to make it straighter, to make it appear more like white folks' hair. This too, like the problem with color, was an aspect of racial hatred. Given these problems, it was very difficult for a black person to grow up loving his black, kinky-haired self. Malcolm X indicated the great pain and agony he endured trying to make his kinky hair straight, and after his friend Shorty gave him that first conk he was amazed at how straight his hair was, "as straight as any white man's."[8]

When I was a student at Morehouse, some of my schoolmates wore stocking caps to bed, presumably to achieve waves and turn their natural hair into "good hair." And as I've previously noted, any blacks who have so-called good hair often have a heritage of American Indian ancestry.

The entrepreneur Madame C. J. Walker, who founded a beauty- and hair-products company, turned the quest for straight hair into a multimillion-dollar enterprise. She was, in fact, not only the first black millionaire; she was the first woman millionaire, period.

PLAYING THE DOZENS

Langston Hughes had his character Simple give a clear and simple definition of the dozens. He says that "white folks really don't know what the dozens is—which means talking bad, sex-like, about someone else's mama."[9] This verbal sparring game was heard on street corners, on playgrounds, and in cafés—wherever, in short, that blacks, usually men, congregated. The scene is played out by two men in front of a group of interested bystanders serving as judges who note whose words seem to have the greater effect on his opponent. The target of derision is the opponent's mother. To strike out against one's mother is, in the African American community, to hit at the heart of a young man's love and affection. The more graphic and descriptive one can make the alleged sexual encounter appear, the further one moves into the realm of the dirty dozens. It was a contest of one-upmanship where the winner was the one who landed the most decisive verbal jab, causing his opponent to lose equilibrium and become angry, cry, or simply walk away. Being brought to tears was perhaps the greatest humiliation a young man could suffer. In such a case, he might have to fight to restore any degree of self-respect.

Some of my classmates, I believe, actually spent more time thinking about the dozens and practicing the rhythm and cadence necessary to defeat an able opponent than they did on their school work. There were those, in fact, who could present the case against your mama so convincingly that you had to pause briefly and wonder whether the assertions were in any way true. A couple of students known as Goggle-Eye and Trick Greene were the acknowledged champions at our school. If either one made a first strike at you, it would well be wise to surrender quickly by suggesting that the game was beneath you and walking away. I used this technique myself.

The following simulated exchange between two individuals using well-known and less-well-known dirty dozens offers some sense of this art form:

> I can tell by your knees
> Your mother eats surplus cheese
> I can tell by your knees
> Your mother climbs trees

> Your mama's like a birthday cake
> Easy to slice and everybody gets a piece
>
> At least my mother ain't no doorknob—
> Everybody gets a turn

Some dirty dozens include the phrase "I fucked your mother" as part of a rhyming couplet, as in:

> I fucked your mother on City Hall.
> William Penn said, "Don't take it all."

What accounts for the popularity of this form, particularly among poor African Americans? Is it just a carryover from Africa, as some argue, or is there a deeper psychological reason behind the game? Two earlier essays on the form may assist readers in coming to their own conclusion on the matter: John Dollard's "The Dozens: Dialectic of Insult" and Roger D. Abrahams's "Playing the Dozens." While I don't have a theory of my own, I'm not certain that I agree with Abrahams's argument that playing the dozens was a ritual that reflected the tensions caused by the structure of the black family. "As an institutionalized mechanism," Abrahams concludes, "the dozens is most important to the lower-class Negro youth in search of his masculine identity. It represents a transition point in his life, that place at which he casts off a woman's world for a man's, and begins to develop the tools by which he is to implement his new found position, in a member of a gang existence."[10]

I have difficulty connecting this practice to gang activity in any way. For one thing, the dozens were played in the South long before that region became associated with gangs. Though incomplete, Dollard's argument that the ritual is a way of releasing racial frustration against whites by attacking blacks may be closer to the point.[11]

NOTES

1. Malcolm X (with the assistance of Alex Haley), *The Autobiography of Malcolm X* (New York: Grove Press, 1965), 4.

2. Ibid.

3. Ibid., 7.

4. Wallace Thurman, *The Blacker the Berry: A Novel of Negro Life* (1929; repr., New York: AMS Press, 1972), 9.

5. Ibid.

6. Ibid., 10.

7. Much of Garvey's feud with W. E. B. Du Bois, an older contemporary and one of the founders of the NAACP, stemmed from the problem of skin color. In criticizing Garvey's Universal Negro Improvement Association (UNIA), Du Bois referred to Garvey as a "little, fat, ugly black man; ugly, but with intelligent eyes and a big head." Garvey launched a long, scathing attack on Du Bois, calling him a "misleader of his people, who has a hatred for every drop of black blood in his body." He continued:

> It is no wonder that Du Bois seeks the company of white people, because he hates black as being ugly. That is why he likes to dance with white people, and dine with them, and sometimes sleep with them, because from his way of seeing things all that is black is ugly, and all that is white is beautiful. Yet this professor, who sees ugliness in being black, essays to be a leader of the Negro people and has been trying for over fourteen years to deceive them through his connection with the National Association for the Advancement of Colored People. (Marcus Garvey, *Philosophy and Opinions*, ed. Amy Jacques-Garvey [1925; repr., New York: Atheneum, 1982], 311.)

8. Malcolm X, *Autobiography*, 54.

9. Langston Hughes, "New Kind of Dozens," in *Simple Stakes a Claim* (New York: Rinehart and Co., 1957), 111.

10. Roger D. Abrahams, "Playing the Dozens," in *Mother Wit from the Laughing Barrel: Readings in the Interpretation of Afro-American Folklore*, ed. Alan Dundes (Englewood Cliffs, NJ: Prentice Hall, 1973), 307.

11. John Dollard, "The Dozens: Dialectic of Insult," in Dundes, *Mother Wit*, 277–94.

AFRICAN GODS IN MISSISSIPPI

> The most dominant and intact African survival in the black diaspora has proved to be the religion of voodoo.
>
> **Jessie Mulira, "The Case of Voodoo in New Orleans"**

> Very superstitious, writing's on the wall
> Very superstitious, ladder's 'bout to fall
> Thirteen month old baby, broke the lookin' glass
> Seven years of bad luck, the good things in your past.
>
> **Stevie Wonder, "Superstitious"**

It was not until I began the academic study of religion that many of the old customs and superstitions made much sense to me. To my youthful eyes, those practices were simply things the old folks believed and around which they regulated their lives. With the Delta of that time, there were many similarities to tribal or traditional societies, which is not to see them in a negative light. Such societies spend much effort to combat the threat of otherness, whether that otherness is conceived as a natural or manmade force or simply the white man himself, who often appears to southern black children as a bogeyman. Various forms of magic or conjuring helped give people some sense of control over their lives. Taboos were in place and observed to mark what things in the society were considered dangerous. Every black boy in the Delta knew, for example, that white women were taboo. Anyone not observing the taboo, like my friend Joe Lee Lofton on that day he chased some white boys, was asking for trouble or death. The case of Emmett Till stood as a reminder of what might go wrong if you didn't observe taboos.

The customs—and notions of what would happen if you didn't follow them—were many: Don't sweep dust from the house after dark or you'd be sweeping someone's spirit away. Don't walk under a ladder. If my mother sewed something I was wearing, I had to place something in my mouth. Don't let someone sweep your feet with a broom. If a black cat crosses your path, bad luck will follow. Breaking a mirror will bring seven years of bad luck. When walking with a friend or family member, splitting a post will split the relationship. Fish and milk, when consumed together, will kill you, as will watermelon and whiskey. Ashes can't be removed from the fireplace before a baby is one year old.

Many men and women of my parents' and grandparents' generations observed a number of taboos associated with hair. They didn't leave their hair in barber or beauty shops for fear that someone would use it in foul ways. They were also careful to remove any hair from brushes or combs. My mother believed that if your hair wound up in the wrong hands, that person could control all aspects of your life, especially your love life. In one well-known slave narrative, Henry Bibb, who was born on a Kentucky plantation in 1815, related how he thought that if he could get a lock of hair from the woman he desired, she wouldn't be able to resist his advances. However, the opposite outcome occurred:

> After I found there was no virtue in the bone of a frog, I thought I would try some other way to carry out my object. I then sought another counselor among the old superstitious influential slaves; one who professed to be a great friend of mine, told me to get a lock of hair from the head of any girl, and wear it in my shoes: this would cause her to love me above all other persons. As there was another girl whose affections I was anxious to gain, but could not succeed, I thought without trying the experiment of this hair. I slipped off one night to see the girl, and asked her for a lock of her hair; but she refused to give it. Believing that my success depended greatly upon this bunch of hair, I was bent on having a lock before I left that night let it cost what it might. As it was time for me to start home in order to get any sleep that night, I grasped hold of a lock of her hair, which

caused her to screech, but I never let go until I had pulled it out. This of course made the girl mad with me, and I accomplished nothing but gained her displeasure.[1]

This passage is significant in indicating that superstitions regarding hair go back to slavery and, no doubt, to Africa. Note that Bibb said he sought counsel from one among "the old, superstitious *influential slaves*" (my emphasis). This suggests that the practice of conjuring was widespread and that those with a reputation for practicing it were respected and sought after. Practices begun and developed in Africa were thus brought to the new world.

African funeral practices can also be seen throughout the South, including the Mississippi Delta. There is the practice, for example, of burying alongside the deceased something he or she cherished. Should a favorite watch of the deceased be buried with her or passed along to a member of the family? This is a question with which more than one family, including my own, has had to grapple. African influences can be seen in the orientation of caskets in graves, placed so that the deceased's head points east. Admittedly, this practice is so common today that it's difficult to associate its origins with a particular people or place. It can safely be said, however, that in this as in so many other things, Africa was at least an equal partner in the making and exchange of culture. If you were to ask any of the churchgoers about their knowledge of certain beliefs, they would point a finger away from themselves to other, older, less-educated, superstitious folk. But even the most religious among them were not ready to reap the consequences of tempting the gods through a systematic doctrine of unbelief.

There was one custom, in particular, that interested me a great deal. Whenever the skies darkened because of an impending storm—not just a shower, or hard rain even, but a real thunderstorm—my grandmother summoned Fred or Scott to fetch the axe. She had them take the axe into the yard and slam it in the ground. It was not until I read Albert Raboteau's discussion of this practice that I learned it had in fact survived from West Africa.[2] The West African deity Shango is the god of lightning and thunder, whose symbol is the axe. The act of slamming the axe into the ground was an effort to cut the force of Shango's power. Many years later, while visiting the West African country of Ghana, I asked the mother of one of my students whether she had heard of this particular belief. She indicated that it was not simply a belief but a certain fact. This was borne out, she said, in her own experiences with storms.

Despite my grandmother's directives to my uncles, we still had storms in the Delta and violent ones at that. My mother had a great fear of storms. She had us cover all the mirrors in the house and then we all gathered together in one of the subterranean storm pits constructed for shelter. Not everyone had such a pit, so one shelter would have to serve the needs of several families. I was both fascinated and awed by the prospect of sitting in one of those pits, surrounded by darkness. We children often tried to make each other laugh, knowing full well that such activity, or any activity, was frowned upon and strictly forbidden. We, of course, would always disavow responsibility for any untoward behavior, such as pinching or farting. In the quiet darkness, a lone, long poot was bound to bring, first, snickers and then, when we couldn't hold out any longer, bursts of laughter. This distressed the older folks, who had decreed that nothing at all could be done while God was doing his work. Violating this firm rule would surely bring a whipping—if the culprit could be identified—but that would have to wait until the storm had passed and God's task was finished.

NOTES

1. Henry Bibb, *The Life and Adventures of Henry Bibb: An American Slave,* with a new introduction by Charles Heglar (Madison: Univ. of Wisconsin Press, 2001), 31.

2. See Albert Raboteau, *Slave Religion: The Invisible Institution in the Antebellum South* (New York: Oxford Univ. Press, 1978), 81.

A DELTA REVIVAL

> Then I said, I will not make mention of Him nor speak any more in His name. But His Word was in mine heart as a burning fire shut up in my bones and I was weary with forbearing and I could not stay.
>
> **Jeremiah 20:9**

Each year at the end of summer, our church held its revival. I joined Good Hope Missionary Baptist Church when I was about twelve years old. I remember sitting on what we called the mourners' bench,[1] listening to the minister urging us to come to God while we were still young. There were about ten or twelve of us children, sitting there being preached to. While several joined during the first four days, many more waited until the last night to confess Christ. I also went on that Friday night. The minister reserved his best sermon for Friday night, his last opportunity to save souls. Here, he lingered a bit longer after his sermon, entreating the youngsters to come forward with his plea: "Will you trust Him tonight?" It was considered a real coup if the minister could empty the mourners' bench during the week he tended revival. This would most likely get him a return engagement, if not the following year, certainly in the near future.

It was customary for children to give some kind of brief testimony as they came forward to shake the minister's hand. It's interesting how similarly the Holy Spirit worked in us, for most of us gave some slight variation of the "I felt a fire shut up in my bones" speech drawn from Jeremiah. Though I don't recall what I said, it probably was some version of those words, which I had heard all my life. And I can't say that my being moved at this particular time was because of the Holy Spirit or because of the urgency of Friday night, the very last chance to save my soul and avoid having to come back and go through the whole process again the next year.

There was an occurrence on that Sunday, however, which seemed to confirm the matter, in my mother's mind at least, that I had religion. It started raining on Saturday and continued early that Sunday morning. My mother had told me that the baptism would probably have to be postponed. As was the general custom then, we were baptized on the banks of the Yazoo River, which ran through the Buckeye. My mother assured me that being saved was the main thing and that I could be baptized later. In any case, if it continued to rain, the banks would be too hazardous, and no one could be baptized. I predicted to her that around ten o'clock that Sunday morning, the skies would clear and the sun would come out. I promised her that the baptism would take place on time.

When the skies did indeed clear sometime around ten, she was amazed and took this to be a clear sign that her son had found the Lord. As I reflect on it today, I believe that my prediction was based partly on meteorological evidence I had noticed from similar situations in the past and partly on the sincere hope that all aspects of my coming-to-the-Lord might be consummated that single week. But then my mother's joyousness had me convinced that indeed my prediction had come true through divine intervention. Now that the weather had cleared, the deacons and pastor gave their okay to go ahead with the baptism. For the occasion, my mother had purchased a beautiful blue suit for me, which I was to wear at the Sunday service immediately following the baptism. For the baptism itself, all the candidates wore white gowns with a white headpiece that made it hard to tell the boys from the girls. Two or three of us got dressed at the home of Brother Frank Anderson, one of the church deacons, as it was conveniently located between the church and the river. We then all gathered at the church to march the half-mile or so to the river, more quiet than any of us had been in our lives. Reverend W. H. Kingston, our regular pastor, was in charge of the baptism, the revival minister having completed his task of preparing us for the moment. Dressed in a black robe with black cloth headgear, Reverend Kingston took his position. Some of the sisters noted out loud how good the pastor looked on that Baptismal Sunday. On either side were Brother Anderson and Brother Scott Wilson, my uncle and also a deacon. Brother Sonny Garner, another deacon, helped lead the candidates down to the water. The deacons were there to support the minister and aid any candidate who might slip on the muddy banks of the river. Any of the candidates would tell you that their main purpose was to prevent, as much as possible, the beige water of the Yazoo River from filling their mouths and nostrils. One or two other church members stood nearby to keep back debris and discourage any cottonmouths—or water moccasins, as we called those deadly snakes—from taking part in the ceremony.

As each candidate came forward, the preacher, first determining whether the candidate he was baptizing was a boy or girl, intoned in a rich baritone: "Upon your profession of faith, my brother, in the Lord Jesus, I indeed baptize you in the name of the Father, the Son, and the Holy Ghost." Sisters Ceria M. Travis and Effie D. Purnell took turns singing a hymn: "I Love the Lord, He Heard My Cry," or "Ring the Bell, I Done Got Over." We were then wrapped in white sheets to keep us as warm as possible. When all of us were properly baptized—with the notable exception of one candidate, Richard Garner—we began the walk back to Brother Anderson's house to dress for the church service. This walk was swifter and more purposeful, as we had to shed our wet clothes for the dresses and suits our parents had purchased for this special occasion. It was, of course, a time of great seriousness. Our parents made sure of that. They warned us on any number of occasions that, now that we had become Christians, we couldn't take part in the same kinds of mischief and foolishness as before. Religion was the stick used to regulate our behavior.

Reverend Kingston could never count Richard Garner among his success stories. When it came time to dunk his head under that dirty water harboring poisonous snakes and all manner of debris, Richard simply didn't comply, even under the menacing gaze of his father and uncles, all deacons in the church, and his mother, the church secretary. The pastor finally gave up and sprinkled some water in his direction and pronounced the obligatory formula that separated the saved from the unsaved, the good from the bad. Years afterward, whenever the pastor ran into Richard, he reminded him that he had still not been properly baptized.[2]

Notes

1. According to a friend, the Reverend Dr. Earnest Brothers, the name "mourners' bench" probably refers to one of the beatitudes from Christ's Sermon on the Mount: "Blessed are they that mourn: for they shall be comforted" (Matthew 5:4).

2. Many Baptist churches still believe in the doctrine of total immersion.

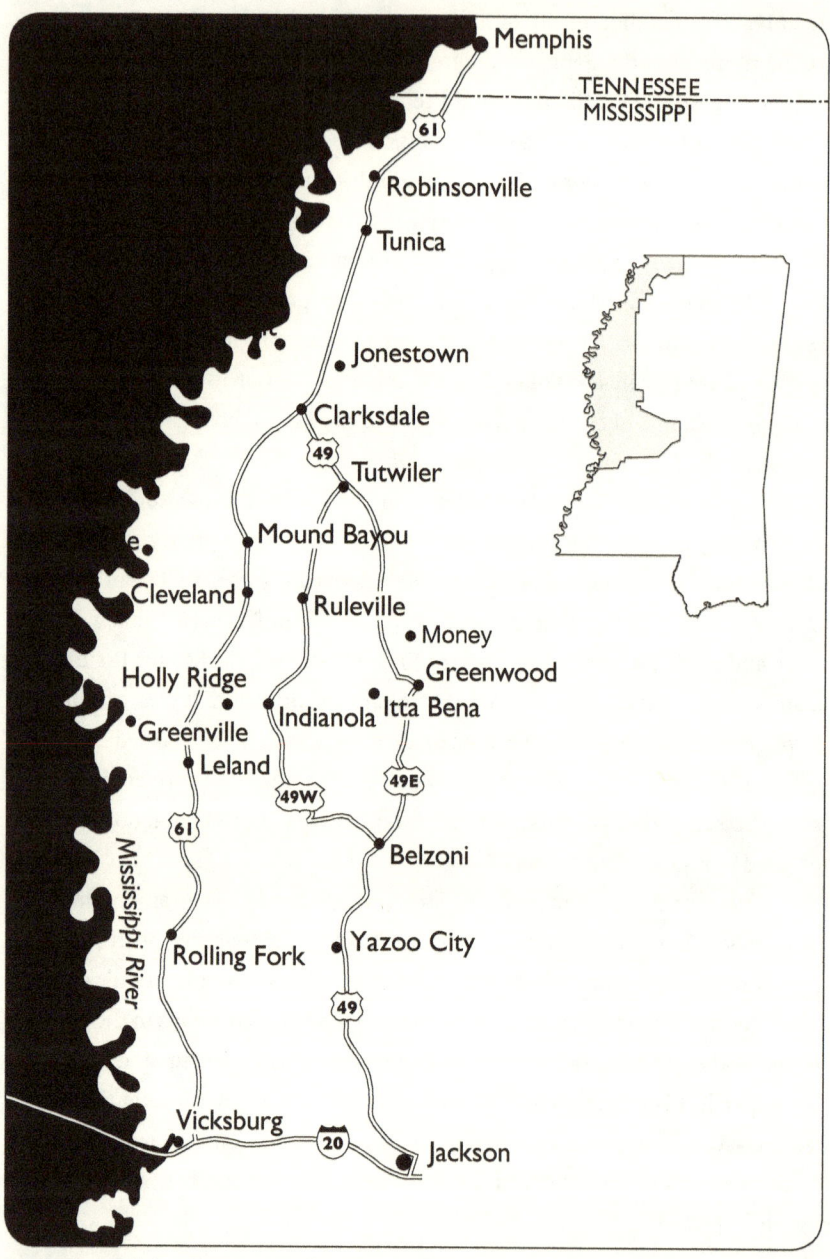

Mississippi and the Mississippi Delta. The shaded area in the smaller map indicates the area shown in the larger map.

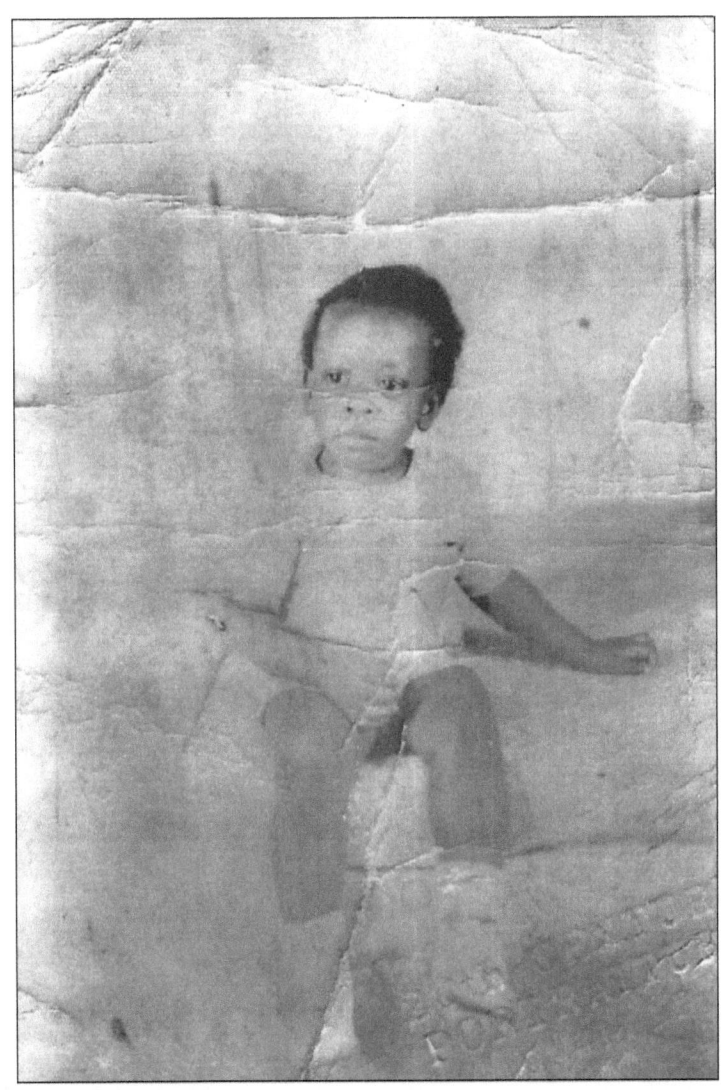

The author at age two.

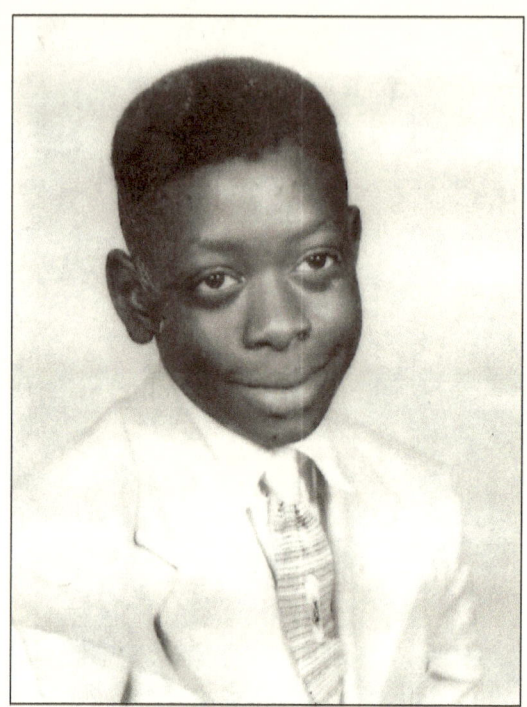

The author at age twelve.

John Hodges, high school graduate (1963).

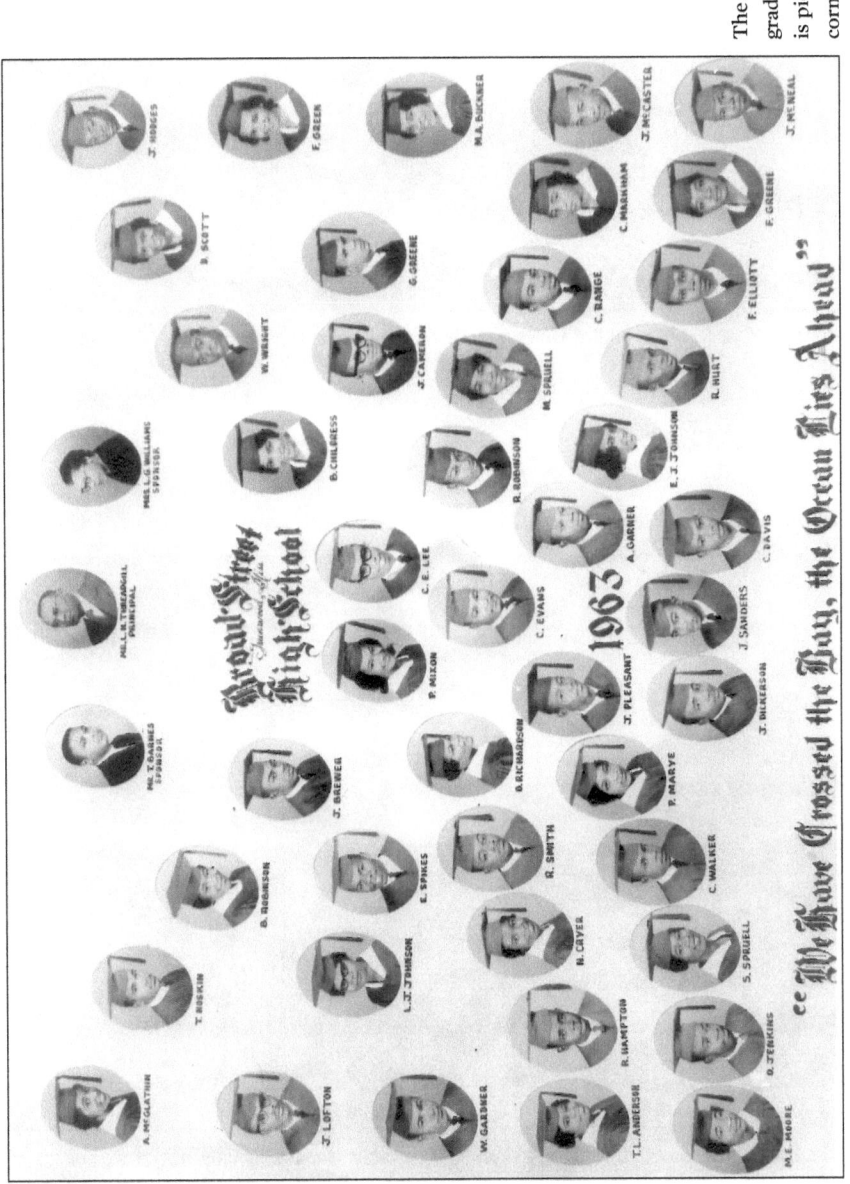

The author's 1963 high school graduating class. The author is pictured in the upper right corner.

G Street Boys: (*from left*) John McNeal, Jeffie McNeal, the author, James O. Elliott, and Roy Elliott.

Home at 804 Avenue G. It is pictured here as later refurbished; originally, half of the house was a store.

The author's mother (*right*) with her friend Mrs. Emma Brown.

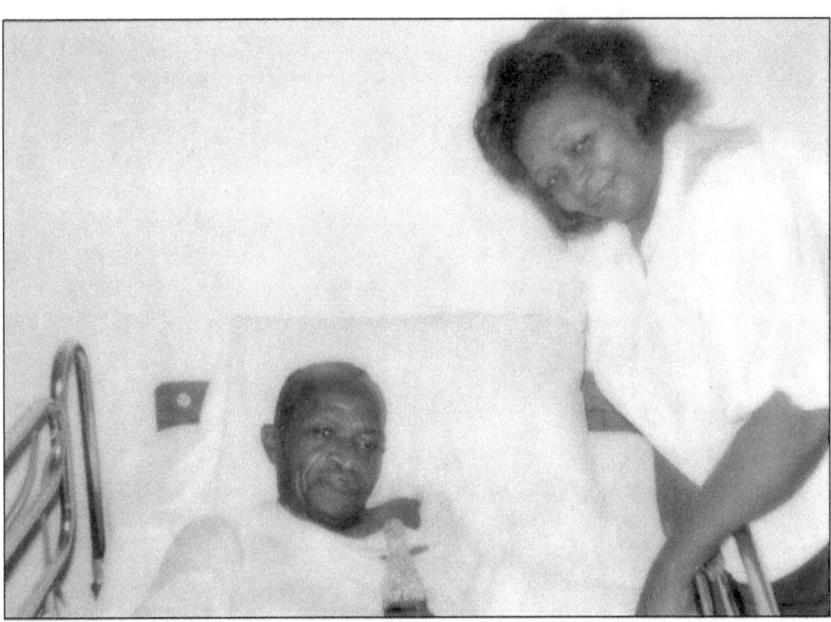

The author's sister Edna and uncle Fred.

Teacher and friend Solomon "Chief" Outlaw.

The author's cousins Lula (*second from left*), Carlos (*third from left*), and Myrtle (*fourth from left*) and their spouses, Andy, Venice, and Maurice.

Uncle Oliver (*center*) and his cousins Arthur "Big Son" Chandler (*left*) and Stone Chandler (*right*).

Classmates at 2007 reunion: (*from left*) Freddie Greene Biddle, Michael Lindsey [deceased], Dollie Scott Mosley, George Greene, Cora Markham Garner, the author, and Jeffie McNeal.

Classmates at 2011 reunion: Shirley Spruell Harris (*left*), the author, and Cora Markham Garner.

Former teachers William Ware, Minnie R. Barfield Baker (*left*), and Helen Griffith Adams.

The author, with Mrs. Ellen Jackson, who shared her home with the G Street Boys.

The Greenes at reunion banquet: (*from left*) Cookie, George, Missy, and Freddie.

My cousin Luevina and her son Nathaniel.

THE BLACK CHURCH

> The Negro church of today is the social centre of Negro life in the United States, and the most characteristic expression of African character.
>
> W. E. B. Du Bois, The Souls of Black Folk

Booker T. Washington once quipped that if you could find a black man who wasn't a Methodist or a Baptist, some white man had been tampering with his religion. Although not generally known for his humor, Washington was giving a fairly accurate picture of the state of religion during his time. With the notable exception of certain new religious movements that have gained some traction in the South, it hasn't changed much since then. In fact, one of the most significant aspects of African American religion is its general constancy through the ages. When I was growing up in the Delta, I thought that the Baptist and Methodist churches were the only two denominations open to blacks. To the predominance of these two groups, we should now certainly add the Church of God in Christ (COGIC).

Yet, in August 1998, on the corner of Bowie Lane and Broad Street in Greenwood, I saw something happening that was both familiar and unusual. A clean-cut, middle-aged black man in coat, shirt, and bowtie was selling newspapers. Dressed as he was in the sweltering, late summer heat, I immediately recognized him as a Muslim. I had often seen Muslims selling papers on busy street corners in places such as Chicago, Atlanta, and even Knoxville, but not in Greenwood, where one was either Baptist, Methodist, or some form of Pentecostal. I paid my dollar for the paper and later had the opportunity to talk with Muhammad, as he now called himself. Standing outside the Wal-Mart and fighting off mosquitos, I listened carefully to his explanation of why he had joined forces with Louis Farrakhan.

Indeed, one of the most significant changes in the region has been the arrival of the Muslims, who can be found in even the smallest communities in the Delta today, places where they wouldn't have been heard of twenty or so years ago. Their growth in the rural South is due to several factors: the widespread impact of television, especially cable television, and the number of blacks who travel from the South to the North on a fairly regular basis. To this must be added the charisma of the leader, together with the general message that Islam offers a better alternative for African Americans. The typical profile of a Muslim in the Delta is this: a young black male in his mid-twenties who has run afoul of the law and quite probably spent some time in prison. In fact, it's usually in prison that such a young man first hears of the teachings of the Honorable Elijah Muhammad (1897–1975), the longtime leader of the Nation of Islam. This, in all likelihood, is not his first exposure to religion. As a child, he likely grew up as a Baptist and attended church, as most of us did, because his parents so dictated. But now he has become convinced that Christianity itself is a tool the white man uses to keep blacks under control. As with many of his brothers, as indeed with the patriarch Elijah Muhammad himself, he has the physical and psychic scars to prove his point.

Islam, in its various forms, has made significant inroads in the Delta. So have several other traditions—so much so that one needs to exercise caution in talking about the black church as if it were a monolithic institution or comprises only two or three major Protestant traditions. Perhaps this has never been the case, and it's certainly even less true today. Yet, it may serve some historical purpose to speak of a religion with deep African roots, one that our forefathers brought with them and that has formed the substance of "the invisible institution"[1] whose features persist in many ways to this day. We may have some difficulty outlining all its contours, but we know it when we hear and see it. It's a tradition that E. Franklin Frazier, Melville Herskovits, W. E. B. Du Bois, Benjamin E. Mays, and James Cone, among other intellectuals, have attempted to describe.

While the Baptist and Methodist strains may be dominant, it transcends any one tradition.

This was the religion of my youth, of which I have been very critical at times, even while recognizing the positive impact it has had on my own life. At times, the church has given blacks the strength to survive, and at others, it seems to have been the chief stumbling block to genuine progress. I will reflect on this negative aspect of the church in other vignettes, but here I wish to speak of its positive impact on me and others in the African American community. Indeed, it was the one institution that gave me the courage, motivation, and confidence to tackle any task large or small. Whenever the South discouraged me, the church was there to prop me up. When society said I couldn't, the black church was the institution that assured me I could do almost anything I set my mind to. It provided this encouragement for countless others also.

As I look back, it seems that I've always been destined to be a teacher, although that wasn't among the professions I initially considered. I simply wanted to make some difference in the lives of others, which I thought could best be accomplished by a career in medicine or law. As I now recall, I got my first opportunity to teach while in Sunday school at Good Hope Missionary Baptist Church around the age of thirteen. I was in charge of providing a review summary of the main points in the lesson for the day. Whenever the lesson demonstration fell on the fourth Sunday, our regular worship day, many churchgoers arrived early for the chance to watch Master Hodges demonstrate the lesson. Apparently, I had some knack for making clear to others what appeared evident to me. After a number of these performances, many thought I was headed for the ministry or a career in teaching. But, as indicated above, I was more interested in doing what I felt at the time was most needed by my people. In whatever I undertook, however, I felt that the mothers, deacons, and regular church members were there to support me. I was never made to feel like a failure in the church, even after one notable incident that might have marked me as such.

On this particular Sunday, the regular pianist did not show, perhaps because of illness or some other reason. Without a pianist, the choir would have to sing *a cappella,* but then someone remembered that Master Hodges had been taking piano lessons and could probably fill in for this emergency. Rather than decline as I should have, I decided to show off my skills. I hadn't practiced with the choir and in fact had never played with any choir before. Truth be told, I wasn't far along in my music lessons. But despite all this, I thought I could do it.

The church told me I could. Needless to say, it didn't go very well at all. My belief that I could pull this off was based on a measure of unchecked confidence and foolhardiness. Though I could read the notes, I was a ways off playing for a black choir that didn't go strictly by the music. There was the swing after each line that wasn't called for in any standard songbook or hymnal, yet so essential to the music. I have no idea how I made it through that performance. I only remember that the church actually paid me, and I graciously accepted the money. Such an incident could easily have been devastating for a child. Yet, I was made to feel no worse than the young boy who forgets his Easter speech but is reassured by the senior mother in the church who says, "That's all right baby, you tried; and anyway, you look so good in your blue suit."

I remember the church during that time as an all-embracing institution that was involved in virtually every aspect of our lives. Since we weren't allowed to have functions at the civic center, or at any public building for that matter, countless activities were held at the church. It was the place where we first met the Lord, as well as our first boyfriend or girlfriend; it was where we went to school, participated in plays, and held our spaghetti dinners and picnics. Here, we were married at the altar and buried in the churchyard cemetery. And it was the place where, along the way, any talent at all was first recognized and encouraged.

Thus, it never occurred to any of us that we should try to attend services at a white church. The black church more than filled the time we had to devote to worship. In any case, we knew we wouldn't be welcome. We seemed resigned to this like that "colored fellow," so the story went, "who was told by Christ that He Himself had been trying without luck to get into that Episcopal church." Integrating white churches became an issue only during the 1960s and 1970s, not so much because we wanted to attend white churches but because we were agitating for acceptance in all arenas and felt that the church, especially, should not be exempt. While most southern whites thought that blacks shouldn't be welcomed at white churches, few were willing to voice their feelings as vehemently as Byron De La Beckwith, the Greenwood white supremacist later convicted for the 1963 murder of Medgar Evers. De La Beckwith swore that no black person would ever attend a church where he was a member. He even carried a pistol to church, letting everyone know that he was prepared to uphold his conviction.

Whites appeared much more interested in maintaining separate churches than did blacks. If whites came to our churches, say, for a funeral, we were pleased and offered them special seats, separate from us. This, in fact, occurred at my mother's funeral, where some whites for whom my mother had worked were given seats normally reserved for deacons and mothers of the church. Although whites seldom attended black churches except for funerals, they had an open invitation to attend our church and were extended every courtesy. The separate seating arrangement was dictated by a higher social law which our church felt that it was either unable or unwilling to challenge, even as late as 1971, the year my mother died.

Our church, like many others, simply stayed away from what some called "that civil rights mess." In return, it was allowed to go its way. It could be a bulwark against racism and intolerance if it could do so without challenging the system. The church would be allowed to support and encourage blacks as long as they stayed in their place. Their place was not to agitate for rights or to try to get into white colleges and universities. They were especially forbidden to become involved with voter-registration matters and were generally expected to ignore anyone who did get involved.

For that reason, you could count on a single hand those churches that opened their doors to mass meetings and other civil rights activities during the 1960s. Several of those that did in the Delta and throughout the South were torched or bombed, some with fatal consequences. Because of its role, the church has always had a place of privilege and power within the African American community, and whites concerned with maintaining the status quo have watched and feared it. So, when the church was attacked, as in certain periods of its life, the violence was meant to strike at the heart and soul of the black community. It was, in fact, an attack upon that very community.

NOTE

1. "The invisible institution" refers to the religion practiced by the slaves outside the mainline churches.

THE BLACK PREACHER

> Young man—
> Young man—
> Your arm's too short to box with God.
>
> James Weldon Johnson, "The Prodigal Son"

As far back as I can remember, folks have told me that I had a mark, or gift, which meant that they felt I had been set apart for some special purpose. No purpose in their minds could be greater than that of becoming a minister of the gospel. Admittedly, there was little in my early or later life that dispelled this notion among those determined to believe it. Family members and close friends claimed they remember me clowning around as a child of three or four imitating preachers I had heard. (As I now recall, I might well have been encouraged in my antics by one of the unsaved, who slipped me a drink of beer or some other spirit.) Then there was the work in Sunday school as a demonstrator of the lesson. Later, in high school, I was called upon to preach the "funeral service" for our football rival, Greenville's Coleman High School, as part of a giant pep rally before the annual Turkey Day classic between Broad Street High and Coleman. My senior class yearbook lists my aspiration as minister. Finally, there was my attendance at the University of Chicago Divinity School, where my interest was in a doctor of philosophy degree and not a degree in ministry or theology.[1] I was following a track that would place me in the classroom rather than in the pulpit. I wound up at Chicago only because the University of Illinois Law School, where I had been accepted, could not grant me a deferment. Once I told my draft board that I was going to a divinity school, they also assumed I was bound for the ministry. I felt no urgent need to clarify matters at that point. It was either divinity school or Vietnam.

So, without asking me, everybody just assumed I would become a minister. I often became hostile and defensive when others made this assumption. More recently, when I again felt the need to correct someone on this point, an old classmate confided in me that if I just studied "The Word," I could very well become a minister. What all this shows is the tremendous respect traditionally accorded the black preacher. Everyone thought I should feel honored to be included among this group. Indeed, the black preacher has often had much more power than his white counterpart. This is certainly true among black Baptists. The reason for this is that, given the structure of the black Baptist Church—or, rather, the lack of it—the black minister is usually left to his own devices to work things out with his congregation. Of course, there is the trustee board, but those individuals are more likely than not to follow the particular wishes of the minister, who, in some cases, inherited the church from his father or grandfather.

Furthermore, whites have shown a measure of respect for the black preacher, whether this is born out of fear or the belief that the preacher is more likely to support than threaten the status quo. Philosopher and theologian Howard Thurman once recalled an incident in which a black man was stopped by a white officer for a routine traffic violation. Just as the policeman took out his billy club, the black man earnestly inquired, "You wouldn't hit a man of the cloth, would you?" The minister was thus spared a certain beating and allowed to continue on his way.[2]

Many ministers are highly educated individuals who are completely engaged in the affairs of their communities and are making a difference on the world stage. They include college presidents, congressmen, businessmen, and the heads of major civic organizations. They wield power in all areas of life, not just in the pulpit. That *Ebony* magazine's list of the most influential African Americans always includes a large percentage of ministers is no accident. Du Bois's comment regarding the power of the black preacher still holds:

> The Preacher is the most unique personality developed by the Negro on American soil. A leader, a politician, an orator, a "boss,"

an intriguer, an idealist, all these he is, and ever, too, the centre of a group of men, now twenty, now a thousand in number. The combination of a certain adroitness with deep-seated earnestness, of tact with consummate ability, gave him his preëminence, and helps him maintain it.[3]

Indeed, as *Ebony* suggests, African Americans are more likely to choose their leaders from this profession than from any other group.

Although the plantation preacher often lacked the sophistication of his northern brother, he was every bit his equal in other aspects of his role. His influence, though more local, was great nevertheless. His primary purpose, of course, was to preach on Sundays, marry church members, visit them when they were sick, and preside at their funerals when they died. During my youth, the small church I attended, like many others, couldn't afford a full-time minister. So, in those situations, the minister might preach on the first and third Sundays, or on the second and fourth Sundays. For many of the plantation churches, preaching occurred on just one Sunday per month. This is how it was at my own church. Sunday school and meetings of the Baptist Young People's Union were held every Sunday, but the regular service was held on the fourth Sunday of the month. Our pastor had at least two other churches to take care of on those other Sundays.

I doubt that the pastor was paid anything like a regular salary. His pay generally came out of the collections for that pastoral Sunday. To make ends meet, he often had to take a job doing some menial labor through the week. He certainly didn't have any regular benefits as many pastors of medium to large churches have today. The membership would, of course, remember him with monetary gifts for Christmas and on his birthday and his anniversary at the church. Compared to members of the congregation, he wore nice clothes and drove a large modern car. He could expect to be served Sunday dinner and be lodged for the night after the evening service at the home of one of the members. Hosting the pastor was quite an honor, which was reserved for the more well-to-do members. For poorer families, such as ours, this wasn't even a consideration. In general, the congregation saw it as an article of faith to take care of "us" pastor, even when this meant that they themselves might go wanting.

In exchange, the members expected to hear a stirring message on pastoral Sunday; the minister's job was to make sure that this happened. His goal was to preach the righteousness of a living God who was able to answer the prayers of the believers. He was prepared to do whatever was necessary for the congregation to realize God's presence among them. "God is not dead," he'd shout, and the congregation took its cue that they were to make a joyful noise in acknowledging this fact. A typical black Baptist church creates a highly charged atmosphere where one can expect to sense God's presence. In my discussion of the folk sermon, I'll endeavor to suggest in greater detail how this is done.

As a child, I remember being mesmerized by the frenzy taking place all around me. Even though I couldn't understand every word the minister was saying, I was nevertheless taken by the spectacle. For example, it was not until I was about nine or ten that I understood that everyone who died was not named Reed or Marie. To my young ears, the minister, in addressing the *bereaved* family, seemed to be saying something like "the Reed family" or "the Marie family." Certainly, the preacher hadn't forgotten the name of the departed member.

My reasons for not pursuing a career in the ministry are perhaps more deep-seated than I realize. But I believe them to be somewhere located in my image of the black preacher of my youth. He was an individual who better fit the description set forth by Frederick Douglass and William Wells Brown than that presented by Du Bois. He was, for the most part, only slightly better educated than those he was attempting to lead. His authority to preach came not from a college or seminary degree but from a certain call he received from God. I saw the minister more as an object of caricature than as an individual of seriousness and gravitas. That those whites for whom my parents worked would suggest that I could be a preacher did very little to dissuade me from the belief that preaching was the one profession I should *not* aspire to. All too often, the average black preacher was not seen as a threat to the power of whites.

While I was impressed with the minister's ability to preach, I wasn't impressed at all with how he handled what I perceived to be his other duties. He was an orator and charmer and, perhaps much too often, ladies' man. There were unconfirmed reports of a certain minister fathering a child out of wedlock and of being involved with one or more of his members. Apparently, he was seen making a number of visits to one or more of these sisters' homes at all times of the day and evening. Generally, such reports should be treated as malicious gossip until they are shown to come from more than one reliable source and suggest some kind of pattern.

During my work with the Greenwood civil rights movement in the early 1960s, I became even more disappointed with the average preacher I saw in the Delta. He was, I'll admit, certainly in a tough spot, required to do something like a tightrope act. How could he allow civil rights workers to speak about voter registration matters to church members who depended on whites for their jobs? Shouldn't he be forgiven for not volunteering his church for a mass meeting when the very land upon which the church stood had been donated by the plantation owner? In those and countless other ways, he often found himself seriously compromised. Whenever he got the notion to support the movement in some way, including registering to vote himself, he was reminded of the tragic case of the Reverend George W. Lee, the Belzoni, Mississippi, NAACP leader who was murdered in 1955. It's for this reason that you could count on one hand the number of preachers who were actively involved in the civil rights movement in Greenwood.

Compromised in his role as a civic leader and often fearful for his life, he had to provide his people with whatever hope he could by preaching sermons designed to numb their pain and suffering in this life while promising an eventual reward in the next, where "they will be done with the troubles of this world."

Notes

1. Chicago, as well as several other major divinity schools, has long offered the PhD in addition to other typical theological degrees.

2. Howard Thurman, *The Luminous Darkness* (New York: Harper & Row, 1965), 22–24.

3. W. E. B. Du Bois, *The Souls of Black Folk* (Chicago: A. C. McClung & Co., 1903), 190–91.

THE FOLK SERMON

> The black and massive form of the preacher swayed and quivered as the words crowded to his lips and flew at us in singular eloquence. The people moaned and fluttered, and then the gaunt-cheeked brown woman beside me suddenly leaped straight into the air and shrieked like a lost soul, while round about came wail and groan and outcry, and a scene of human passion such as I had never conceived before.
>
> W. E. B. Du Bois, The Souls of Black Folk

W. E. B. Du Bois's description of the old-time Negro sermon presented at the dawn of the twentieth century is similar to what I remember as a child growing up in the Mississippi Delta. This type of sermon can still be heard on Sunday mornings in a large number of black churches in Mound Bayou, or Clarksdale, or Greenwood, or in any Delta hamlet or town. Indeed, what appears remarkable is that this art form seems to have remained fairly untouched over the years. Although ministers today are often better educated and have refined their preaching techniques, the substance and purpose of the sermon remain essentially that described by Du Bois over a hundred years ago. Its history, of course, can be traced back much further than that.

Strictly as a work of art, it rivals that of any well-made drama or opera. To speak of it in these terms is perhaps to appear disrespectful or irreverent, if not downright blasphemous. What I wish to convey here is that the performance may be appreciated even if one does not always comprehend or agree with the message.

As I noted in my previous vignette, church members expect to hear a stirring message when they convene, and the minister's job is to deliver it. Although he may not be well educated, he is a master communicator. Growing up in one of those churches, I was always amazed at the ability of the minister to get his members to shout. It seemed that unless he was able to make his congregation "happy," he had failed. They wanted to be transported to a world beyond their daily troubles. I noticed early on that those who shouted tended to be older women who had just gone through a tough period in their lives. That they had made it through their trials with any degree of success was testimony to God's goodness and power to answer prayer.

I noticed how often the minister resorted to using elements of rhyme and rhythm and other poetic techniques. The best ministers were masters in their use of poetry to create visual and auditory imagery. In fact, I became so enthralled with the ministers' ability in this area that I wrote my master's thesis in English at Atlanta University on the subject of "Poetry in the Sermons of Contemporary Black Baptist Preachers." After I began work on the topic, I learned that James Weldon Johnson earlier had noticed this same aspect of black preaching. His 1927 book, *God's Trombones,* is a collection of seven poems written in the style of the black sermon, and after him, a number of others have noted the use of poetic elements to produce what is now often referred to as the chanted sermon.

Johnson's inspiration for writing "The Creation," his best known poem in *God's Trombones,* came from his visit to a black church, where he saw a minister who

> strode the pulpit up and down, and brought into play the full gamut of a voice that excited my envy. He intoned, he moaned, he pleaded—he blared, he crashed, he thundered. A woman sprang to her feet, uttered a piercing scream, threw her handbag to the pulpit, striking the preacher full in the chest, whirled round several times, and fainted. The congregation reached a state of ecstasy. I was fascinated by this exhibition; moreover, something primordial in me was stirred. Before the preacher finished, I took a slip of paper from my pocket and somewhat surreptitiously jotted down some ideas for my first poem.[1]

The scriptural basis for this poem is the first chapter of Genesis. Comparing the poem to the biblical account, we immediately become aware of Johnson's poetic technique, by which he renders the rather unimaginative and staid biblical version more vivid and lifelike. From the time God steps out on space and decides to make a world culminating in the creation of man, *Imago Dei*, the poet, using visual imagery, invites us to take part in that very creation.

Johnson must have been keenly aware of the old-time preacher's ability to re-create experience through a variety of means, notably through imagery, rhythm, personification, and allegory—that is, through some of the basic elements of poetry. The preacher lets his congregation know that God is because He acts. God smiles and the light breaks; He bats his eyes and the lightning flashes; and He blows the breath of life into man, who becomes a living soul. Julius Lester's statement on the black preacher is particularly pertinent here: "God is like a personal friend, an old buddy, whom you walk with and talk to man to man. The black church congregation doesn't want to be told about God, it wants to feel Him, see Him, and touch Him. It is the Preacher's responsibility to see that they do."[2]

Though no description can capture the flavor and fervor of actually seeing and hearing firsthand a preacher deliver his sermon, it might be possible to suggest the ways in which he's able to communicate his message. The sermon has a tripartite structure consisting of an introduction, body, and conclusion.

The preacher starts out slowly and often complains of being under the weather. He certainly needs the Holy Spirit and the congregation to get him through his task. He may say a prayer, invoking God's presence to help "his lowly servant preach His divine Word." He announces the scriptural text for the sermon and gives the subject of his sermon, which he may repeat for effect. In the body of the sermon he endeavors to relate the text and subject to the lives of his congregation. Near the end of this section, the pace quickens, so that by the time the preacher arrives at his conclusion, his light canter has become a full gallop. Now overtaken by the Holy Spirit, he cannot contain himself, and neither can the congregation. He now has abandoned his subject so that he can proclaim God's love and grace generally. He is now preaching and relying on everything in his arsenal to do so. His whoop now becomes more audible, rhythmic patterns develop, and imagery becomes more noticeable. A look at excerpts from sermons I heard and recorded during the 1960s will help make the point. It should become apparent that the preacher depends as much on his congregation as they on him to make sure that the message is properly communicated.

The Reverend W. H. Kingston makes use of certain poetic devices in this excerpt from his sermon "The Prince of Peace":

> Don't you remember last Sunday night? The winds were
> rising, the thunder were roaring, the lightning were
> playing a limber game on the bosom of the cloud.

The parallel structure created by repetition helps create a rhythmic pattern. The preacher's intonation and inflection are also important as he produces an image of a storm the members can hear and see.

Another minister, the Reverend Jasper Williams, uses a similar pattern to show Jesus's love for humankind:

> Look at Him, my dying bed-maker;
> Jesus, my Rose of Sharon,
> Jesus, my rock in a weary land.
> Come on down to this sinful world.
>
> Born in another man's stable
> Grew up in another man's town
> Walked another man's streets
> Went to another man's school
> Preached in another man's book
> Bore another man's cross
> Died for another man's sin
> Rose for another man's salvation
> He did it because he loved us. Yes He did!

The Reverend Williams here uses repetition of parallel lines to create a rhythmic pattern that takes us from Jesus's birth to His death and resurrection. Not until we consider the above pattern spoken with perfect timing and phrasing by a consummately skilled orator can we begin to understand the overall effectiveness of this passage.

The preacher may also show Jesus's love through a simple yet vivid image. According to one minister, Jesus told God, "Give me a man robe, let me dress myself up in humanity." What better way is there to express the idea of an anthropomorphic God than in this image of a "man robe"? A troubled people must be convinced of God's love and concern and His willingness to come to earth for their sake.

The incidents surrounding the death and resurrection are often dramatized to make the congregation identify more closely with the agony and suffering of Christ. Consider this excerpt from Reverend Williams's sermon "Jesus on the Cross":

> While He was carrying the cross, Death began to talk with Him, Death said, "Jesus you ought to come on and die now." But Jesus said, "No, it ain't time for me to die. Get back Death leave me alone." He went on up a little higher and after while Death came running back and said, "Jesus, come on and die now, I've been tracking you down for thirty-three long years. I thought I had you out on the stormy sea, but you walked away, knocked the sea from your eyes and said, "Peace be still and I had to go and leave you alone . . ." Death came back and said, "Jesus, come on and die now." Jesus said, "Death you leave me alone; you can't take my life, but I'll lay my life down." He looked toward heaven and said, "Father in thy hands I commend my spirit."

Since Death is personified, the above drama appears real because it is an actual dialogue between two real characters, Death and Jesus. The drama is narrated so skillfully that the preacher draws little attention to himself, allowing the congregation to focus its attention on the central figures. The congregation witnesses and even takes part in the Crucifixion. Furthermore, through the use of visual imagery, the minister attempts to make the congregation not only see but even touch the wounds of Jesus, as is apparent in the following lines:

> Nails were in his hands and feet. Blood, because of a thorny crown, was gouging from his brow, running into the lock of his shoulders.

The word *gouging* is particularly effective, as it suggests a rapid uneven flow. This image in its intensity moves beyond the mere visual level. It touches upon the inner life of feeling.

No doubt the most persistent element found in the black sermon is the pattern of call and response. By this means, the preacher is able to carry on a conversation with the congregation, as this brief excerpt makes clear:

MINISTER: Can there be peace on earth? Oh have mercy Lord!
CONGREGATION: Have mercy Lord!
MINISTER: Help your servant preach Your eternal word. Oh! Oh! Lord.
CONGREGATION: Oh! Lord!

But there is another type of call-and-response pattern, one that takes place between the preacher and other ministers in the pulpit. This help from the pulpit happens at the same time as the call and response between the minister and the congregation. Rather than create confusion, it contributes to the overall effectiveness of the sermon:

MINISTER: I'm going to talk this morning about a Waymaker.
PULPIT MINISTER: Yeah! A Waymaker!
MINISTER: Jesus may not have made no way for you. But Jesus has made a way for me.
PULPIT: Yeah! Go 'head now.
MINISTER: So many times.
PULPIT: So many times. Yeah! Yeah!
MINISTER: When I didn't know the way.
PULPIT: Yeah! Yeah!
MINISTER: The way was dark.
PULPIT: Yeah Dark.
MINISTER: Sometimes the hills were high.
PULPIT: Yeah! Yeah! High!
MINISTER: Sometime the valleys were low.
PULPIT: Yeah! Yeah! Low!
MINISTER: But He made a way.
PULPIT: Made a way! Yeah!

I could give numerous examples of the various ways in which the preacher conveys his message to his congregation. The essential point is that, in attending one of these services, one does so not so much as an observer but as an active participant. I'll consider later the usual content of these messages. But for now we need only note that, having gotten their batteries recharged, the congregation seems refreshed and strengthened to the point that they can endure another round of hardships, sorrows, and disappointments.

NOTES

1. James Weldon Johnson, *God's Trombones* (New York: Viking Press, 1927), 6–7.

2. Julius Lester, *Look Out, Whitey! Black Power is Gon Get Your Mama* (New York: Grove Press, 1968), 87.

IS GOD GOOD?

> O God? How long shall the mounting flood of innocent blood roar in Thine ears and pound in our hearts for vengeance? ... Forgive us, good Lord, we know not what we say! Bewildered we are and passion-tossed, mad with the madness of a mobbed and mocked and murdered people; straining at the armposts of Thy throne, we raise our shackled hands and charge Thee, God, by the bones of our stolen fathers, by the tears of our dead mothers, by the very blood of Thy crucified Christ: What meaneth this? Tell us the plan; give us the sign!
>
> **W. E. B. Du Bois,** *Darkwater*

On the second and fourth Sunday of each month, the members of a typical black rural church in the Mississippi Delta congregate to reassure themselves that, despite their hardships (one almost feels because of them), God is "a good God," who will "in His own time" deliver them from their sufferings. "He knows," the minister intones, "just how much we can bear." A large chorus of "amens" rings throughout this church of about sixty or so worshipers. This scene is repeated at almost every black church in the Mississippi Delta, if not on the second and fourth Sundays, then on the first and third. For the smaller assemblies, a service is held only once a month.

Across town, the scene is markedly different. The whites in this community, though convinced of God's goodness, don't seem to go to the lengths their black brethren go to in attempting to reconcile the fact of their suffering with the intrinsic goodness of God. I've often wondered why this seems to be the case. Are the reasons ethnic or economic or some combination of both? Is there some relationship between one's economic level and his or her intensity of faith?[1] While it must be acknowledged that whites experience suffering just as blacks do, the nature and intensity of the suffering are different. Black suffering, especially in the Mississippi Delta, is so often economically based. There is one premise my research and observations have confirmed: those who suffer greater economic hardships are the ones most likely to proclaim God's goodness and to defend Him/Her against charges of indifference or injustice. The sermons I've observed appear to accept suffering either as normative or compensatory, as having some intrinsic value. They thus hearken back to Jupiter Hammon's "Address to the Negroes in the State of New York (1787)," which argued that blacks should accept suffering in this life in exchange for an eternal life of happiness.[2] Similarly, Martin Luther King Jr. promoted a notion of the redemptive value of black suffering, a view that placed him closer to Hammon than he likely would have cared to acknowledge. Could one of the major stumbling blocks be that, as Christians, these ministers had to work from a paradigm that pigeonholed them into certain doctrines tending either toward fatalism or a compensatory view of the world? In either case, individuals are encouraged to accept their situation of suffering blindly rather than to attempt to ameliorate it. Richard Wright, while not providing any solutions himself, does offer a challenge to those ministers who seem, so easily, to find meaning in what appears to be meaningless suffering—a critique that I'll address more fully in a moment.

Admittedly, suffering is a difficult term to grasp. It may be generally defined as the enduring of extraordinary pain, loss, deprivation, or hardship. While we normally understand suffering as something endured against an individual's will, we must acknowledge that one may suffer willingly. The masochist who seeks pleasure from pain; the individual who fasts for religious or political reasons, depriving himself of food or drink; the Shiite who flogs himself to re-create the martyrdom of Husayn—all are examples of willing sufferers. This type of suffering may be considered positive in that it is endured willingly and has some desired goal that is determined and controlled by the one who endures the pain or deprivation.

An intriguing understanding of suffering is that which Martin Luther King calls creative suffering. King's success, in great part, depended on his ability to submit himself and to have others submit themselves to the kind of brutality that blacks faced on a daily basis. Pictures of vicious dogs attacking blacks, of fire hoses turned on children, for example, were used in positive, creative ways to call attention to the suffering of blacks in general. King speaks of this type of suffering in his "I Have a Dream" speech, delivered on August 28, 1963:

> I am not unmindful that some of you have come here out of excessive trials and tribulation. Some of you have come fresh from narrow jail cells. Some of you have come from areas where your quest for freedom left you battered by the storms of persecution and staggered by the winds of police brutality. You have been the veterans of creative suffering. Continue to work with the faith that unearned suffering is redemptive.[3]

Whether or not this type or any type of suffering can be considered redemptive is an issue I'll briefly touch on in a moment, but let's first consider negative suffering, to which one doesn't submit willingly and over which one has little or no control. Consider especially its impact on communities rather than on particular individuals. This kind of suffering is best understood in relation to some normative condition. That is, when we say that some individual or community is suffering, we mean that their pains or losses or hardships are much more extreme than those of others. In speaking of the suffering of whole communities, we also recognize a causal factor, in that one group's suffering results, either directly or indirectly, from the actions of another group, which stands to gain socially, economically, or emotionally from the plight of the suffering group. In arguing that blacks in the Mississippi Delta suffer,[4] I mean that they experience hardships far greater than their white counterparts, who, as a community, stand to benefit from the suffering and oppression of blacks.

While whites outnumber blacks in the state of Mississippi as a whole, in each of the counties that make up the Delta blacks outnumber whites by a significant margin. And in many of these municipalities, the percentage of blacks now exceeds 70 percent. The 2010 U.S. Census indicates that these Delta counties lead the state in individuals below the poverty level—and this in a state leading the nation in that statistic. Charles S. Aiken, a professor of geography at the University of Tennessee, points to a disturbing pattern of rural ghettos throughout the Delta, created in great part by white flight. He writes:

> Black ghetto towns have characteristics that are similar to those of metropolitan black ghettos, including a high poverty rate, federal housing that has contributed to the concentration of a minority population, and lack of employment opportunities.... Despite their importance as spatial concentrations of a minority population, black ghetto towns are obscure places that face bleak futures.[5]

Accompanying the high level of poverty is a host of related problems, including poor health care, higher illiteracy, shorter life expectancies, drug addiction, and a higher rate of infant mortality. Blacks are also more likely to be victims of crimes and random violence. There can be little doubt that in this area blacks suffer disproportionately to whites. Yet, it's in communities such as these that on the second and fourth Sundays, or on the first and third, that the members follow their ministers' lead in proclaiming the goodness of God.

The novelist Richard Wright, who grew up in Mississippi and lived for a while in Greenwood, provides an important critique of the kind of religion he saw practiced in the South of a few generations ago. In many ways, it is similar to that found in Mississippi today. The symbols of the Christian faith that seemed to nourish members of Wright's immediate family were for him but another cruel reminder of the power whites exercised over blacks. In his home, he noticed how regularly the worst atrocities seemed always to "walk in the wake of a hymn." The Seventh Day Adventist religion of his grandmother not only failed to address the larger issues of racial injustice and suffering but seemed itself to be a weapon in the arsenal of the white power brokers.

In his essay "Tradition and Industrialization," Wright discusses his Protestant upbringing in some detail, noting:

> I lived my childhood under a racial code, brutal and bloody, that white men proclaimed was made mandatory by the nature of their religion. Naturally, I rejected that religion and would reject any religion which prescribes for me an inferior position in life; I reject that tradition or any tradition which proscribes my humanity.[6]

Isn't this precisely what Bigger Thomas, in Wright's novel *Native Son*, does as he sits in his jail cell awaiting execution? He rejects the vicarious view of suffering offered by Reverend Hammond. As the family minister pleads with him to accept the cross and the victory through death it symbolizes, Bigger's mind flashes back to the cross he saw burned by the Ku Klux Klan just outside the courthouse as part of its regular ritual of racial and religious hatred. In his anguish and confusion, he cries, "I can die without a cross."

Wright, therefore, unlike King, refuses to take the cross upon himself. For Wright, suffering has no apparent value, no real meaning. In his autobiography, *Black Boy*, he recalls the message he gave to the boy whom his grandmother had sent to him in the hope of softening his position on religion. Wright remembers telling the boy: "If laying down my life could stop the suffering in the world, I'd do it. But I don't believe anything can stop it."[7]

While I wouldn't go to the extent Wright does in rejecting the religion he saw practiced regularly in the South of his time, I do support him in the view that there is no value in black suffering. I don't believe that God wants blacks to suffer any more than any of His other children. And those sermons that seem to accept suffering as normative do a great disservice to the African American community. This theology, if followed, too often leads to stagnation and procrastination, to the individual accepting his or her suffering as ordained by God.

In thus criticizing the message I so often heard in sermons is not to say that the sermons have no value. Indeed, they may provide some kind of catharsis or release valve when the pressures of life are too great. I've already mentioned their importance as works of art. But there is no reason that the sermons cannot serve those purposes, as well as provide guidelines for taking full advantage of a world "charged with the grandeur of God."[8]

NOTES

1. Maya Angelou's thoughts on this subject are most pertinent: "I find it interesting that the meanest life, the poorest existence, is attributed to God's will, but as human beings become more affluent, as their living standard and style begin to ascend the material scale, God descends the scale of responsibility at a commensurate speed." *I Know Why the Caged Bird Sings* (New York: Bantam Books, 1971), 120–21.

2. Hammon's address can be downloaded as a PDF from DigitalCommons@University of Nebraska–Lincoln: http://digitalcommons.unl.edu/etas/12/.

3. Many commentators on Martin Luther King, including Vincent Harding, James Baldwin, and James Cone, have noted a shift in King's philosophy beginning around 1966. Although technically holding to principles of nonviolence, he began to stress issues related to economic justice. The notion of the redemptive value of unearned suffering appears to be absent from his later writings.

4. It must be acknowledged that some individuals who, by any objective standard, appear to be suffering may not see themselves as being particularly disadvantaged (or, at least, won't admit this to others). Can the category of suffering, then, be presupposed for individuals who don't feel that the term applies to them? I believe that it can, for the nature of their oppression may be such that they aren't fully aware of their own situation.

5. Charles S. Aiken, "A New Type of Black Ghetto in the Plantation South," *Annals of the Association of American Geographers* 80, no. 2 (1990): 224–46.

6. Richard Wright, "Tradition and Industrialization," in *White Man Listen!* (New York: Doubleday, 1957), 86.

7. Richard Wright, *Black Boy* (New York: Harper & Row, 1945), 127–28.

8. This phrase comes from Gerard Manly Hopkins's 1877 poem "God's Grandeur."

THE COLOR LINE

> To live anywhere in the world of A.D. 1955 and be against equality because of race or color, is like living in Alaska and being against snow.
> **William Faulkner, address to the Southern Historical Association**

> The problem of the twentieth century is the problem of the color-line.
> **W. E. B. Du Bois,** *The Souls of Black Folk*

W. E. B. Du Bois wrote more than a century ago that in most American cities you'd find nine-tenths of blacks separated from nine-tenths of whites by a color line. Still evident to a large degree today, this line was a tangible partition between the races, which separated them in all aspects of social, political, and religious life. In one city it might be a creek, in another a street, and in still another a railroad track. But whatever it might be, it was a clear demarcation separating two worlds: those within and those outside the veil. Originally intended to regulate the relationship and conduct between blacks and whites after slavery, the color line has, in more recent times in the Delta, become the single greatest stumbling block to racial harmony and genuine progress.

This doctrine was given official sanction in the Supreme Court case *Plessy v. Ferguson* in 1896. On the short train ride from New Orleans to Covington, Louisiana, Homer Plessy, who was one-eighth black and seven-eighths white, sat in the car reserved for whites. In so doing, he violated the 1890 Louisiana Railways Accommodations Act, which stipulated that white and black passengers should sit in separate compartments.[1] Only those blacks who were clearly serving white passengers, such as nurses and personal maids, were permitted to sit in the white section. Plessy's attorneys argued, with no success, that this law violated rights granted to him under the Thirteenth and Fourteenth Amendments.

The court held that it was indeed reasonable to separate black and white passengers and that such laws contravened neither of the two constitutional amendments.[2] The court thus institutionalized the doctrine of "separate but equal" under which this nation operated for well over fifty years. Booker T. Washington, a year earlier in 1895, had assured whites in his famous Atlanta Exposition address that blacks would not clamor for social and political equality and that he would do what he could to persuade his people of the folly of such agitation. Wasn't it better to have the opportunity to earn a dollar in a factory than to spend a dollar in an opera house? He thus concluded that blacks and whites could be "as separate as the fingers" in social and political matters, "yet one as the hand" in economic matters that would benefit both races.

W. E. B. Du Bois, who had earlier penned a note to Washington commending him for the eloquence of his words in Atlanta, would by 1903 see this compromise as something of a Faustian bargain. Had Washington given away too much in his effort to assure blacks a fair share of the country's economic pie? Furthermore, Du Bois and some others wondered whether whites had fastened their attention more on the separate fingers than on the single hand in Washington's paradigm. It became painfully obvious that in the period preceding the Great Depression, southern blacks didn't benefit nearly as much as their white neighbors did in the cotton economy.[3]

Throughout Mississippi and in the Delta in particular, enforced segregation not only embarrassed blacks and relegated them to an inferior status, it also embarrassed the entire state and prevented it from taking full advantage of its rich resources and talents. Reviewing a few well-known examples may help prove the point. The state spent untold millions creating a dual educational system for blacks and whites because of the perceived necessity to keep the races separate. This resulted not only in black grade schools and black high schools but black colleges as well.[4] Thus, limited resources for education became even more strained, which may be partly responsible for Mississippi ranking near the bottom in terms of literacy and the overall educational level of its citizens.

Education is but one example of how forced segregation proved costly, embarrassing, and absurd. In periods of national and regional crises, the state found its efforts to offer relief to all its citizens compromised by a policy that mandated separate facilities and accommodations for blacks and whites. This occurred during the great flu epidemic in 1918 and again during the great flood that hit the Delta in 1927. In casting about for ways to handle these crises, everything was placed on the table except the policy of racial apartheid.

Over the years, governors and state officials not only refused to question whether segregation was a sensible policy, but they often used state revenues to support various groups, both legal and extralegal, that were determined to strengthen segregation's grip.[5] Whenever they felt segregation was being threatened or undermined, governors from James Vardaman to Theodore Bilbo to Ross Barnett were there to reassure white citizens that, despite federal and judicial intervention, separation of the races was still the law in the state.

The ruling in *Brown v. Board of Education* proved especially challenging. The Supreme Court's unanimous finding that segregated schools were inherently unequal was quite a blow to those who considered it reasonable to separate individuals along the lines of color so long as "equal" facilities were provided to both groups. Now this notion had been completely upended by a court decision leaving no doubt that state-sponsored segregation was unconstitutional.[6]

The court relied on the findings of psychologists Kenneth and Mamie Clark, who proved through their doll test that segregation had such a demeaning impact on minority children that it was difficult for them to learn and compete with students of the majority group.[7] Now, I readily admit that segregation has had a negative impact on me and other blacks as well, but I don't believe its negative impact has been limited to blacks. I've noted how segregation proved to be an albatross around the necks of Mississippians trying to make the best use of scarce resources and compete with other states in regard to education and economic development. Now, I wish to consider some personal experiences that, I believe, show the psychological effects on me and others caused by strict enforcement of the color bar.

Long after the Supreme Court had ordered the removal of those "colored only" signs over water fountains, bathrooms, and waiting rooms, blacks still went to those familiar areas to use the facilities previously designated for them. African Americans had learned their lessons so well that the authorities knew that if they kept the facilities—whether there were signs or not—most blacks would still observe the rules of apartheid. Even when I returned to Greenwood long after the period of enforced segregation, I found myself subconsciously changing my own conduct to conform to the mores of the South in which I had been brought up. And, of course, I wasn't alone in this. It was noticeable aboard buses, as black and white interstate passengers seemed to change in their relationship to one another once they reached Memphis. If they were headed south, that relationship became more strained; if they were headed north, the opposite occurred. Perry Lymon, my cousin Luevina's husband, indicated that many buses had a curtain that could be lowered or raised at a given point, depending on whether the bus was headed south or north.

The old laws segregating whites and blacks seemed immutable, and officials often went to great lengths to carry them out regardless of cost or inconvenience. More than one black entertainer coming to the South faced the prospect of presenting his or her act to an all-white or all-black audience unless some satisfactory seating arrangements could be made to respect the city's segregation codes. I faced a rather uncomfortable situation in 1963 when, as president of the Magnolia State Association of Student Councils, I was invited along with other state presidents to Colonial Williamsburg. It didn't take long for us to realize that some states had two representatives and that they were all southern states. So I, along with a white counterpart, represented Mississippi. I suppose that he represented the white citizens, and I the black citizens. The southern states found an ingenious way to have two representatives, while much larger states, such as California, New York, and Illinois, had only one.

In the Delta, as in other places in the South, the color line decreed that blacks use the back door. If we wanted to sell our produce to whites, we had to use the back door. No one thought twice about breaking this rule. A riddle supposedly popular among whites of a few generations ago posed the question, "Why do whites in the South find it necessary to lock only their back door?" The assumption, of course, was that blacks didn't use the front door and that whites didn't steal.[8] The hideousness of this code was brought home to me a number of years after I had left the South. It was in 1971 following my mother's death, when I was studying for my doctorate at the University of Chicago. My mother always insisted on paying all just debts. So, after she died, I wanted very much to honor her by paying her doctor bills. As I approached the doctor's office, the secretary or nurse, in a pleasant but insistent voice, said that I needed to come to the back. Already saddened by my mother's death, I didn't need this added insult. "If you want this money," I said most firmly, "you will take it from me where I stand." She didn't like this at all and accepted the money with a huff.

The above incident proves that the color bar in the South was so stringent and had so much traction that, even by the early seventies, some still tried to enforce its principles. Few, if any, exceptions were allowed. It governed all aspects of life in the Mississippi Delta, and the South in general to the point of absurdity. In arguing Homer Plessy's case, his lead attorney, Albion Tourgé, posed several questions designed to show how unreasonable the Louisiana law was and how it violated basic rights of free association. Would a white mother traveling with her infant black child be forced to separate herself from her own child? What if black and white passengers of their own volition decided they wanted to sit together?

In discussing the *Brown* case, I touched on some of the psychological effects of a systematic policy of segregation. I may never fully realize, for instance, the psychological damage I suffered when I felt I had to leave whenever Vicki Jo Laurent's white friends came over to see him. I knew how I felt when I couldn't play with him anymore, but how did he himself feel? If I developed an unconscious sense of inferiority, wasn't it also damaging to develop an unconscious sense of one's superiority? If in the one it leads to self-doubt, might it in the other lead to haughtiness? Neither trait is admirable.

I recall a Martin Luther King Day celebration, at which various speakers talked about what the day meant to each of them. A white man roughly my age took the podium and described an incident from his childhood involving a segregated drinking fountain. He was told he could contract some deadly contagion if he took a drink from the black fountain. He noticed, however, that the black children appeared rejuvenated after drinking from their fountain, seeming to suffer no ill effects. Confronted in his young mind with a challenge, he decided at last to take a chance and drink from the fountain. He discovered that the water tasted just the same as the whites' water. And, of course, he lived to tell his story. The color line not only denied black boys and girls opportunities, it also denied opportunities to whites, except that such disadvantages were presented as privileges. So, at that celebration of the King holiday, the speaker and I both reflected on how King's vision was liberating to blacks and whites alike.

Much of what I remember about the color line, of course, isn't pleasant, but some of it is humorous. For a very long time I thought that a particular sign on buses—"Passengers must stand behind the white line"—to be a stern admonition applying only to black people. I actually looked for a line of white folks to stand behind. It was most liberating one day as I happened to glance at the floor, perhaps to retrieve something I had dropped, to see an actual white line. I smiled and took my seat near the front of the bus. Growing up around signs, realizing their power to separate the human family into black and white, and being told early on of the stern and often brutal penalties that could befall anyone who might disobey them, I looked for ways to stay out of trouble. I often read more into signs than was actually there: "Greenwood Separate School District," "Mississippi Law: STOP."

NOTES

1. Plessy participated in an orchestrated test to determine whether the law violated the Constitution's Thirteenth Amendment, which outlawed slavery, and Fourteenth Amendment, which (among other provisions) broadened the definition of citizenship to include blacks and guaranteed due process and equal protection under the law.

2. The court dismissed Plessy's claim that the law reduced him to a slave in violation of the Thirteenth Amendment and that the Fourteenth Amendment was never meant to guarantee social equality. Justice Henry B. Brown issued the 7–1 majority opinion: "Legislation is powerless to eradicate racial instincts or to abolish distinctions based on physical differences, and the attempt to do so can only result in accentuating the differences of the present situation. If the civil and political rights of both races be equal, one cannot be inferior to the other civilly or politically. If one race be inferior to the other socially, the Constitution of the United States cannot put them on the same plane." Justice John Marshall Harlan gave the now-famous dissenting opinion. While agreeing that the white race was the dominant race in this country, he wrote, "But in view of the constitution, in the eye of the law, there is in this country no superior, dominant, ruling class of citizens. There is no caste here. Our constitution is color-blind, and neither knows nor tolerates classes among citizens. In respect of civil rights, all citizens are equal before the law."

3. From the late 1800s through the early 1900s, Mississippi was one of the richest states in the nation. During that same period, blacks in the Delta lived in poverty. See Sharon Wright Austin, *The Transformation of Plantation Politics* (Albany: State Univ. of New York Press, 2006), 32.

4. In Mississippi, for example, schools such as Jackson State, Alcorn, and Mississippi Valley State were created to serve blacks citizens.

5. I have in mind such groups as the White Citizen Councils and the Mississippi State Sovereignty Commission.

6. A summary of the court's finding in the case reads as follows:

> Does segregation of children in public schools solely on the basis of race, even though the physical facilities and other 'tangible' factors may be equal, deprive the children of the minority group of equal educational opportunities? We believe that it

does.... Segregation of white and colored children in public schools has a detrimental effect upon the colored children. The impact is greater when it has the sanction of the law, for the policy of separating the races is usually interpreted as denoting the inferiority of the [N]egro group. A sense of inferiority affects the motivation of a child to learn. Segregation with the sanction of law, therefore, has a tendency to [retard] the educational and mental development of [N]egro children and to deprive them of some of the benefits they would receive in a racial[ly] integrated school system.... We conclude that, in the field of public education, the doctrine of "separate but equal" has no place. Separate educational facilities are inherently unequal. Therefore, we hold that the plaintiffs and others similarly situated for whom the actions have been brought are, by reason of the segregation complained of, deprived of the equal protection of the laws guaranteed by the Fourteenth Amendment. (See Abraham L. Davis and Barbara Luck Graham, *The Supreme Court, Race, and Civil Rights* [Thousand Oaks, CA: Sage Publications, 1995], 164–66.)

7. A group of black elementary students were given several dolls that were identical in every respect but color. The children were asked which dolls were uglier, which more beautiful, and which looked like them. That most of the students found the white dolls to be more beautiful and said that they looked like the black dolls seemed to suggest that the students had already developed a sense of inferiority and self-hatred. Ibid., 122.

8. David M. Oshinsky, *Worse Than Slavery: Parchman Farm and the Ordeal of Jim Crow Justice* (New York: Simon & Schuster, 1996), 123.

EMMETT TILL

> The majority—by no means all, but the majority—of the white people in Mississippi 1) either approve Big Milam's action or else 2) they don't disapprove enough to risk giving their "enemies" the satisfaction of a conviction.
>
> **William Bradford Huie,** *Look* **magazine**

Without a doubt, the most significant event of my youth was the lynching of Emmett Till, a fourteen-year-old Chicago boy, in August 1955. At first, the anger and horror were directed not so much at the perpetrators of this heinous act as they were toward Emmett Till and his family. What seemed even more appalling was that the reaction of the black community didn't seem to be that much different from that in the white neighborhoods. The case provided a clear object lesson on the importance of staying in one's place. Black mothers reassured themselves that this couldn't happen to any of their children because they knew better. "Poor Emmett Till," we heard people say. "His parents should have taught him how to behave in the South." Blacks and whites could at least agree on this one thing: "That boy couldn't have been from around here." His mother, who was born in the Delta, of course, had warned him about white women in the South. She specifically told him that if he were to cross paths with a white woman, he should cross the street and drop his head. In no case should he make eye contact.

What else could a parent do? Perhaps, she might have done what a number of our parents actually did: scold and whip us as a reminder that coming into contact with a white woman was a certain death sentence.

I was eleven years old at the time but had learned what Richard Wright called "the ethics of living Jim Crow" so well that the fate that had befallen Emmett Till most likely would not have been mine.[1] My mother used this case as yet another reminder of how to act around white folks. In speaking of the murder in these terms, I realize that I run the risk of justifying this despicable act or, at least, of placing as much blame for it on Till as on his confessed killers, Roy Bryant and J. W. Milam. This is certainly not my intention. The real culprit was a code that locked individuals into such predetermined roles that the slightest deviation from them was considered an unpardonable sin. There were certain cardinal features of the code that had to be observed by all players in the southern drama, black or white:

(1) Individuals were not equal: whites were superior, blacks inferior.
(2) There was a preordained place for the two races. Everyone had to stay in his or her place.
(3) White women were sacred, and black men naturally lusted after them. They had to be kept apart by any and all means.

This groundless and indefensible code, together with its various corollaries, determined all interaction between blacks and whites in the Mississippi Delta.

Perhaps Milam and Bryant felt they were acting within this code, which they understood and thought that Emmett Till should have known and understood as well. So, when Till was unrepentant and said that he was as good as they were and that he had, indeed, "had" white women, Milam and Bryant saw this breach of southern ethics as intolerable. They had no choice but to act.[2]

While there are conflicting reports regarding certain details, there seems to be enough agreement about the case that a general picture emerges. In August 1955, Emmett Till, called "Bobo" by his mother, went to visit his great-uncle, Mose Wright, in Money, Mississippi, a small hamlet about eleven miles from Greenwood. In so doing, the young teenager made a journey that many others before and after him made. Since the Great Migration of the twentieth century, Chicago has been a second home or haven for blacks from the Mississippi

Delta and other parts of the South. Almost every black in Chicago has relatives in the South and vice-versa, and travel between the two regions is common.

On Wednesday, August 25, 1955, around 7:30 PM, a group of eight teenagers, including one girl, arrived at the store where Carolyn Bryant, the twenty-one-year-old wife of Roy Bryant, was working. Apparently, black kids often gathered at the store to play checkers and frolic about. The boys were wrestling and kidding around about girls, when Emmett happened to brag about his having dated a white girl and showed a picture of a white girl he kept in his wallet. Not believing him, one of the boys dared Till to see if he could get a date with the white woman working in the store. Emmett entered the store alone and purchased two cents' worth of bubble gum. When Bryant handed it to him, he squeezed her hand and said, "How about a date, baby?" When she jerked loose, he assured her that "she needn't worry and that he'd been with white girls before." As one of Till's cousins pulled him out the store, Bryant went to fetch a gun from a car belonging to J. W. Milam, her husband's half-brother. Reportedly, as the teenagers rushed off, Emmett made a wolf whistle. Carolyn and her sister-in-law, Juanita, determined that they wouldn't let their husbands know about the incident, but talk was getting around when a local African American man told Roy Bryant exactly what the talk was about and that the young Chicago visitor was staying with Mose "Preacher" Wright. With this information, especially since it came from a black man, did Bryant feel compelled by the mores of his culture that something had to be done?

Bryant and Milam went to Preacher's home "to talk to that boy who did all that talking in Money." Wright pleaded with the men that Emmett was not from the area and offered to whip his nephew there on the spot for his indiscretion. Bryant and Milam, however, took the youth with them after telling the sixty-four-year-old Wright that he should keep quiet about the abduction if he wanted to live to be sixty-five. The two men later insisted that they only intended to whip the boy and scare him but that Emmett was not sufficiently penitent in their eyes, declaring to the end that he wasn't afraid of them and that "yeah, he had 'had' white women." After repeated beatings he was dropped by a bullet to his right ear from Milam's .45-caliber gun. Till apparently never realized the extent to which some would go to defend a way of life they believed was sacred.

Till's disfigured body was found a few days later by a fisherman in the Tallahatchie River. Weighted down by a seventy-five-pound cotton gin fan tied to it by barbed wire, the boy's badly decomposed body was hardly recognizable. The defense, in fact, argued that the body was not that of Emmett Till. Mamie Till Bradley's ability to identify her son by a ring his father had given him seemed to have no sway on the all-white male jury. In their closing remarks at the trial, the defense attorneys had no qualms about openly appealing to their southern white brothers along racial lines. Certainly they could not convict any of their brothers for such a crime. Their forefathers would roll over in their graves if such a thing happened. Under no circumstances could these defenders of the faith be considered murderers.

The jury took just over an hour to deliver its not-guilty verdict, a period they spent not in deliberating the case, as was later revealed, but in chatting and drinking sodas. Even the various news media throughout the South seemed to conspire in the court's verdict. Newspapers generally showed the Bryants and Milams as innocent family people, whose only interest was in protecting the lovely, twenty-one-year-old beauty queen from the advances of a northern, street-smart, uppity Negro man, who was made to appear far more mature than his fourteen years. Without fear of being retried for the crime, Bryant and Milam sold their story for four thousand dollars to *Look* magazine. Not only were the men acquitted, they actually benefited financially from murdering Emmett Till.

As some have suggested, perhaps the men benefited in other ways as well. Were there considerations other than the obvious financial ones that prompted the men to give their confession to *Look*? Was this cleverly crafted confession designed to conceal and obfuscate more than it revealed? Recent reports suggest strongly that the men didn't act alone. Their confession, then, may amount to something like a preemptive move to keep several other, more powerful citizens from being brought to justice. Also, were black men involved in assisting Mylam and Bryant in much the same way that masters used their slaves to whip and torture other blacks? We may never know the full details of this case. But those of my generation know of its impact on our lives. The novelist John Edgar Wideman, who was Till's age, speaks for many of us when he confessed that "a nightmare from my childhood still haunts my sleep."[3]

The nature of the gruesome murder and the subsequent acquittal of the white perpetrators by an all-white male jury certainly served as one of the chief catalysts for the civil rights and protest movements of the 1960s. This case gave the movement a much-needed shock after the landmark *Brown* decision had led blacks into a false sense of security. In May 1954, the Supreme Court reached its unanimous decision striking down the doctrine of "separate but equal," established in the 1896 *Plessy v. Ferguson* case. "In the field of public education the doctrine of 'separate but equal' has no place," the Warren Court concluded. "Separate educational facilities are inherently unequal." Blacks and progressive whites hailed the decision as a victory, only to realize later that the court's phrase "with all deliberate speed" was sufficiently ambiguous to give proponents of the status quo what they needed to establish a gradual desegregation plan that had the effect of all but nullifying the court's ruling. More than one observer noticed that there was far too much deliberation and not enough speed.

In any case, movements are born not out of victories but out of insults, humiliation, and violence. And in the Emmett Till case all these elements were present, signaling to blacks that real change would come only through their efforts to change the system at its core. The outrageous nature of the case generated national and international support for civil rights and helped loosen the heretofore firm segregationist soil. The Montgomery Bus Boycott, which occurred just four months later, clearly signaled that blacks were now prepared to move beyond the courts to achieve their demands for a truly just society. Voter-registration drives and boycotts in Birmingham, Selma, Little Rock, and other places in the South can be traced to the events in August 1955.

NOTES

1. I borrow a phrase here from the title of Richard Wright's essay "The Ethics of Living Jim Crow."

2. Till reportedly told his tormentors, "You bastards, I'm not afraid of you. I'm as good as you are. I've 'had' white women. My grandmother was a white woman." Milam described his response as follows:

> Well, what else could we do? He was hopeless. I'm no bully; I never hurt a nigger in my life. I like niggers—in their place—I know how to work 'em. But I just decided it was time a few people got put on notice. As long as I live and can do anything about it, niggers are gonna stay in their place. Niggers ain't gonna vote where I live. If they did, they'd control the government. They ain't gonna go to school with my kids. And when a nigger gets close to mentioning sex with a white woman, he's tired o' livin'. I'm likely to kill him. Me and my folks fought for this country, and we got some rights. I stood there in that shed and listened to that nigger throw that poison at me, and I just made up my mind. "Chicago boy," I said, "I'm tired of 'em sending your kind down here to stir up trouble. Goddam you, I'm going to make an example

of you—just so everybody can know how me and my folks stand." (William Bradford Huie, "Approved Killing in Mississippi," *Look,* Jan. 24, 1956, 46–50. My account of the circumstances of the case generally follows that presented by Huie.)

3. John Edgar Wideman, "The Killing of Black Boys," in *The Lynching of Emmett Till: A Documentary Narrative,* ed. Christopher Metress (Charlottesville: Univ. of Virginia Press, 2002), 278.

RULEVILLE REVISITED: REFLECTIONS FIFTY YEARS AFTER MARIUS

> We were a backdoor people.
> We knew our place. It was
> Behind the nearest white man, on
> The back of the bus
> Through the kitchen, waiting
> Until table cleaning time for
> Cold rolls spatter with coffee grounds,
> And meat left on T-bones for Negroes
> Racing with dogs.
>
> John Milton Wesley, "Son Child"

"It can be worth your life these days to work for civil rights in Mississippi." So begins an article, "Ruleville: Reminiscence and Reflection," by the late historian and novelist Richard C. Marius, published in the September 23, 1964, issue of the *Christian Century* (pp. 1169–71). Marius's comments were spurred by the then-recent flurry of civil rights activities that had engulfed Mississippi in the early 1960s and had reached a peak in Freedom Summer, 1964. Against the backdrop of this tension-filled period, Marius recalled his stay in Mississippi nine years earlier, where he preached on weekends for the better part of a year. As a ministerial student at the New Orleans Baptist Theological Seminary, he went to Mississippi to heed the school's evangelical mission to preach the gospel and save souls. In February 1955, he preached in a weeklong revival in Ruleville, in the heart of the Mississippi Delta, a designation the town has earned, one feels, not only because of its central location but because its ideals and values are representative of the entire region.

A town split along the lines of color, Ruleville can boast of being the home of both Senator James O. Eastland and civil rights activist Fannie Lou Hamer. It was Eastland who asserted in 1945, "The Negro Race is an inferior race. The doctrine of white supremacy is one which, if adhered to, will save America."[1] After suffering for many years under the Eastland doctrine, Fannie Lou Hamer finally declared that she was "sick and tired of being sick and tired." She was among the first to go to the courthouse to register to vote in 1962, an act considered both courageous and foolhardy. As a result she was jailed, beaten, and fired from her plantation job. Those of us involved in voter-registration drives to insure that blacks would not be disfranchised by intimidation and such unjust measures as poll taxes and literacy tests knew just how dangerous it was to labor for civil rights during that time. A number of individuals, black and white, died in that struggle throughout Mississippi and the South.

So, when my colleague in religious studies, Ralph Norman, thrust into my hands a copy of Marius's article and asked whether I had heard of Ruleville, I nodded yes and then began to read what Marius had said about this small town. Ruleville was familiar to me not only because of its proximity to Greenwood but also because I had been arrested there in the summer of 1962 while participating in a voter-registration campaign throughout Sunflower County, the same campaign that attempted to register Fannie Lou Hamer and other blacks. My classmate Albert Garner and I, along with several others, were arrested for distributing handbills without a permit, a statute that was certainly on the books but never enforced except in special situations like this. (See appendix 2 for details of my arrest.) Coming from Leflore County, Garner and I were considered outside agitators, despite the fact that Leflore County adjoins Sunflower on the east and that we were only about twenty-six miles from home. Our parents, understandably concerned about our safety, spent most of a restless night on the phone trying to comfort one another. Our arrest (for which we posted a one-hundred-dollar bond, fined fifty dollars at the trial, and released) caused quite a furor in

Greenwood, not only because of our youth but also because Garner and I were prominent students in the black high school. As we were just beginning our senior year, there was some question about whether we would be allowed to finish school. The principal received calls asking what he planned to do about "those boys," which put him in an awkward situation since Garner had been elected senior class president and I had been elected president of the student council. With his own job and reputation in the community on the line, he realized that he had to handle the matter with the utmost diplomacy, which he evidently did. We both graduated with our class at the end of the academic year. I suppose, however, that my mother was relieved that I decided to attend Morehouse College in Atlanta, rather than follow my friend Garner to Tougaloo, which had quite a reputation for civil rights agitation in those days.

But it was evangelism, not activism, that brought Richard Marius to Ruleville. I was especially taken with the vivid description he gave of the church where he had preached: "It was a white frame church," which "stood in a grove of trees alongside the road which ran from Ruleville to Cleveland." This church, he continued, "tilted dangerously. But it stood fast, and it had stood in that precarious position for as long as anyone could remember." With his suggestion that the church might still be there, I became increasingly interested in returning to Ruleville to see if this was in fact the case, now fifty years after Marius had arrived there. I was well on my way to Ruleville before I admitted the folly of searching for a structure that had been tilting for so long. By now, the city or county building inspectors would certainly have declared such a structure unsafe and had it demolished. But there were other issues Marius raised in his article that needed to be addressed. Marius expressed the belief that the Christian Church would slowly but steadily make progress in the area of race relations. Having spent my formative years in the Mississippi Delta, I found this view of things much too optimistic. Quite frankly, I wondered if he had been so taken in by the hospitality and genteel manners of whites in the Mississippi Delta that he couldn't understand that a number of these churchmen and their relatives and friends were largely responsible for the wretched condition of blacks in the region. This certainly was the view that blacks held some fifty years ago. How had the churches in Ruleville and the rest of the South changed in all these years on issues of race? Had they finally taken their place as an agent for reconciliation between the races? More important for me personally, I wanted to see for myself how far Ruleville had come since my arrest there as an eighteen-year-old high school student in 1962. The more I thought about these matters, the more convinced I became in justifying my trip back to Ruleville.

So, for the first time since my visit as part of a voter-registration effort during the civil rights era, I arrived in downtown Ruleville. It was early December 2004, and I was armed only with Marius's article and a set of questions I had drawn up. Having grown up in the Mississippi Delta, I had no fear at all for my safety, for I knew how to act and how to stay in my place. The public library would be my first stop. Academics always feel that the library will house the answers to most of their questions. Alas, the library was closed on Mondays; it was open only on alternate days. The public service assistant, as she was called because she had no library science degree, also ran the library up the road in Drew on those days when she was not in Ruleville. Sensing my frustration, a white gentleman asked how he could help and then suggested I go to City Hall and talk to the folks there.

"I am from the University of Tennessee," I announced, as if that fact would open doors for me. Waving Marius's article in my hand and using his description, I told them that I was trying to find some information on a "leaning" church located on a large plantation on the road, Highway 8, that runs from Ruleville to Cleveland. The three women in the office immediately recognized this as the old Dockery Church, and one even knew one of its members who was still living. She called this woman and handed me the phone. After I explained that I was trying to locate this church and perhaps its pastor from the time Marius was there, the woman promptly invited me to come to her home to talk to her. The two black women in the office seemed particularly amused by all this, for they were certain that this white woman had assumed that I was also white. Their feelings were verified the moment I stepped out of my car at the woman's house. "Oh!" she said. "You must be looking for a colored church." I told her that I was indeed looking for a white church and apologized if she had been misled but hoped that she would still talk with me, which she agreed to do. She showed me the special program booklet the church had put together in 2002 to mark its centennial anniversary. It contained much of the valuable information I had been hunting. The booklet featured pictures of the church then and now, a brief history, and a list of all the pastors with the dates of their service. There was no doubt that the Dockery Church, established in 1902, was the nameless church in Marius's article. I wasn't surprised that the building where Marius had preached in 1955 was no longer standing, though I did have a picture of how it looked before it started to lean. Another picture on the inside cover showed the church as it had begun to tilt; cables were used to keep the structure upright. It finally had to be demolished in the 1960s, and the present structure was built on the lot. I've since learned the name of the church's young pastor in 1955, a man still living but who had moved away from Ruleville. Mission accomplished!

While I didn't want to overstay my welcome, I sensed an excellent opportunity to ask this octogenarian questions about race relations in Ruleville. Although not born in Ruleville, she had lived there since the 1930s. Yes, she knew Fannie Lou Hamer quite well, before she got married, when her name was Townsend and before she got involved in those civil rights activities. She indicated that she had no problems with blacks and noted, "When we all get to heaven, there will be no separation of the races into black and white."

When I returned to City Hall a few days later, I learned that one of the black women working at a typewriter on my first visit was actually the mayor of Ruleville. She had the distinction of being the first woman and first black person to hold that office in this town. Notably, with seventy-three black mayors, Mississippi has more black mayors than any other state in the union, and a number of these are in the Mississippi Delta. Although it could hardly be called a scientific sample, it did appear to me, after talking with black and white citizens in Ruleville, that there are individuals now willing to discuss issues of race in an open and direct way. I can only hope that the citizens themselves are willing to talk to each other in such a frank manner.

If you ask the white citizens of Ruleville about the state of race relations in their city, they will tell you that, although Ruleville is not perfect, blacks and whites get along very well. When you suggest that this picture seems inconsistent with that of fifty or even forty years ago, you'll hear that Ruleville had some problems in the past, but those problems were often caused by outsiders and magnified by the media. Ruleville now not only has a black mayor but a black police chief, a black assistant police chief, and a black superintendent of education as well. Blacks also constitute a majority on the City Council. It even has a monument honoring the late local civil rights heroine, Fannie Lou Hamer, who successfully challenged the all-white Mississippi delegation to the 1964 Democratic Convention. The post office and a street have been named for her. Quite clearly, this is not the same place that the black native son John Milton Wesley memorializes in his poem "Son Child":

> Ruleville, a main street town
> North on 49-W, one policeman
> Khaki and fat, spat on Negroes,
> Ate their cooking, beat their men,
> Loved their women, robbed their children,
> Then gave us their old clothes.[2]

During that time the population was more evenly divided between blacks and whites. Now the city is 85 percent black. Then, blacks there held no major public or political offices. By any objective measure, Ruleville has made tremendous progress from the period of the 1950s and 1960s. Blacks, while acknowledging progress in certain areas, feel that vestiges of racism remain and that they are all but shut out of certain job opportunities. The progress, largely in the political and public-accommodations arenas, however, must be credited to the civil rights movement and generally not to the white church, a fact Marius would find disturbing. Marius knew, of course, that any southern white minister working for civil rights in the 1960s would soon find himself without a church and probably be forced to leave the South. The white minister's public stance on race matters was determined not by his own views but by those of his congregation. In this, he was not as free as his black counterpart, whose opinion was almost always supported by his members. But could this still be true some fifty years later?

To gain some insight into this issue, I made another trip to Ruleville to visit a white Baptist church. I had never gone to a white church in Mississippi before. In fact, such an act during the 1950s and 1960s would have been seen as an act of protest. Blacks simply were not welcome at white churches then. According to my respondents, with the possible exception of funerals and revivals, blacks and whites still don't worship together on anything close to a regular basis.

I arrived at the church around 11:05 AM, a time I thought was safe for an 11:00 o'clock service, only to discover that the service actually began a bit before 11:00, giving the pastor some wiggle room should his sermon go on a bit long. The service was never to go beyond noon. This was quite different from the services I remember in the black Baptist churches in the Delta. There, services might start around 11:00 AM but could extend well beyond 1:00 in the afternoon. Assuming that the Holy Ghost works in both churches, it must get its job done by noon in the white church and may need to take a bit longer in the black church.

I sat behind two rather hefty young men I assumed were football players, only to be told later that that wasn't the case. Upon closer examination, I noticed that one of them was black, and I was both relieved and disappointed by this fact. On the one hand, I wanted to see just how I would be treated as the only black person in the congregation. On the other, however, I was a bit relieved that there was at least one other brother in attendance to help ease any angst I might experience. This young man, I discovered, had been invited by his white friend from college. They had both grown up in the area and became friends while working together in Washington, D.C.

Other than the starting and ending time, there is much else that differentiates the typical white Baptist church from its black counterpart. The white church is typically not marked by the kind of religious frenzy that one notes in the black church. Among black congregations, only the Episcopalians can claim to be as quiet as this white Baptist church in Ruleville. Blacks generally consider such a service to be dead. During my youth, it seemed that no black preacher could get through his sermon without the active participation of a loud congregation that actually talked back to him. I don't think the lecture type of sermon would have worked at a black church on a regular basis, although I must confess I found this white pastor's message informative and even inspirational.

Some might argue that the differences in style of worship are the main reason that even today, 11:00 AM on Sunday morning is the most segregated hour of the week. The church, and here I speak of the church not only in the South but also throughout America, tends to be divided along the color line. The two young college friends perhaps didn't attach as much importance to their act as I did. Who cares if their own parents couldn't have done what they were doing? They weren't trying to prove anything to anyone, as indeed I was. They were friends and didn't see the need to leave their friendship at the steps of the church.

I am not so naïve as to believe that by worshipping together blacks and whites can solve the major problems that confront folks in Ruleville and other communities in the Mississippi Delta. Only through serious dialogue and cooperation and willingness to put aside personal differences for the common good can meaningful things be accomplished here. Churches that are completely open to all will send a powerful signal that blacks and whites are ready to engage each other on issues affecting the entire community. Crime, a worsening economy, poor health care, and lack of public school funding are several of the issues the black and white citizens of Ruleville face. These problems can't be solved by individuals going their separate ways or by staying out of one another's path.

Will the Christian church deal with these critical issues in the future? Or will it continue to be, as W. E. B. Du Bois argued in the 1920s, "just another social club" and not an agent for positive social change? While I'm not as optimistic as Marius was in 1964, the thought of those two young friends, one black and one white, worshipping together does give me hope. We all sat there, hearing the words of the minister reading from the Book of James: "Now faith without works is dead." I believe those two young men got the message.

Notes

1. *Congressional Record,* 79th Congress (June 29, 1945).

2. John Milton Wesley, "Son Child," http://usadeepsouth.ms11.net/ruleville.html.

CIVIL RIGHTS

> Those who profess to favor freedom, and yet deprecate agitation, are men who want crops without plowing up the ground. They want rain without thunder and lightning. . . . This struggle may be a moral one; or it may be physical; but it must be a struggle. Power concedes nothing without a demand. It never did and it never will.
>
> **Frederick Douglass, "West India Emancipation" speech (1857)**

We were neither shocked nor surprised when our civics instructor in high school failed to pass the literacy test necessary to become a registered voter in Leflore County. We knew that he was bright enough. After all, he was teaching us government, which meant he at least had a college education. But when he went to register, he was not able to pass a test that required him to copy a section of the state constitution and then, and here is the problem, to interpret the same passage in front of the registrar.[1] It didn't matter what blacks said; the clerk always indicated that the response was wrong. We teased our teacher for a long time, asking him how he could teach us something about the constitution he didn't know himself.

Another hindrance to voting was the poll tax. When I was a child, the amount was two dollars. This, I admit, is not a large sum by today's standards. But in the 1950s and 1960s it was an entire day's pay for some people. The amount notwithstanding, it was a real nuisance to pay any sum to vote for a candidate who would not be significantly different from his opponent.

One of the aims of the voter-registration project was to increase the number of registered black voters. In 1962, according to government statistics, six Mississippi counties had 38,772 of 53,742 eligible whites registered to vote and only 1,955 of 49,998 black eligible voters were registered.[2] That is, of those eligible to vote, 4 percent of blacks were registered, as compared to 72 percent of whites. Furthermore, a larger percentage of blacks than whites were ruled ineligible. The figures are astounding and, if one assumes that blacks were attempting to vote, offer evidence that blacks were systematically being disfranchised.

The literacy requirement and poll taxes were not the only hurdle; on November 8, 1960, the legislature added good moral character as a requirement for voter registration. These restrictions, although they technically applied to all applicants, actually were used as a means of maintaining white racial supremacy by insuring a white electorate.

In addition to these "legal" means, intimidation and reprisals also kept blacks from registering to vote. The newspapers, which didn't normally print anything positive about blacks, made sure that it recorded for public information those blacks who had attempted to register to vote, along with their addresses. Once their names were published in the papers, they could expect to receive phone calls or visits that encouraged them to withdraw their names from the rolls. Employers were routinely contacted whenever any of their black employees showed up to register to vote.[3]

In short, there were very few blacks who were registered voters in the Mississippi of my youth. My parents never registered; neither did those of most of my schoolmates. I doubt that many of our teachers or ministers were registered. Blacks thus had no voice in the political affairs of the state or the nation. Unabashed and unashamed, white candidates tried to outdo each other in their promises to maintain white supremacy and keep blacks under foot. They followed the trail blazed by the "Great White Chief," James Kimble Vardaman, who served as Mississippi governor and later senator early in the twentieth century; among his openly racist campaign slogans was this: "A VOTE FOR VARDAMAN IS A VOTE FOR WHITE SUPREMACY, THE SAFETY OF THE HOME, AND THE PROTECTION OF OUR WOMEN AND CHILDREN."[4] The right of blacks to vote would not only mean that more blacks could run for political office and stand a chance of winning but, even more important, that candidates could no longer make such blatant racist appeals with impunity.

Getting more blacks to vote in the Mississippi Delta was a most difficult task. When the Reverend George Lee of Belzoni tried to do that in 1955, it cost him his life. Blacks knew that second only to the commandment forbidding black men from consorting with white women was the one that prohibited them from voting. So when civil rights activists Bob Moses, Sam Block, and Willie Peacock, among others, arrived in the Delta in the summer of 1962, African Americans didn't at first welcome them with open arms. There were suspicions and fears that had to be overcome. Were the workers there to cause trouble and then leave town as quickly as they had arrived? How could these outsiders possibly understand what it was like to live in Greenwood and Leflore County? Slowly, however, by working with the people, socializing with them, and attending their churches, they won their trust. This was aided in great part by a number of younger people in the area who had determined that they wouldn't live in fear as had many of their parents.[5] Indeed, it was something like this that attracted me to the movement. Furthermore, an unexpected boost came from a group of black ministers who, after being chastised by comedian and activist Dick Gregory, finally indicated their support for civil rights.[6]

No one needed to prod Mrs. Laura McGhee, however, who was an early and staunch supporter of the movement. While only a few people outside Greenwood may have ever heard of Mrs. McGhee, she is certainly one of the unsung heroines of the civil rights movement in the Delta. Her brother, Gus Courts, was president of the Belzoni Chapter of the NAACP and worked alongside Reverend Lee to register black voters in that town. Because she had the reputation for standing up to anyone, white or black, word got around that she was a bit "off." Rumors circulated that she had been taken to Whitfield, the state mental institution, on several occasions. Mrs. McGhee and her four boys and daughter lived on a farm in Browning, a predominantly black subdivision outside of Greenwood. On a number of occasions, she was urged to sell her property to whites who wanted the rich farmland next to Highway 82. She held on to her property until her death, when her children continued to honor their mother's defiance. The sixty or so acres still belong to the family, I'm told.

When a number of other black parents were discouraging any participation in "dat mess," Mrs. McGhee, though certainly anxious about the safety of her own children, supported their participation in the movement. She had always taught her children to respect and love—yes, even love—everyone despite their color. She simply demanded the same for herself and for her children. That was evidenced one time when she refused to allow her children to call a white playmate "sir." The McGhees regularly rented their farmland out to whites. On this occasion, Mrs. McGhee was renting her land to a farmer whose child was about the same age as two of her boys, Silas and Jake. As youngsters, the children often played together, but as they matured, the farmer thought it appropriate to draw the color line. He demanded that the children, if not Mrs. McGhee herself, start addressing his son as "sir." It wouldn't do for his friends to know that he had a son who was not respected by colored people. When Mrs. McGhee flatly refused, she knew she was committing a serious breach of Jim Crow etiquette.

Or another occasion, after a white officer shoved her as she tried to see the sheriff to ask why her son Jake had been put in jail and what she might do to get him released, she immediately punched him in the nose. And when he in turn reached for his pistol, he was grabbed by two of the civil rights workers who had accompanied her to post bond. Though shots were fired into her house and her family constantly received threats, she never wavered in her support of the movement. This type of defiance, no doubt, was passed along to her sons, Ben, Silas, Jake, and Clarence, which fed the belief that the whole family was a bit "touched." How else could one explain this total disregard for the power of white folks?

Silas was in the forefront of the efforts to desegregate facilities in Greenwood, seeking to test the recently passed 1964 Civil Rights Accommodations Act. Unlike some small towns, Greenwood had a movie theater for blacks and a theater for whites. There was no arrangement, common in some places, whereby blacks and whites shared the same theaters by having blacks sit in the balcony. In July 1964, a day or so after the act was signed into law by President Johnson, Silas wanted to see if the city would follow the law and whether the government would prosecute any infractions of the code. When Silas struck out on foot alone that hot July morning from Browning to Greenwood, he wasn't bound for the whites-only Leflore Theater. He was headed to the Crystal Grill, an establishment known for serving good food—but not to blacks, except from a "to go" window. Under no circumstances could blacks be seated among the white patrons. That the meals were prepared and served by black help mattered not at all.

When Silas finally arrived, he found the restaurant closed. Disappointed and dismayed, but not deterred from testing the efficacy of the new law, he continued his solo walk to the Leflore Theater. When he approached the ticket window, the woman at the box office, not knowing what to do, called the manager, who told her to sell Silas the ticket. The man's decision, Silas believed, was a business one.

Though Silas didn't remember the name of the movie, he did remember that it starred Jerry Lewis. (Silas later confided to me that he wasn't a particular fan of Jerry Lewis's films.) When he took his seat, not far from the aisle, he was approached by several whites, who wanted to know what he was doing there. When he told them he was there to see the movie, they poured a soft drink down his back. When this didn't succeed in getting him to move, they became more forceful and threatened to remove him physically from the theater. Silas vowed that he wouldn't leave on his own. At this time Silas was not yet a member of the Student Nonviolent Coordinating Committee and hadn't made a pledge to nonviolence, so he decided to fight back. The manager called the police, who urged the man to file a complaint against Silas for disturbing the peace. The manager refused to do so, saying that Silas was the one who was attacked. Yet, no charges were filed against the four whites, who were allowed to go their way. Silas was taken to the police station and eventually released since no charges had been filed against him. In the normal course of things in the Delta, a white person would have preferred charges against any black person in such an incident, even if it meant manufacturing them, but the theater manager was different. Silas continued on several occasions to go to the theater, and the manager, no doubt gritting his teeth, continued to sell him tickets. Because of this, the manager was threatened, and his theater was boycotted and eventually shut down.

In a separate incident a week or so after the attack at the theater but certainly related to it, Silas was beaten by three white men. While walking home from a voter-registration drive at the old post office, he was abducted at gunpoint and forced into their truck. After assuring themselves that he was "the nigger" who had been going to the Leflore Theater, they took him to a shed where they beat him across the head with a metal pipe. Silas was eventually able to free himself and report the incident to the FBI. He gave the authorities a clear description of his attackers, who were eventually picked up and charged with the incident. I don't know whether the men were found guilty and had to spend time in jail.

On the evening of August 15, as the students participating in Freedom Summer in Greenwood were heading back to college, they had to withstand one last jolt. There was to be a kind of celebration that day to mark a fitting end to the hard-fought if not hard-won struggles. The event was intended as a tribute to blacks and whites working together in the South to help end racial apartheid.

What happened instead was another brutal crime perpetrated by their opponents. At the center of the event was again Silas McGhee. As he waited in his car outside a café where the freedom fighters were hosting a party for those returning to their books, Silas was shot in the head, the bullet traveling down his neck. He had to be taken all the way to Jackson, a distance of about a hundred miles, to be treated. It was the particular angle of the bullet as it entered his skull that saved his life—maybe because of the way the shooter held the gun, or maybe because of the rolled-up window that deflected the shot just enough so that it missed his brain or another vital organ, or maybe because of Silas's position in the seat, his head slightly tilted to the side. The black folks knew that it could only be God's grace, for surviving a bullet fired at your head from point-blank range seemed nothing less than miraculous. Those whites who saw Silas also shook their heads and perhaps thought to themselves that God might indeed be on the side of blacks. After the shot was heard in the café, several individuals used their shirts to help bandage Silas's wound and then took him directly to the hospital, deciding they couldn't wait on an ambulance. When they arrived, the civil rights workers weren't allowed to enter the hospital with Silas because they had taken off their shirts to use as bandages. Silas didn't want the nurse to give him a shot, so fearful he was that any assistance he might receive would just assist him "away from here." But he did listen to the black doctor who was called in and agreed to accompany him to Jackson, where there were facilities to treat his type of injury.

The kind of heroism displayed by the McGhees was also evident among the Greenes and Sanderses and Johnsons and several other families in Greenwood. Dewey R. Greene Sr., for example, was a leader of the local NAACP and its first president in Greenwood. A painter by trade, he had established a reputation for doing excellent work for both black and white homeowners. While he wasn't wealthy, he certainly could be counted among the well-to-do of Greenwood's black citizenry, a status that placed him alongside some of the more prominent black teachers, ministers, and funeral directors. His business suffered mightily, however, as a result of his open support of voter-registration activities during the early 1960s.

Like Laura McGhee, Dewey Greene never discouraged his children from taking part in the movement, a matter that unsettled many whites. He certainly did all he could to shelter his daughters from any dangers that civil rights work often brought, especially his youngest daughter, Dorothy. But even "Cookie," as she was called, could be found canvassing blacks in her neighborhood and urging them to get out and vote. The more heavy lifting, however, was left to the boys, George and Dewey Junior. The younger Dewey caused quite a stir in his efforts to apply to Ole Miss. On October 24, 1962, Dewey Junior wrote to L. H. Threadgill, the principal of Broad Street High School, requesting that a transcript be sent to the University of Mississippi, with a copy to Lillian Louie, his legal counsel in this matter. As a result, the whole family was subjected to recriminations from the White Citizens Council and to intense investigations by the Mississippi State Sovereignty Commission. The commission ran a thorough check of Dewey Senior and his family, which involved credit reports and police records. Threadgill was asked for his assessment of the Greenes as students at Broad Street. But through all the checks and reports, nothing untoward could be found regarding Dewey Greene or his family. The investigator did find that Dewey Senior and his wife, Freddie, had registered to vote in 1954 but had not paid poll taxes or attempted to vote. The report also stated that on one occasion, Dewey Senior attempted to get Threadgill fired and that the parents "always upheld the children for what devilment they got into at school." Shots were fired into the Greenes' home in late March 1963, and they suffered additional recriminations. So did others.

Dave Sanders, the grandfather of one of my classmates, rented space to the movement for a library and citizenship-training classes. His place was constantly threatened. But Mr. Sanders, who had once put a bullet into a white man who wanted to take his cotton, was not about to buckle under threats from anonymous whites who were afraid to show their faces.

And there was Rev. Aaron Johnson, who offered his church on more than one occasion for mass meetings. What these individuals had in common, other than being fed up with the system, was economic independence. Since they were not dependent on whites for their livelihood, they were not likely to suffer the same kind of recriminations that my parents and many others suffered. But as most would readily acknowledge, the success of the freedom movement in Greenwood and in other communities depended on the efforts and cooperation of such local people—both those who took more active roles and those willing to follow.

Notes

1. One popular application to vote consisted of twenty questions, of which the last three were the most significant. For question 18, the applicant was asked to copy a section of the state constitution designated by the registrar. Question 19 required the applicant to write "a reasonable interpretation (the meaning) of the section of the Constitution of Mississippi which you have just copied." For question 20, the applicant had to write "a statement setting forth your understanding of the duties and obligations of citizenship under a constitutional form of government." See John Dittmer, *Local People: The Struggle for Civil Rights in Mississippi* (Urbana: Univ. of Illinois Press, 1995), 71.

2. These statistics are given in an editorial appearing in the *Greenwood Commonwealth*, August 28, 1962.

3. For example, the name of Joe Lofton, an older classmate of mine, was published in the paper so that others, including his employer, could contact him as part of this program of intimidation.

4. David M. Oshinsky, *Worse Than Slavery: Parchman Farm and the Ordeal of Jim Crow Justice* (New York: Simon & Schuster, 1996), 90.

5. Several commentators on the civil rights movement in the Delta and in Mississippi have documented the work of many of the younger activists. See Dittmer, *Local People*; Charles Payne, *I've Got the Light of Freedom: The Organizing Tradition and the Mississippi Freedom Struggle* (Berkeley: Univ. of California Press, 1995); and Endesha Ida Mae Holland, *From the Mississippi Delta: A Memoir* (New York: Simon & Schuster, 1997).

6. Dick Gregory chided preachers and teachers for their lack of active support for the Greenwood movement. Perhaps as a result of Gregory's scathing words, a group of thirty-one black ministers endorsed the following statement: "We the undersigned Pastors and Ministers of the city of Greenwood and Leflore County do hereby endorse the Freedom Movement one-hundred percent and urge our members and friends of Leflore County and the state of Mississippi to register and become first-class citizens." Quoted in Payne, *I've Got the Light of Freedom*, 198–99.

MEDGAR

> We believe that there are white Mississippians who want to go forward on the race question. Their religion tells them there is something wrong with the old system. Their sense of justice and fair play sends them the same message. But whether Jackson and the State choose to change or not, the years of change are upon us. In the racial picture, things will never be as they once were.
>
> **Medgar Evers, in a radio address a few weeks before his shooting**

I first met Medgar Evers around 1959 or 1960. As the newly elected field secretary of the NAACP, he traveled the state organizing youth chapters of the organization. My friend Albert Garner was the president of our chapter, and I worked alongside him. We usually met upstairs in his room at Hotel Plaza, a black-owned business in Greenwood that catered exclusively to African Americans, as its sign clearly stated: "Hotel Plaza for Colored." Located near the junction of Highways 49 and 82, the hotel was one of the main hangouts for blacks at the time. I remember Medgar to be a gentle, unassuming, and soft-spoken man, not at all bombastic. He made his points without resorting to loud or flowery language. He was clear and organized. But one could tell that he was determined and motivated to get done whatever job lay before him.

Medgar, at thirty-seven years of age in 1963, was the first and youngest of the major civil rights leaders to be assassinated. Certainly Malcolm X and

Martin Luther King were more visible on the national stage. Medgar limited his activities for the most part to Mississippi. He was our own homeboy, who loved his native state. "There's land here," he said in an interview for *Ebony* magazine, "where a man can raise cattle and I'm going to do that some day." No one could accuse him of being an outsider, as King was often labeled in his campaigns for racial justice throughout the South and nation. Born in Decatur, Mississippi, in 1925, Medgar saw violence by whites against blacks at an early age. He told Jack Mendelsohn, author of *The Martyrs*, that white kids used to throw rocks at him and called him and other blacks filthy names. At around eleven or twelve years of age, he witnessed the lynching of a family friend because the man had "sassed a white woman." The victim's bloody clothes were left on a post as a reminder to any other blacks who might think of getting out of place.

As a young man, Medgar served his country in World War II, only to find upon his return that he had more formidable foes in Mississippi than he had found among the Germans and Japanese. Following his honorable service to his country, he decided to register to vote. The registration went all right, but when he tried to actually cast a ballot, a gang of whites stood in his way. He recalled the incident to Mendelsohn: "We fought during the war for America, and Mississippi was included. Now after the Germans and the Japanese hadn't killed us, it looked as though the white Mississippians would." Evers concluded, "I was born in Decatur, was raised there, but I never in my life was permitted to vote there."[1]

It was as a student at Alcorn State University in Lorman, Mississippi, that he met his future wife, Myrlie Beasley. After graduation, Medgar became a salesman for an insurance company, which paid him a salary sufficient to support his wife and himself. Around this time, he joined the NAACP to attempt to pave the way for other blacks to vote. Indeed, when we consider the full range of protests and boycotts in which he was involved, it was the right to vote that lay closest to his heart. This was in line with the objective identified by the Mississippi Ministerial Improvement Association as early as 1958. Their primary goal was to use every legal means to encourage registration and voting. Certainly it was in an attempt to secure voting rights for blacks that brought Medgar and other activists to Greenwood. And it was on this issue that he faced his greatest threats and challenges from whites.

As Albert Garner and I talked to Medgar, we didn't realize then that he was under constant surveillance. Everything he did from around 1956 until his death in 1963 was carefully monitored. It was on March 29, 1956, by an act of the

Mississippi legislature, that the Mississippi State Sovereignty Commission was created. As a means of responding to and reckoning with the 1954 *Brown* decision, which outlawed segregation in public schools, the commission had fairly broad powers. Its mission was to "do and perform any and all acts deemed necessary and proper to protect the sovereignty of the state of Mississippi and her sister states" from perceived "encroachment thereon by the Federal government or any branch, department or agency thereof."[2] The commission had extensive investigative powers and had been granted a yearly sum of $250,000 to get its work underway. The governor sat as ex officio chairman, together with other high-ranking state officials.

Gov. J. P. Coleman had flatly stated his belief that the "Negro [was] not ready" to vote in Mississippi. Since various activist groups had determined that black registration and voting were priorities, the Mississippi State Sovereignty Commission had to consider its options to counter such efforts. It did note that Mississippi at the time had a literacy requirement that called for reading and interpreting a section of the state constitution to the satisfaction of the registrar. Since there were no Negro registrars in Mississippi, it reasoned, it was only a matter of seeing that white registrars did their jobs by making sure blacks didn't pass the test. The Voting Rights Law passed a year earlier in 1957 was largely ineffectual because it lacked the teeth to enforce its mandates. Yet, the commission members felt that the presence of long voter-registration lines was a challenge to their authority. They chose to reduce the number of individuals at the polls through threats and reprisals. Names of individuals attempting to vote were published in the local newspaper with their addresses. They were warned that attempting to register could cost them their employment or worse. Fannie Lou Hamer's story in Ruleville is typical of many. She was given the choice of rescinding her application to vote or else losing her job on the plantation where she had worked for years. The investigative arm of the Mississippi State Sovereignty Commission played a major role in uncovering information on both those trying to vote and those activists urging blacks to register.

The file on Medgar Evers was especially thick. In perusing the files, I found more entries on him than on any other single individual. This speaks to both Medgar's activism and the insistence of the commission to document every move he made. He was a marked man from the beginning of his work with the NAACP until his death. It's now clear that many of the details about Medgar were handed over by paid and unpaid informants, individuals close to him who knew his schedule and had no qualms about reporting on his activities. In various mass meetings (led mostly by the Student Nonviolent Coordinating Committee) that I sat through, I often heard speakers chide these black informants with the words: "Now, run and tell that!" It never really occurred to me until reviewing the files that there were actually individuals there being paid to spy on their brothers and sisters. Charles Payne in *I've Got the Light of Freedom* indicates that there were several known spies in Greenwood and in other Delta towns.

It's not surprising, then, that Byron De La Beckwith would know about Medgar's whereabouts as did everyone in the Klan. Medgar was on a short hit list that the Klan had prepared; he reported to the FBI that he was being followed by police during the week leading up to his assassination. On that fateful early morning of June 12, around 12:30, Myrlie and her three children waited in their home for Medgar to return from a meeting with NAACP lawyers. Myrlie had been heartened by John F. Kennedy's speech a few hours earlier when he declared that the nation was involved in a moral crisis and that as president he would send to the Congress legislation aimed at securing rights for all American citizens.

"There's Daddy!" one of the children shouted as Medgar's Oldsmobile pulled into the driveway of his Jackson home. Just after Medgar got out of his car, the sound of a single shot that "smashed into Evers's back, just below the right shoulder blade" rang out.[3] He was still breathing as he was rushed to University Hospital, but he had lost too much blood and could not survive his wounds.

Almost immediately, Byron De La Beckwith became the number-one suspect in Medgar's death. For one thing, the murder weapon, the rifle, could be traced to him, and, further, he was known to be a diehard segregationist who would stop at nothing to make sure that integration was never achieved in Mississippi. He had once applied to J. P. Coleman for a position with the Mississippi State Sovereignty Commission, stating in his application that he "WAS RABID ON THE SUBJECT OF SEGREGATION." It would take two mistrials, a third trial, and over thirty years for De La Beckwith to be brought to justice for the murder of Medgar Evers. Because of the perseverance of Medgar's widow, Myrlie, who had remarried by 1993, Byron De La Beckwith was finally tried and convicted for the murder of her first husband.

De La Beckwith was reportedly a loudmouth who, on more than one occasion, indirectly suggested that he was responsible for Medgar's death. Various individuals who had been reluctant to testify at the earlier trials for the prosecution were called to do so at the 1993–94 trial. The testimony of two witnesses, Dan Prince and Peggy Morgan, were especially damning. According to journalist Maryanne Vollers, who wrote the book *Ghosts of Mississippi* about the Evers assassination and the trials that followed, "Once in a casual conversation, De La Beckwith had told Prince that he had been tried twice in Mississippi 'for killing that nigger. . . . I had a job to do and I did it and I didn't suffer any more than your wife if she was going to have a baby.'"[4] Peggy Morgan said that she heard De La Beckwith state that "he had killed Medgar Evers, a nigger, and he wasn't scared to kill again."[5] De La Beckwith never took the stand in his own defense. His lawyers felt that he wouldn't be able to withstand a rigorous cross-examination. On Saturday, February 5, 1994, a jury of eight blacks and four whites found Byron De La Beckwith guilty of the murder of Medgar Evers.

This third trial was a significant moment in Mississippi's history and not just because De La Beckwith was finally convicted of his crime. Everyone associated with the case knew from the outset that he was guilty: not only did he often talk openly about the murder to his friends, but he even seemed to seek acclaim for it. When he ran for lieutenant governor in 1967, his campaign slogan touted him as a "straight shooter"—a not-so-veiled reference to the assassination. What was most significant about the conviction was that it was the first time since Reconstruction that a white man was successfully prosecuted for killing a black man in the state. No longer could such murders be carried out with the assurance once afforded by a code that stated essentially: "We whites have a right to do whatever we want with niggers in Mississippi." For the Evers family, the conviction brought a measure of solace, and for the South, it relieved the burden of loyalty to a vicious racial code.[6]

NOTES

1. Jack Mendelsohn, *The Martyrs: Sixteen Who Gave Their Lives for Racial Justice* (New York: Harper & Row, 1966), 65–66.

2. Yasuhiro Katagiri, *The Mississippi State Sovereignty Commission* (Jackson: Univ. Press of Mississippi, 2001), 6.

3. Maryanne Vollers, *Ghosts of Mississippi* (Boston: Little, Brown, 1995), 126–27.

4. Ibid., 356–57.

5. Ibid., 358.

6. In the Emmett Till case, for example, the defense attorneys appealed to racial loyalty: J. W. Kellum warned that the jurors' forefathers "would turn in their graves" at a guilty verdict, while John Witten declared his faith that "every last Anglo-Saxon one of you men in this jury has the courage to set these men free." See Dan Wakefield, "Justice in Summer," in *The Lynching of Emmett Till: A Documentary Narrative,* ed. Christopher Metress (Charlottesville: Univ. of Virginia Press, 2002), 121.

1963

> One hundred years of delay have passed since President Lincoln freed the slaves, yet their heirs, their grandsons, are not fully free. They are not yet freed from the bonds of injustice. They are not yet freed from social and economic oppression. And this Nation, for all its hopes and all its boasts, will not be fully free until all its citizens are free.
>
> **John F. Kennedy, June 11, 1963**

By most accounts, 1963 was the most significant year of the civil rights movement. It was also the bloodiest. The previous summer I had been involved in a number of voter-registration campaigns throughout the Delta, and I've indicated how those activities put my parents on edge. They knew how dangerous participating in civil rights activities could be. If I didn't take a break from my activities, I ran the risk of not completing my senior year. My mother also stood to lose her job as a maid in the Greenwood public school system. Although I continued to support the movement, I could not be such an active participant as I had been earlier on. So my mother seemed relieved when I decided to spend the summer of 1963 visiting my father in Portland, Oregon. I would get to meet a father whom I didn't really know and, I hoped, find a job to help meet the expenses of my first year at Morehouse. But the activities of 1963 were so tumultuous that they resounded throughout the nation and indeed the world. When I enrolled at Morehouse,

I kept up my participation, though in a more limited way, in desegregation protests in Atlanta.

The year of my graduation from high school was such a pivotal year because it was the centennial of the signing of the Emancipation Proclamation, granting freedom to millions of individuals in bondage. Lincoln made it clear that his primary purpose was to save the union, for he believed that the nation could not long endure half slave and half free. The president's motivation notwithstanding, African Americans saw this as a beneficent act that would grant them the same rights and privileges enjoyed by white Americans. Nothing could be further from the truth. One hundred years had passed and blacks were still facing injustices in all aspects of public life. Despite the passage of the Fourteenth Amendment in 1868 and the Fifteenth Amendment in 1870, blacks weren't allowed to vote in most areas in the South. They couldn't use countless public facilities, including restaurants, theaters, parks, and libraries. A document alone, they learned, without the determination of a nation to back its claims was like receiving a check with insufficient funds. This was, at least, the case that Martin Luther King Jr. attempted to press in his speech on August 28, 1963.

Indeed, King wanted to heighten and prick the conscience of a nation that didn't fully realize the plight of its black citizens. It was by all reckoning a year of *Kairos*, as the theologian Paul Tillich put it in his *Protestant Era*. *Kairos* refers to a moment that is rich in content and significance, a time laden with possibilities and ripe for some important undertaking. Nineteen sixty-three was such a year. The events of that year were so powerful they demanded each of us to answer the question, "Where were you?"

On the other side were intransigent individuals who were determined to maintain the status quo of keeping blacks in an inferior position relative to whites. These individuals spoke vaguely of state rights and sovereignty and southern heritage. Seldom were the words "white supremacy" spoken among elected officials, but those who heard Alabama Governor George C. Wallace deliver his inaugural address on January 14, 1963, got a clear message: "Today I have stood, where once Jefferson Davis stood, and took an oath to my people.... In the name of the greatest people that have trod this earth, I draw the line in the dust and toss the gauntlet before the feet of tyranny... and I say... segregation today... segregation tomorrow... segregation forever."[1]

In no single year were forces more clearly aligned on either side. The outcome of this tug-of-war was more often than not violent. While King didn't advocate violence in the least, he recognized fairly early on that making sure the other side's violence was visible for the entire world to see could be a positive force in his overall strategy. The images of defenseless children attacked by dogs and hosed by water from powerful fire hydrants did more to prick the conscience of the nation and world than a speech on injustice could ever accomplish.

Protests for equal rights and justice were followed almost immediately by some violent act. The bombing of the 16th Street Baptist Church in Birmingham, Alabama, and the assassinations of Medgar Evers and John F. Kennedy could all be viewed, whether directly or indirectly, as responses to civil rights agitation. King was well aware that any protests could lead to violence by staunch segregationists who felt they had to defend their way of life and preserve what they considered a sacred heritage. For the young civil rights leader, however, the increased attacks on innocent, nonviolent protestors were a kind of victory in that the protests had the desired effect of bringing tensions out into the open. The violence that civil rights activists faced, in King's view, made the case for more, not less, agitation. Through 1963, therefore, protests for jobs and access to public facilities swept the South from St. Augustine, Florida, to Albany, Georgia, to Birmingham, Alabama.

King called Birmingham the most segregated city in America. Those in other deeply segregated cities were willing to nominate their own city for this distinction. Birmingham became the focal point of the movement because there were a number of unsolved bombings in the city, prompting many to call it "Bombingham." Blacks were not hired as clerks in any of the department stores, though they spent large portions of their incomes shopping at these places. Furthermore, they were not allowed to use the fitting rooms to try on clothing they wished to purchase. It was generally understood that no white person would want to buy a garment that a black person had tried on.

Birmingham was chosen as well because the movement desperately needed a victory after Albany. There King had not successfully aroused the national consciousness to the problems blacks were facing. Things had gone too smoothly. Where there was no upheaval, there was no victory. The movement depended on white racists acting in the way they normally acted. The drama was to be played out on a stage where the world could see just how blacks were routinely treated in the South. The Reverend Fred Shuttlesworth, a leading Birmingham activist, assured King that the city would not act with the restraint that had all but paralyzed the movement in Albany. The dogs and fire hoses turned on students proved Shuttlesworth's point.

On May 10, a settlement was reached in Birmingham. It called for a ninety-day cooling-off period, the removal of "WHITES ONLY" signs and the hiring of a black clerk in a downtown store. Though perhaps not enough, it was at least something positive on which the movement could build. Before the leaders could take a well-deserved respite, King's house was bombed the very next day.

The demonstrations in Birmingham gave birth to one of the most significant documents of the entire civil rights movement: King's "Letter from a Birmingham Jail," a response to a letter by eight white clergymen who criticized his demonstrations in Birmingham. In their statement, the ministers had asked the citizens of the city to withdraw their support from what they contended was an ill-timed movement led by outsiders. The letter urged King to allow the matter to be settled in the courts rather than in the streets. The clergymen argued that King was moving too hastily and that the newly elected mayor should be given a chance to consider the matter. King carefully responded to each of the concerns raised in the ministers' statement. Further, he gave a strong defense of his methods of nonviolent direct action by citing both Thoreau and Gandhi. Drawing a distinction between unjust human laws and the laws of God, he countered the tenets of segregation by showing that all Jim Crow laws were unjust, denigrating rather than uplifting the human personality. While King's letter did little to quell the violence—in fact, the opposite may be argued—it began to set the moral tone and elevate the discussion beyond civil rights to human rights.

That tone was continued two months later in John F. Kennedy's speech on June 11. Clearly frustrated with the attempts by George Wallace and others to defy a clear mandate to register two black students at the University of Alabama, Kennedy made his appeal directly to the American people. Whereas King's letter could be considered self-serving in that it was written by a black man defending his nonviolent campaign, Kennedy as a white man and president could speak more on how segregation had put the entire nation, black and white, in a moral crisis. He cited statistics to show the large gulf between blacks and whites:

> The Negro baby born in America today ... has about one-half as much chance of completing high school as a white baby born in the same place on the same day, one-third as much chance of completing college, one-third as much chance of becoming a professional man, twice as much chance of becoming unemployed, about one-seventh

as much chance of earning $10,000 a year, a life expectancy which is
7 years shorter, and the prospects of earning only half as much.

Given these sobering statistics, the president asked simply, "Who among us would be content to have the color of his skin changed and stand in his place?" Certainly this expression of the Golden Rule to "do unto others as you would have them do unto you" would resonate among Christians and other religious people and especially in that section of the country—the South—which held this most basic of Sunday school teachings in such high regard. "In short," Kennedy said, "every American ought to have the right to be treated as he would wish to be treated, as one would wish his children to be treated, but this is not the case."[2] Again, the president was right. The very next day—actually within hours—Medgar Evers was assassinated in his own driveway.

It was only afterwards that my high school classmates and I would reflect on the deeper significance of graduating in 1963, a year associated with both hope and disillusionment. The activities of that year led to the passage of the momentous Civil Rights Act of 1964, which was enacted despite the commitment of certain southern senators to "filibuster the bill to death." This act had provisions that would begin dismantling Jim Crow throughout our nation. There would be time to weigh the gains and losses and to count the cost in lives lost. We sat there in our blue robes on that last Thursday evening in May listening to hopeful speeches given by various classmates, glancing often at the class motto: "We have crossed the bay, the ocean lies ahead."

NOTES

1. Quoted in Peter B. Levy, *The Civil Rights Movement* (Westport, CT: Greenwood Press, 1998), 169.

2. John F. Kennedy, "Radio and Television Address," June 11, 1963. See *Congressional Record*, 88th Congress, 1st session, 10965–10966.

ENDESHA: A NEW WALK FOR FREEDOM

> Where the old Cat had walked her "walk," sensuous and slow and wanting only to attract the longing gaze of hungry men, this new Cat had no time for that kind of nonsense. I raced to get where I needed to go, even arriving early, eager to get a head start on the day's work. I couldn't wait for freedom to come to me; I was poised to take elusive freedom in one long leap. For the first time in my life I knew who I was.
>
> **Endesha Ida Mae Holland,** *From the Mississippi Delta*

One of the most significant, yet overlooked, aspects of the civil rights movement of the 1950s and 1960s was the role it played in instilling in blacks a sense of pride and dignity that inspired them to overcome circumstances of birth, race, and place to achieve something in life. A number of the movement's lieutenants went on to impressive public careers. I have in mind such individuals as Jesse Jackson, Julian Bond, Maya Angelou, Andrew Young, Fannie Lou Hamer, and John Lewis, all of whom were nourished in some way or form by the movement. They developed leadership and organizational skills that proved invaluable in their careers as social and political leaders. Yet there were countless other average citizens who gained a sense of their value as individuals and refused to submit to the indignities heaped upon them by the stewards of American apartheid.

Charles Payne's wonderful book *I've Got the Light of Freedom* chronicles many of the stories of those individuals. For, in the final analysis, this was a movement that attempted to dismantle not only the outer barriers of racism and bigotry but also the inner barriers of fear and diffidence. In fact, giving blacks a deeper sense of their value as human beings may be seen in the long run as one of the greatest contributions of the civil rights movement.

Among the more remarkable of these personal stories is that of Endesha Ida Mae Holland, who was born in my hometown of Greenwood and was known to all of us as Cat. No doubt a talented, street-smart girl, she seemed to be headed toward, at best, a life of poverty not unlike that of many other girls and, at worst, a prison sentence or death. Hers is a completely engaging and captivating story, that of an individual who rose from a life of petty crime and hustling to a career as a college professor and playwright—a pilgrimage from the meanest of circumstances to a quality existence. It is not unlike the one that Malcolm X made, and indeed, both Endesha and Malcolm came to tell their stories not so much to celebrate their own lives but to show the possibilities for human advancement in the face of oppression. True to her adopted Swahili name, Endesha—which means "to steer, to lead, to guide"—she wanted to drive both herself and others forward. How else are we to account for the many incidents of deeply personal testimony that we see on almost every page of her memoir?

She was a class or two ahead of me in school, so I didn't know firsthand of her hustling. In any case, I would have been quite out of place among those youngsters who played hooky and exhibited rebellious behavior. There were a number of others, including my sister, who could confirm Endesha's stories. They remember Cat picking up tricks on McLaurin Street and in the 82 Grill. It's not a stretch, then, to proffer that of all of us growing up in Greenwood, she would be among the least likely to go on to earn a PhD. That she did in fact complete her degree speaks volumes about her native intelligence and her motivation and perseverance. It also speaks a great deal about the influence of the movement on the lives of many individuals in Greenwood.

The parallel with Maya Angelou may be even more immediate, for she, like Ida, was raped at an early age, though the circumstances were quite different. We may remember that Marguerite (Maya) was raped by her stepfather when she was only eight years old. This was such a profound moment in her young life that it led to her inability to speak for several years. It would be difficult to imagine any event silencing Cat at that age or later. In her own case, she was raped on her eleventh birthday by her white employer. After consummating this foul act, the man gave her a five-dollar bill and wished her a happy birthday.

What are we to make of this incident? Most important, it suggests the inability of black girls, or black women for that matter, to protect themselves against the sexual advances of whites with whom they come into intimate contact. Many blacks during that time worked as maids in the homes of whites. While it certainly was not the case that every white man raped his employee, he knew that if he did, he could easily get away with it.[1] In this respect, the situation of blacks during the 1950s and 1960s was not very different from that which blacks faced during slavery. As Endesha put it, every white man considered getting some "colored pussy" as part of his rite of passage. How often were we asked by white men, "Where could I find me some colored pussy?"

In his essay "The Ethics of Living Jim Crow," Richard Wright noted that this was precisely the kind of indignity a black boy of his generation had to endure. While working in a hotel in Jackson, he regularly saw white prostitutes and their tricks lie nude as he made deliveries to their rooms. He had to pretend that he didn't notice them and to avert his eyes to avoid a scolding or worse. Nor could he show outrage at seeing a white man slap the backside of a young black woman with whom he was walking. Wright simply had to accept it as just another lesson in learning to live Jim Crow.

So, as we look back on that period, we realize that the movement was about more than achieving the right to vote and the right to use public facilities: it was also about the right to walk with pride and dignity. This is truly one of the great lessons we learn from Endesha's story.

When her mother lay dying of burns she suffered in a house fire believed to have been set by the Ku Klux Klan, Endesha promised her that she was "gonna make something" of her life. And sure enough, the onetime streetwalker earned her doctorate and became a professor at the University of Buffalo and later the University of Southern California, one of the nation's leading universities; she also saw her play *From the Mississippi Delta* performed off Broadway to great acclaim. Hers was a remarkable story. Indeed, Cat Holland kept her promise to her mother. On October 18, 1991, she was invited back to Greenwood to receive various commendations, including a brass key to the city. Her entourage passed by many accommodations where she had been denied admission as a youngster as well as the place where the police beat her as she attempted to register blacks to vote. Mississippi now had well over eight hundred black elected officials, more than any other state. Endesha could take some satisfaction that her voter-registration efforts had achieved some tangible results. Her mother would certainly have been proud.

Now walking with a noticeable limp, the result of the crippling neurological disease ataxia, which had already claimed the life of an older brother, Endesha needed the aid of a cane to make her way to the podium to accept her honors. That evening after the celebrations, she took a moment to reflect on her journey. Like her hometown, she had come a long way. The words of the certificate presented to her by then governor Ray Mabus held a special meaning for Endesha: "Her history has served as a model for all people and shows how, with determination, we can overcome obstacles for a better life." To that she could say, "Amen."[2]

Notes

1. David Cohn and William Alexander Percy, among others, indicate that white men would go to any lengths to enforce the taboo against black male and white woman relationships—even to the extent of murdering the black male. The relationship between white men and black women was taken for granted and went unpunished.

2. Dr. Endesha Ida Mae Holland died in a nursing home in Santa Monica, California, from complications of ataxia on January 25, 2006. She was sixty-one years old.

WHITES IN THE STRUGGLE

> While life in Mississippi can be languid and pleasant, certain hazards confront the dissenter who would disparage the local customs. Mississippi is famous for a past of police brutality, and for the sure harassment, even to death, of those who defy the code.... Today [1964] the press has become even less bothered about reporting brutality than it was shown to be by a down-played news story in the Raymond Gazette on July 18, 1885: "Four negroes were lynched at Grenada last week; also one at Oxford."
>
> **James W. Silver,** *Mississippi: The Closed Society*

> Wherever there is a human being, I see God-given rights inherent in that being, whatever may be the sex or complexion.
>
> **William Lloyd Garrison,** *The Story of His Life*

I could see it on their faces, the polite smiles that couldn't completely mask the sense of frustration and bewilderment they were feeling. "Knowing your students" means that you can pick up on such things. Then comes the question that is on many of their minds: "Dr. Hodges, do you believe all whites hate blacks?" I have learned from years of hearing this question in various forms not to answer with the quick retort: "Of course not, and I never said that!" Nor would they, nor should they, be satisfied when I mention John Brown or William Lloyd Garrison or any number of other whites who devoted much of their lives and careers in pursuit of justice for all citizens. At the same time, I don't want to give the erroneous impression, suggested in so many films and documentaries, that no progress at all would have occurred without the assistance of whites.

The students who have enrolled in this class on African American religion are a diverse group: blacks and whites, males and females, a few international students. They have majors ranging from business and engineering to English and political science. Most are from the South but not all. Most have taken my class because they need it to fulfill a requirement to graduate. Some are there to learn something about African American religion and whatever that entails. Others are there because they feel their attendance and membership in a black church has given them a head start in the class. They are, for the most part, deeply religious and conservative. Many of the black students also evince a conservatism that at first may appear disarming. Perhaps no one is completely prepared for a class in which the instructor needs the students as much as they need him. I am sincere when I admit that I seek to have the kind of dialogue with them that I wish I could have had with their parents and grandparents.

So these students, while conservative in many ways, know well that the circumstances of my background have placed me in a different political camp than they; yet they haven't been able to reconcile the treatment of African Americans and others in the South with their understanding of what it means to be a Christian. Certainly, there must have been others who felt as they do. So why wasn't there even a greater outcry among those Christians who were having their religion hijacked in the name of states' rights and southern heritage? The students deserve a much more nuanced response to their questions than I might be able to give them on the spot. Perhaps I need a whole class—or even a course—to discuss the complex and interesting dynamics involving the participation of whites in the civil rights movement. Since I've been so close to the problem, maybe I'm incapable of giving an unbiased opinion, but they do expect and deserve some response.

Whites participated at all stages of the freedom movement during the 1950s and 1960s. This includes laying the groundwork for legal challenges to segregation as in *Brown v. Board of Education,* the Freedom Rides, sit-ins, voter registration campaigns, protest marches, and demonstrations. The one reason that there was not more of a hue and cry from white citizens is that those in charge of maintaining the status quo made the participation of whites such a perilous affair. In many ways, it was much more dangerous for whites to participate than blacks, although it was dangerous for both. This is shown in so many instances.

Consider, for example, the story of Bob Zellner. Born April 5, 1939, the son of a Methodist minister and a school teacher, Robert Zellner became involved in the civil rights movement as a student at Huntington College in Montgomery, Alabama. He surely seemed an unlikely candidate at first, given his background as a southerner and the fact that his grandfather was a Klansman and probably his great-grandfather as well. At Huntington, he was assigned a paper in which he was to present his ideas on solving the racial problem. He not only searched books like a good scholar but also found that Montgomery, the heart of what once was the Confederacy, offered an opportunity to gain more first-hand information. Information from the local Klu Klux Klan and White Citizens Council was readily available, as was information from the Montgomery Improvement Association, which had led the fight to desegregate buses in that city in 1955. When he wished to become even more involved with the MIA and attend various workshops, he was warned that his involvement would certainly lead to his being arrested. The young Zellner couldn't understand at the time that he wasn't just a student who wanted to exercise his rights as any citizen would. The truth was that he was a white student seeking involvement with the freedom movement. He was asked to resign from the school because of his activities, which at that time only consisted of attending a rally sponsored by a civil rights organization. Later on, as the first white chairman of the Student Nonviolent Coordinating Committee (SNCC), he was arrested on several spurious charges and beaten on a number of occasions for his participation.

At least Zellner lived to tell his story. There were others who were killed as a result of their participation in the movement. The Reverend James Reeb, a Unitarian minister from Boston, was among many white clergymen who joined the Selma marchers after the attack by state troopers at the Edmund Pettus bridge. Reeb was beaten to death by white men while he walked down a Selma street. Jonathan Myrick Daniels, an Episcopal seminary student in Boston, went to Alabama to help with black voter registration in Lowndes County. He was arrested at a demonstration, jailed in Hayneville, and then suddenly released. Moments after his release, he was shot to death by a deputy sheriff. Then there is the case of Mrs. Viola Gregg Liuzzo, a housewife and mother, who made the trip alone from her home in Detroit to Alabama. She had seen on television the brutality and intransigence of police officers attacking marchers at the Pettus bridge. She was there simply to help. But while driving marchers back to Selma from Montgomery, she was shot and killed by a Klansmen in a passing car.[1] In the initial trial at the state level, the defense attorney appealed directly to the all-white jury with inflammatory racist language, characterizing Mrs. Liuzzo as "'a white nigger' who turned her car over to a 'black nigger' for the purpose of 'hauling' niggers and Communists back and forth.'"[2]

No case during that period was more calculated in its planning and gruesome in its execution than that of three civil rights workers who went missing in Neshoba County near Philadelphia, Mississippi, in June 1964. By the time the dust had settled and most of the details were in and the major parties identified, one saw a clear example of how local law enforcement officials often cooperated with such groups as the Ku Klux Klan and White Citizens Councils to "deprive" activists of their civil rights—which in this instance was just so much federal legalese for murder.

While returning to Meridian on June 21 after investigating the recent firebombing of the Mt. Zion Methodist Church in Philadelphia, the three young men were pulled over by Deputy Cecil Price. James Chaney, a twenty-one-year-old African American from Meridian, was charged with speeding, while Michael Schwerner and Andrew Goodman, both white and both from New York, were charged with "investigation." They were held in jail and not permitted to make phone calls. Both the sheriff and his deputy were Klansmen and had agreed to deliver the young men to other Klansmen who were to carry out the planned execution. Released from jail, the three activists resumed their drive to Meridian, only to be chased down and kidnapped by the Klansmen. Federal transcripts of the trial indicate that Schwerner and Goodman were both shot once in the heart and that Chaney was first beaten and then shot three times. The Klan drove the 1963 Ford station wagon into Bogue Chitto Swamp before setting it on fire. The bodies were buried in an earthen dam and discovered forty-four days later.[3] One of the assassins had reportedly taunted the victims: "So, you wanted to come to Mississippi? Well, now we're gonna let you stay here. We're not even gonna run you out. We're gonna let you stay here with us."[4]

The individuals I've discussed thus far were activists who were well aware of the type of resistance they might encounter in the South. There is ample evidence, however, to show that the racist program of intimidation and terrorism was not just limited to these professional agitators but to their neighbors and ordinary citizens. If you were white, you were either a supporter of white supremacy or "a nigger lover." There was no room anywhere in between. Hodding Carter, editor of the *Delta Democrat* in Greenville, was often counted among the latter because he refused to do the bidding of the Klan and other organizations that attempted to control the media in the South. The same is true for a number of ordinary citizens who were determined to do their jobs in a responsible way. A white librarian who allowed blacks to check out books because "they pay taxes too" had to be reminded of the local policy. A Presbyterian minister in Greenwood was told he needed to send his children to a private school rather than to the recently integrated public schools. A white businessman who advertised in a black newspaper sympathetic to the NAACP was told that the paper was controlled by Communists and suggested that he discontinue his ads. The Catholic Church in Greenwood and in other Delta towns was targeted for sponsoring activities for blacks, especially giving them access to books and publishing their accomplishments in its newspaper.

Mayrene Washington Jones, one of the first black students to integrate Greenwood High School in the fall of 1966, can speak firsthand of the courage of a few white individuals who were willing to denounce bigotry and racial hatred. She and other black students had a difficult time enduring the racial slurs directed at them. She found many of the white students to be simply mean and nasty to her, letting her know that she wasn't welcome in the previously all-white school. Even on the day she graduated, the white male who was to march alongside her (because of the alphabetical listing of their names) refused to do so, choosing instead to march alone at the end of the line. (I understand that both this young man and his father later regretted this decision.) But there were whites who refused to join in with the others. They were not trying to make any particular case. They just wanted to be decent, civil, and humane. The principal, Seth Dillon, was credited with doing all he could to keep the situation under control. There were teachers, such as Beverly Smith, who tried to treat Mayrene and the other black students with the kindness and charity afforded to all students. Then there was Bobby Miller, as Mayrene recalls, "who would stick up for me—even though he had to fuss with some of the others." The cost of being civil was to be regarded as a "nigger lover."

All of these cases and so many more point to just how often whites were pressured to follow the dictates and dogma of the Klan and Citizens Councils instead of their own instincts to do what was right and decent. Anyone who could not be counted on openly to carry out the party line was ostracized or in some cases banished completely from the community. There were those who found subtle ways to continue being human during this time. That there weren't more must be attributed to the reign of terror that engulfed a South imprisoning blacks and seriously limiting the freedom of whites as well.

NOTES

1. Seth Cogan and Philip Dray, *We Are Not Afraid: The Story of Goodman, Schwerner, and Chaney, and the Civil Rights Campaign for Mississippi* (New York: Nation Books, 2006), 442.

2. Ibid.

3. Ibid., 364–402

4. Ibid., 46.

REUNION AS PILGRIMAGE

> Home is the place where, when you have to go there,
> They have to take you in.
>
> **Robert Frost, "The Death of the Hired Man"**

Most of us have been away from Greenwood now for forty, fifty, sixty years, or more, reside in various places throughout the United States and abroad, and perhaps have no real desire to return to this place as permanent residents. The question so often posed by outlanders who wish to make our acquaintance is, "Where is home?" We respond with a question intended to make a clarifying distinction: "Do you mean where I now live, or where I'm from?" To make the distinction between where one lives and where one calls home is not to quibble over semantics. To the "where I'm from" question, I and so many other schoolmates refer to this town at the eastern edge of the Yazoo-Mississippi Delta named for the Choctaw chief Greenwood LeFlore. The matter of where I'm from strikes at the very core of who I am as an individual and as a member of a particular community. Although education, family, work, and other circumstances have taken me to other places, I still see Greenwood and the Delta as home. It's not so much a matter of whether I was treated well or ill there, it's more a matter of finding a locus for my own personal and communal story that is at stake. Where I'm from, therefore, has everything to do with who I am now and what prospects my future holds—even, and perhaps especially, if it has served as my primary motivation for rising beyond those prospects bequeathed at birth.

For me, then, the Delta is a sacred place—a notion at which some might bristle. But the graduates of Stone Street, Broad Street, and Threadgill High Schools who return there for the class reunion every odd year during the week of the Fourth of July or the following week understand this to be the case. Class reunions, whether for high school or college, are, of course, periodic rites that take place throughout the nation, perhaps even throughout the world. But it seems to me that the reunion that happens in the Mississippi Delta every couple of years holds significance beyond the average class reunion. In the first place, it very well may be the best modern example of the need and obligation to return to a special place or home—a defining characteristic of both traditional and modern societies. Those of us who return become part of a pilgrimage to a sacred place that held some important meaning in the beginning, when we were young and starting out in life. The biennial pilgrimage to Greenwood is an effort to take hold of one's story and find meaning among others similarly situated. Most of my classmates may wish to stop short of seeing it the way I do—as a deeply spiritual act. They may simply see it as a way of meeting old friends and talking about old times, but there is a reason that the meetings and associations reenergize and restore us individually and as members of a community.

If we consider some of the most sacred places throughout the world, such as Jerusalem, Mecca, Delphi, or the Black Hills, we know that on certain occasions they seem to acquire even greater sacredness. It's not when we visit them as single individuals on a sightseeing trip; it is rather when we go as part of a community, as pilgrims among other pilgrims taking part in special ceremonies, that we enter them as holy places. I visited Nigeria in 2001 along with several colleagues from the University of Tennessee. One of the highlights of the trip was a festival held at Ile-Ife about eighty miles or so from where we were staying in Lagos. The Yoruba see this place as sacred because it is the home of their ancestors and, they claim, the home of humankind in general. For those outside the Yoruba community, it was just another beautiful festival with great food and drink. But for the Yoruba and those blacks who could trace their lineage back to them, it took on a much greater significance that was partly captured in their warm greeting, "Welcome home."

Now, perhaps such a large claim shouldn't be made for the reunions in Greenwood, but it does strike me that the festivities occurring during those weekends are meant to bring us to a better understanding of who we are as a group of African Americans from a place that held great meaning for us at some earlier time. It is a return home, to a place with memories of a past struggle, that continues to bind us together. When we return to Greenwood, we return to the past, to our roots, to our beginnings. This is the reason we couldn't hold the affair in Chicago or Pittsburgh or Los Angeles, despite the many amenities these cities offer and the fact that many of our graduates have wound up in one of these major hubs. A meeting outside the home place wouldn't carry the same significance.

The biennial reunion is limited to the classes from the 1930s to the 1960s and early years of the 1970s. Classes from later years will petition to be included in future reunions, especially as many of the older schoolmates pass away. While those coming later have a story, it simply is not the story of those of us who came from segregated high schools to forge a future for ourselves and our children despite the hardships imposed by a rigid and intractable color line. I imagine those who were the first to go to the newly integrated schools have an equally compelling narrative; it's just not ours. The power of the reunion—indeed, that which makes it special—lies in the fact that it brings together individuals who have a common history and a common purpose.

The function of the ceremony is to remind us of that history by transporting us back to a sacred place and time, which the historian of religions Mircea Eliade refers to as *Illo Tempore*. The skits, songs, dances, and even the food are carefully selected for their power to transport us back to that special time. Moreover, a great effort is made to recall specific incidents that situate us in that time. Of course, it's unrealistic to assume we haven't changed at all during a period of forty years or more removed from high school. Our graying hair and expanding girths remind us that we aren't quite the same as we were back then, though there is a genuine attempt, it seems, to abolish that space between then and now and create an eternal present where we remember "the way we were" and, for the moment at least, are again.

One of the most significant rituals is the Golden Graduates ceremony that takes place on Saturday evening. Here the fifty-year graduates are honored with the opportunity to march and receive their "diplomas," certificates that commemorate this significant moment and are designed to look like real diplomas. There is genuine joy and excitement as Dr. Pauline Pearson Stamps, the Reunion Committee co-chair, reminds the "golden" graduates, with her characteristic wit and humor, of their activities and accomplishments of fifty years ago. John Johnson and others of the Reunion Committee pass out the diplomas that mark this important passage in the lives of the graduates.

Reunion as Pilgrimage

The reunions have brought our classes more closely together than ever before. Cliques and small jealousies have all but disappeared as we realize a greater purpose. We've survived and what brings us together is greater than anything that might keep us apart.

The various reunion chairs perhaps haven't received enough credit for putting together an event so full of significance. It must be a gigantic undertaking. Though I haven't spoken about this with any of the chairs, I imagine that one of the committee's main tasks is figuring out how to match a given activity to the theme of a particular reunion. And one of the major ways of determining that appropriateness, I suspect, is to consider how effective the activity is in locating us back in that time.

Even the golf tournament, a regular feature of so many class reunions around the country, has a special meaning for my schoolmates. Generally held on Saturday morning, this activity represents more than just another occasion to hit the links with friends. Rather, it enables the participants to remember and reclaim a past when playing golf, because of expense and opportunity, was out of reach for most young black men and women. Many learned the game while working as caddies and then playing with inferior equipment on that one day of the week when the course was open to them. But they did learn to play and now return to the course to celebrate the accomplishment.

After the graduation ceremony and banquet dinner, it's time for dancing and socializing. We listen to the music we enjoyed when we fell in and out of love. This is a music that really said something, inspiring and lifting us "higher and higher." It isn't the vapid and degrading "Gansta Rap" of our children and grandchildren; it's Jerry Butler, the Temptations, and Gladys Knight.

The closing church service on Reunion Sunday provides a fitting conclusion to a weekend filled with significant rituals. While this is the most ostensibly religious activity of the reunion, it mustn't be understood as the primary reason why I consider our reunions sacred or spiritual events. As I've argued here, it is the reuniting of a community above all that gives these gatherings their special significance.

The church service is every bit the same type of service I remember from my youth—complete with a choir, ushers, a preacher, and pleas for a generous offering. Those schoolmates who were ushers serve in that capacity again, directing us to our seats. The choir members get to sing with some of their old friends just as they did forty or fifty years ago. (What a special treat it was to have our former teacher and choir director, Mrs. Lynn Twyner, return in 2011 to direct a choir composed of some of the same students she taught and directed back in the early sixties.)

Finally, one of our schoolmates returns to deliver a rousing sermon—prepared, it seems, just for the occasion. We see the preacher not so much as the distinguished pastor he or she has become but as Eugene or Dorothy or by some nickname we used as youngsters back then.

While listening to the inspirational singing, the patterns of call and response, I think not so much of the distance I've had to cover in coming back home but just how much I'm put in mind of my past in Greenwood. I realize in that moment that we've indeed become our parents and grandparents. Our past and present seem to have been fused in some eternal PRESENT. Perhaps that's the real meaning of reunion.

EPILOGUE: THE DELTA THEN AND NOW

> Black people are the magical faces at the bottom of society's well. Even the poorest whites, those who must live their lives only a few levels above, gain their self-esteem by gazing down on us. Surely, they must know that their deliverance depends on letting down their ropes. Only by working together is escape possible.
>
> **Derrick Bell,** *Faces at the Bottom of the Well*

> All God's dangers ain't a white man.
>
> **Nate Shaw, from** *All God's Dangers:*
> *The Autobiography of Nate Shaw* by Theodore Rosengarten

In bringing these fragments to a close, it is important to remind myself and my readers of that poignant statement by Nate Shaw (whose real name was Ned Cobb). I've endeavored to tell my story honestly and truthfully. Yet, there might be those who find in my recounting of the injustices I experienced coming of age in the Delta an effort to lay all the problems I faced at the feet of the southern white man. If Nate Shaw could conclude after all the hardships he encountered, including a twelve-year prison sentence, that there were evils at work other than those posed by the white man, certainly I, facing fewer cruelties, should admit the essential truth of this point. Yet blacks of Shaw's generation and of my own know well that most of the problems we faced could be traced back to a few whites determined to uphold a brutal and stifling system of racial apartheid. Nate Shaw was an Alabama farmer and a younger contemporary of my Mississippi-raised grandfather. They would find much in common in their stories. Much of the prejudice they faced was still present during my youth.

The Delta of my childhood, in important ways, is now but a distant memory. Indeed, the Delta and the South in general have made notable strides in the area of civil rights, but it's fair to point out that it had a very long way to go. Today, thankfully, the "WHITES ONLY" and "COLORED" signs are permanently archived in museums and libraries for students of this region's history. No blacks are denied admission to restaurants, hotels, and theaters based on the color of their skin, and the public libraries, once off-limits to blacks, are now truly public.

The changes in the political arena are even more dramatic. In my youth, there were no African American police officers and firefighters. The first black officers had to call a white policeman before they could arrest a white person. Now, Greenwood has both a black police chief and a black fire chief. The city also has had in its recent past a black mayor. These are changes I couldn't have dreamed of as a boy in Greenwood. Whenever I allowed myself to dream about the future, I thought about how great it would be for me to be Greenwood's first black mayor. At the time, I thought the goal of becoming president of the United States was more attainable. Now, Mississippi has more black mayors than any state in the union.

The progress that blacks have attained in the political arena, of course, may be attributed to their having finally achieved the franchise first guaranteed under the Fifteenth Amendment but not enforced until the passage of the Voting Rights Act of 1965. When I look back on the number of marches and the amount of canvassing we did to help get the voting rights and public accommodations bills passed, I take a great deal of satisfaction from those efforts.

In recording the progress that has been made, it's also fair to say that the Delta, as James Cobb declared some years ago, remains "the most southern place on earth." Here, habits die hard, especially those involving race relations. While official apartheid has ended, as well as Jim Crow laws restricting access to public facilities, there is still an unspoken tension as regards racial mores in the Delta. Richard Wright in the early years of the twentieth century was perplexed at the existence of "two races that never touched it seemed, except in violence." Blacks don't face the violence from whites that was once a daily occurrence;

however, they still don't touch in any meaningful way. Blacks and whites work alongside each other and tend to be cordial in the workplace. Yet, I've failed to see much interaction between the races on a truly social level. Indeed, blacks and whites have attempted to solve the race problem by staying out of each other's way. We know that hasn't worked in the past, and it won't work today.

On October 19, 2010, the Greenwood City Council adopted the Greenwood Comprehensive Plan that was meant to serve as the "city's blueprint for the economic, social and physical development" for the next thirty years. The final plan replaces similar plans adopted by the mayor and City Council in 1963, 1970, and 1978. It's a bold plan that was put together by a steering committee composed of some of the leading black and white citizens of the community. There are ten significant findings that must be addressed if the city is to reach its goals in the coming years.[1] If the city can meet those goals, Greenwood will be a better city, but it still will not have addressed all those issues that must be examined for it to become a great city. While the areas mentioned in the plan certainly need attention, only one seems to speak to what I consider Greenwood's major problems: a weak educational system, a poor economic system, and a rising crime rate among teenagers and young adults. The eighth strategic goal does call for promoting economic development and indicates that establishing a high-quality educational system is important to this outcome. Even in the area of economics and education, I don't get the impression that blacks and whites are working together to solve the problems. But much more attention has to be focused on education itself. While I admit that the three areas are interrelated, I wish to shed light on the problems by taking a brief glance at each.

We must note from the outset that the major stumbling block to solving these problems has been the effort to find a solution to them that doesn't involve integration. Too often the city leaders see a particular problem as a black problem or a white problem and fail to work together to solve what is a community problem. The public school system offers a good example of this. After the 1954 *Brown* decision and its implementation decree a year later, local officials did everything imaginable to make sure that black and white children didn't go to school together. When Greenwood High School was finally desegregated in the late 1960s, few whites remained in the public school system. Within a few years, a school that had been 100 percent white became over 95 percent black. The public school system remains to this day overwhelmingly black and, we must add, poor. The situation in Greenwood is replicated in every city throughout the Mississippi Delta. Whites who take their children out of the public schools withdraw their financial and spiritual support as well. Trying to run what in effect is a dual school system is too expensive, especially for a region that suffers from such low economic growth. As a result, both black and white children continue to suffer.

Thus, we have the rise of the private academies in the South. Even today, whites who want to send their children to public schools are roundly criticized, pressured, and threatened, even though they may not have the financial resources or the will to place their children in private schools. The rise of these private academies, I contend, has had a negative impact on education in the state and perhaps on race relations as well. Since state funding is based on a formula that considers the total number of students, the absence of white students has caused a decrease in allocations to these school districts. Since whites don't have their children in these schools, there is no incentive for them to look for ways to improve them, either through their own personal financial support or by lobbying the state legislature for increased funding. And making matters worse is that very few white teachers in the public schools send their own children to those schools. I see that as a serious problem.

This touches on ethical and moral issues that are just as compelling. White and black parents who fail to allow their children to go to school together are ill-equipping them to become citizens in a world that is becoming increasingly global and diverse. In college and the workplace, they won't be so isolated. Learning to appreciate and deal with difference is an important lesson in life that should be learned as early as possible. I'm not unmindful of the fear that persists among some individuals that truly integrated schools lead inevitably to interracial dating and marriage. This is a concern held by blacks as well as whites but perhaps most commonly among southern white men. The whole bugaboo of race mixing is at best a pseudo-problem based on stereotypes and deep prejudices. If blacks and whites are determined to form liaisons, the matter of attending different schools is hardly sufficient to keep them from doing so. We all know that, historically, white men haven't been so concerned with the issue of racial purity when it comes to affairs with black women. Yet, even today, after antimiscegenation laws have been struck down in the South and interracial marriages are much more common, some still think any relationship between black men and white women is the result of force on the part of black men.[2]

The issue of economics is a major one in the Delta and is related to the problem of education. Mississippi, despite its casinos, is one of the poorest states in the union. And the Delta is the poorest region in the state. Educated blacks and whites often find it necessary to leave the state to find employment commensurate with their training, thus creating a serious talent drain that only exacerbates the economic problem. Those who wish to remain in the state face an ever-rising unemployment rate. While the average unemployment rate for 2009 stood at 12.7 percent, by March 2010 it had reached 15.1 percent. Figures for both years exceed the national rate of unemployment over the same period. To avoid unemployment, individuals find themselves accepting whatever jobs they can. This problem of underemployment has led to the following startling statistics. According to the 2010 census, 21.2 percent of Mississippians were below the poverty level as compared to 13.8 percent nationwide. In Leflore County, 39.7 percent of the population fell below the poverty level. This is astounding, especially when you consider that the figure is about twice the poverty level in the state as a whole and almost three times higher than the national average. It's no wonder that while the state grew slightly in population from 2000 to 2010 (by 4.3 percent), Leflore County has decreased in population by 14.8 percent.

Clearly the Greenwood Comprehensive Plan steering committee was correct in identifying economic development as a major issue. But this issue, like other issues, cannot be adequately addressed as long as vestiges of segregation remain. It's unrealistic to ask blacks and whites to sit across from each other in the boardrooms if they aren't allowed to sit across from each other in the classroom or to play alongside each other on the golf course.

Finally, there is the issue of violence, especially among youth throughout the Delta. Recently, a great-nephew of mine was gunned down in the streets of Greenwood. A code of silence has prevented the murderer from being brought to justice. While blacks don't face violence from whites to nearly the same degree as in the past, blacks are now being terrorized by those within their own community.[3] Crimes brought on by the presence of dope, prostitution, and gang activity, which we once thought were the province of the North, have come to plague the South to a much greater degree than was the case during the 1950s and 1960s. But I don't see this as just a black problem. It should be tackled by both blacks and whites, who must resolve that Greenwood won't be turned over to gangsters and thugs, black or white.

Along with this tough stance must be an equal determination and commitment to create more opportunities for youth in Greenwood and throughout the Delta. These opportunities must be made available to students on a nonsegregated basis and must have the support of blacks and whites alike. Some youth, though not all, get into trouble and run afoul of the law because they have found nothing to do—an oversimplification perhaps, but a matter that needs to be addressed nonetheless. Convening a summit to discuss the various issues involved would be a step in the right direction. Again, it must involve both white and black citizens, who should realize that the issue of violence poses a problem for everyone and that it relates to economic issues as well. If companies, for example, feel that the city doesn't provide a safe environment for its employees, they will be reluctant to locate there. Of course, they will be equally hesitant to locate in a place where there is concern regarding equal educational opportunities for all individuals. So, again, we see the interrelatedness of the problems facing the Delta.

In the late 1940s, the Delta-born writer David Cohn—for all his insight about his native region—couldn't foresee a time when segregation might be questioned. He was wrong, of course, and segregation in many forms *has* ended. But de facto segregation remains a serious problem, a set of codes and circumstances that works no better now than it did when it was entirely legal. Thus, the time has come again—it's long overdue, in fact—for blacks and whites to have serious dialogues about the problems facing all citizens. And this should be done in a completely open manner.

A closing note: Recently, those of my generation witnessed what we thought we would never see in our lifetime: the ascendance of an African American to the presidency of the United States. But despite Barack Obama's historic election in 2008, I don't believe it provides clear evidence that we've entered a "postracial" era. No one can deny that, with the end of legal segregation and the passage of the Civil Rights Accommodation Act of 1964 and the Voting Rights Act of 1965, there has been tremendous progress in the country. And that, of course, includes the Mississippi Delta. But just when we seem prepared to celebrate a new millennium of race relations in this country, we are brought back to the sobering reality that race still matters in the United States.

A recent incident in Crystal Springs, Mississippi, offers a case in point. There, a black couple, Charles and Te'Andrea Wilson, were not allowed to hold their wedding in the white church they had been attending and where the bride's father was a member. Charles and Te'Andrea had to change the venue just because a few in the congregation opposed their having the ceremony there. It didn't seem to matter that most members of the church felt the opposite. This incident shows how a few powerful individuals could still have their way despite the overwhelming presence of Crystal Springs's forward-thinking community.[4] In the South, especially in the Mississippi Delta, strains of racism clearly persist, and they are all the more virulent because we treat the illness with weak, sugar-coated pills. That is, we still tend to talk around issues of racial prejudice rather than to confront them head-on. Only by acknowledging that prejudices remain can blacks and whites in the Delta work together to solve the pressing problems of education, poverty, and crime.

NOTES

1. The Greenwood Comprehensive Plan, 2010–2040, was adopted by the Greenwood City Council on October 19, 2010. It was prepared by the Greenwood Comprehensive Steering Committee with technical assistance from Johnstone and Associates Planning and Marketing Consultants of Hernando, Mississippi. The plan can be accessed online at http://www.cityofgreenwood.org/plan/greenwood_comprehensive_plan.pdf.

2. As of 1967, sixteen states had laws prohibiting interracial marriages. In the case of *Loving v. Virginia*, the U.S. Supreme Court held that the freedom to marry is "one of the vital personal rights essential to the orderly pursuit of happiness by free men. This fundamental right cannot be infringed by the state." For a summary and brief discussion of the case, see Abraham L. Davis and Barbara Luck Graham, *The Supreme Court, Race, and Civil Rights* (Thousand Oaks, CA: Sage Publications, 1995), 214–16.

3. One hopeful note: Most white citizens today are just as appalled as blacks have been over the way justice was dispensed at one time in the South. In fact, efforts have been made and others are ongoing to bring to justice those who once thought their skin allowed them to evade punishment. The efforts, in many cases, are being led by whites themselves, as in the case of Byron De La Beckwith, who was finally convicted of the murder of Medgar Evers. One of De La Beckwith's nephews, Reed Massengill, provided key testimony that helped convict him.

4. Governor Phil Bryant is to be commended for calling the incident "unfortunate" in a statement he made to reporters at the Neshoba County Fair in Philadelphia, Mississippi, on August 2, 2012. Earlier, on July 30, the citizens of Crystal Springs held a unity rally to show support for the couple.

APPENDIX 1

TABLE OF BLACK AND WHITE PERSONS IN THE DELTA BY POPULATION, EDUCATION, AND INCOME

	Population	White Persons	Black Persons	High School Graduates	Median Household Income	Persons Below Poverty Level
United States	308,745,538	72.40%	12.60%	85.00%	$51,914	13.80%
Mississippi	2,967,297	59.10%	37.00%	79.60%	$37,881	21.20%
Bolivar County	34,145	33.50%	64.20%	71.50%	$26,005	35.70%
Coahoma County	26,151	22.90%	75.50%	74.20%	$24,726	35.50%
Humphreys County	9,375	23.50%	74.50%	62.90%	$25,131	42.90%
Issaquena County	1,406	34.60%	64.40%	59.70%	$21,360	39.70%
Leflore County	32,317	24.90%	72.20%	68.80%	$22,020	39.70%
Quitman County	8,223	29.00%	69.60%	63.60%	$24,169	34.80%
Sharkey County	4,916	27.90%	71.00%	70.60%	$30,129	34.90%
Sunflower County	29,450	25.40%	72.90%	69.80%	$25,012	33.30%
Tallahatchie County	15,378	38.90%	56.40%	65.50%	$24,668	32.50%
Tunica County	10,778	23.70%	73.50%	72.40%	$29,994	25.70%
Washington County	51,137	27.00%	71.30%	72.50%	$27,797	34.80%

The ten counties lying completely or largely within the Delta are: Bolivar, Coahoma, Humphreys, Isaquena, LeFlore, Quitman, Sharkey, Sunflower, Tunica, and Washington. Since a significant portion of Tallahatchie County lies within the Delta, it is often considered in discussions about this region.
Source: 2010 U.S. Census

APPENDIX 2

REPORTS RELATING TO 1962 CIVIL RIGHTS ACTIVITIES IN WHICH AUTHOR WAS INVOLVED

AUTHOR'S NOTE: This appendix reproduces three official investigation reports that were filed by the Mississippi Sovereignty Commission and dealt with voter-registration activities in which I was involved in Sunflower County, Mississippi, in 1962. They can be accessed online at the website of the Mississippi Department of Archives and History (http://mdah.state.ms.us/arrec/digital_archives/sovcom/index.php) by searching on "John Hodges," "John O. Hodges," "John Oliver Hodges," and "James O. Hodges" (as I was incorrectly identified in a couple of the reports). These documents are important in that they demonstrate the lengths to which the commission would go to spy on citizens. They clearly reflect the prejudices of the investigators; the misspellings of names suggest that they are questionable even at the level of basic factual accuracy.

In addition to these documents, the online archive includes reproductions of a pair of United Press International news stories that briefly detail encounters with law enforcement that I and several of my fellow activists endured. In one incident, we were arrested in Indianola for distributing voter-registration leaflets without a permit, and in the other, we were arrested in Clarksdale for a midnight-curfew violation, which was said to have "nothing to do" with a voter-registration meeting we had attended earlier that evening.

Title: Sunflower County—Negro Voter Agitators—Robert Moses, Samuel Block, John O. Hodges, Albert Garner, Charles R. McLauren, Lafayette [S]urney (a 17-year old Negro boy)
Date of Investigation: September 7, 1962
Investigated By: Tom Scarbrough, Investigator
Date of Report: September 11, 1962
Typed By: H. Stietenroth

Pursuant to orders from Director Albert Jones to proceed to Bolivar, Leflore and Sunflower Counties to make an investigation on outside-the-State voters registration agitators, I journeyed to Indianola, Mississippi, County seat of Sunflower County, on September 6, 1962.

Appendix 2

Upon my arrival there, I contacted Sheriff Woodley Carr and Chief of Police Will Love. I learned from these two gentlemen that the trial of five Negro males who were charged with handing out literature without a city permit would be held at 7:30 A. M., September 7, 1962. I spent the remainder of the night in Indianola and returned to the Mayor's office the next morning around 7:00 to attend the trial of the five Negroes, namely,

Robert Moses, 17 W. 39th Street, New York, New York. I was advised that this address is located two doors from the Communist Party's newspaper, The Daily Worker.

Samuel Theodore Block, Jr., 206 Washington Street, Cleveland, Mississippi. This Negro has been getting benefits through the State Vocational Rehabilitation. He has lost one eye. He graduated from the East Side Negro High School in 1959. This is the same Negro on whom I made an investigation in the early part of August in Greenwood, Mississippi.

John O. Hodges, who is President of the Student Body of the Greenwood, Mississippi, High School.

Albert Garner, who is a student at Greenwood, Mississippi, and the leader of a Negro high school band in Greenwood. [AUTHOR'S NOTE: Albert was not the "leader of a Negro high school band" as reported here. Rather, he was the incoming president of the senior class.]

Charles R. McLauren, who gave his address only as Jackson, Mississippi, and a Negro youth who was released from his charges by the name of Lafayette Surney, seventeen years old, address, Greenwood, Mississippi.

Title: Sunflower County
Date of Investigation: September 14, 1962
Investigated by: Tom Scarbrough, Investigator
Date of Report: September 26, 1962
Typed by: H. Stietenroth

Pursuant to directions from Director Jones to proceed to Sunflower County to assist county and city officials in combating racial troubles which were being brought about Robert Moses, James Bevels [Bevel], and a number of other racial agitators in and around Ruleville, Mississippi, I journeyed to Sunflower County on September 14, 1962.

Appendix 2

Upon my arrival there I checked with Sheriff Woodley Carr, Deputy Sheriff T. A. Flemings, the Marshall of Ruleville, Mr. Will Love, and the Mayor of Ruleville, Charles Dorrough.

I was advised by city and county officials that they were very happy to have a friendly investigator from the State with them as racial troubles have been flaring up almost daily and nightly in Sunflower County for the past week, brought about by outside Negro agitators, namely, Robert Moses, James Bevels [sic], his wife Diane Nash Bevels [sic], Charles Ray McLaurin, address 2226 Meadow Street, Jackson, Mississippi, but according to a Washington, D.C. Post newspaper McLaurin resides in St. Louis, Missouri, Charles Cobb, Samuel T. Block, James [John] O. Hodges, Albert Garner, and Lawrence Guyot, (Guyot is a Negro attorney from Atlanta, Georgia), all of whom are Negroes, and perhaps Carl Braden, white male. It was further determined that this group of agitators was having meetings at a Negro Baptist Church by the name of Williams Chapel and that these outside agitators have succeeded in getting a few local Negroes interested in their agitative program, namely, Lafayette Searney [Surney], a Negro boy, address Ruleville, Mississippi, age 18 (Searney [sic] finished the Negro school in Ruleville in the Spring of 1962), Joe McDonald and his wife, Herman (Jack) Sisson and his wife, as well as ten or twelve other Negroes, all of whom live in Ruleville, Mississippi, whose names I did not get.

Title: Sunflower County
Date of Investigation: October 30, 1962
Date of Report: November 9, 1962
Investigated By: Tom Scarbrough, Investigator
Typed By: M. Rayfield

This report is made in conjunction with orders which I received from Director Jones to make an investigation on Dewey Roosevelt Green, Jr., Negro male, age 21—address, Greenwood, Mississippi. A separate report has been filed on the above subject in the Leflore County files.

In the course of my investigation of Dewey Greene in Sunflower County, I determined that Robert Moses, James Bevels, Charles Ray McLaurin, Samuel Block, James [John] O. Hodges, and in all probability, Carl Braden are working in four or five counties holding secret meetings with Negroes trying to encourage them to register to vote or to do anything else which will cause discord and strife among the Negro race. These counties in which the above mentioned subjects are now working are Leflore, Sunflower, Coahoma, Quitman and Bolivar Counties.

I also determined that Reverend D. W. Darby, Negro minister, who filed the voter registration suit against the circuit clerk in Jefferson Davis County, at Prentiss, Mississippi, is now located at Marks, Mississippi and has been holding some secret meetings in Quitman County.

Furthermore, I determined that the NAACP AND CIVIL RIGHTS ATTORNEYS OUT OF WASHINGTON, D.C. are working hand-in-glove in encouraging Negroes to try to register to vote and these same civil rights attorneys are offering assistance, encouragement and help in defending any Negro on any frivolous charge which they can be justified in claiming civil rights violations.

SELECTED BIBLIOGRAPHY

The materials in this bibliography are grouped under major topics found in this book. This format will make it easier for the researcher or student to locate those works most pertinent to a particular area. While a number of works may well be placed under more than one category, I have resisted the temptation to list a work more than once. This is especially true of works included under the "general" category.

GENERAL

Anderson, Terry H. *The Sixties*. 3rd ed. New York: Pearson Longman, 2007.

Carpenter, Barbara, ed. *Ethnic Heritage in Mississippi*. Jackson: University Press of Mississippi, 1992.

Cobb, James C. *The Most Southern Place on Earth: The Mississippi Delta and the Roots of Regional Identity*. New York: Oxford University Press, 1992.

De Rosier, Arthur H., Jr. *The Removal of the Choctaw Indians*. Knoxville: University of Tennessee Press, 1970.

Dollard, John. *Caste and Class in a Southern Town*. 1949. Reprint, Garden City, NY: Doubleday, 1957.

Eliade, Mircea. *The Myth of the Eternal Return*. Princeton, NJ: Princeton University Press, 1998.

———. *The Sacred and the Profane: The Nature of Religion*. New York: Harper & Brothers, 1961.

Fairclough, Adam. *A Class of Their Own: Black Teachers in the Segregated South*. Cambridge, MA: Belknap/Harvard University Press, 2007.

Franklin, John Hope. *From Slavery to Freedom: A History of African Americans*. 8th ed. New York: McGraw Hill, 2000.

Johnson, Charles S. *Shadow of the Plantation*. 1934. Reprint, New Brunswick, NJ: Transaction Publishers, 1996.

McMillen, Neil R. *Dark Journey: Black Mississippians in the Age of Jim Crow*. Urbana: University of Illinois Press, 1989.

Norris, Randall, ed., with photographs by Jean-Philippe Cypres. *Highway 61: Heart of the Delta*. Knoxville: University of Tennessee Press, 2008.

Powdermaker, Hortense. *After Freedom*. 1939. Reprint, New York: Russell & Russell, 1968.

Rankin, Tom. *Sacred Space: Photographs from the Mississippi Delta*. Jackson: University of Mississippi Press, 1993.

Richardson, Harry V. *Dark Glory*. New York: Friendship Press, 1947.

Smith, Frank E. *The Yazoo River*. 1954. Reprint, Jackson: University Press of Mississippi, 1988.

Spann, Christopher M. *From Cotton Field to Schoolhouse: African American Education in Mississippi, 1862–1875*. Chapel Hill: University of North Carolina Press, 2009.

Wright Austin, Sharon D. *The Transformation of Plantation Politics: Black Politics, Concentrated Poverty, and Social Capital in the Mississippi Delta*. Albany: State University of New York Press, 2006.

Autobiographies and Biographies

Angelou, Maya. *I Know Why the Caged Bird Sings*. New York: Random House, 1970.

Bibb, Henry. *The Life and Adventures of Henry Bibb: An American Slave*. With a new introduction by Charles Heglar. Madison: University of Wisconsin Press, 2001.

Bolsterli, Margaret Jones. *Born in the Delta: Reflections on the Making of a Southern White Sensibility*. Knoxville: University of Tennessee Press, 1991.

Cohn, David L. *Where I Was Born and Raised*. 1948. Reprint, Notre Dame, IN: University of Notre Dame Press, 1967.

Edwards, David Honeyboy. *The World Don't Owe Me Nothing: The Life and Times of Delta Bluesman Honeyboy Edwards*. Chicago: Chicago Review Press, 1997.

Holland, Endesha Ida Mae. *From the Mississippi Delta*. New York: Simon & Schuster, 1997.

Malcolm X, with the assistance of Alex Haley. *The Autobiography of Malcolm X*. New York: Grove Press, 1965.

Moody, Anne. *Coming of Age in Mississippi*. New York: Dial Press, 1968.

Percy, William Alexander. *Lanterns on the Levee: Recollections of a Planter's Son*. 1941. Reprint, Louisiana State University Press, 1966.

Rosengarten, Theodore. *All God's Dangers: The Autobiography of Nate Shaw*. New York: Knopf, 1974.

Taulbert, Clifton L. *The Last Train North*. Tulsa, OK: Council Oak Books, 1992.

———. *Once Upon a Time When We Were Colored*. Tulsa, OK: Council Oaks Books, 1989.

Washington, Booker T. *Up From Slavery*. New York: Doubleday, Page & Co., 1925.

Wright, Richard. *Black Boy*. New York, Harper & Row, 1945; Perennial Classics, 1966.

African American Religion

Billingsley, Andrew. *Mighty Like a River: The Black Church and Social Reform.* New York: Oxford University Press, 1999.

Cone, James H. *For My People: Black Theology and the Black Church.* Maryknoll, NY: Orbis Books, 1984.

Davis, Gerald L. *I Got the Word in Me and I Can Sing It, You Know: A Study of the Performed African-American Sermon.* Philadelphia: University of Pennsylvania Press, 1985.

Frazier, E. Franklin. *The Negro Church in America.* New York: Schocken Books, 1974.

Fulop, Timothy E., and Raboteau, Albert J., eds. *African-American Religion: Interpretive Essays in History and Culture.* New York: Routledge, 1997.

Hopkins, Dwight H. *Down, Up, and Over: Slave Religion and Black Theology.* Minneapolis: Fortress Press, 2000.

Hubbard, Dolan. *The Sermon and the African American Literary Imagination.* Columbia: University of Missouri Press, 1994.

Johnson, James Weldon. *God's Trombones.* New York: Viking Press, 1927.

King, Martin L. *Strength to Love.* New York: Harper & Row, 1963.

Lincoln, C. Eric, and Lawrence H. Mamiya. *The Black Church in the African American Experience.* Durham: Duke University Press, 1990.

Mays, Benjamin E. *The Negro's God as Reflected in His Literature.* New York: Atheneum, 1969.

Mays, Benjamin E., and Joseph W. Nicholson. *The Negro's Church.* New York: Russell & Russell, 1969.

Mitchell, Henry H. *Black Preaching.* Philadelphia: J. B. Lippincott Co., 1970.

Raboteau, Albert J. *Canaan Land: A Religious History of African Americans.* New York: Oxford University Press, 2001.

———. *A Fire in the Bones: Reflections on African American Religious History.* Boston: Beacon Press, 1995.

———. *Slave Religion: The Invisible Institution in the Antebellum South.* New York: Oxford University Press, 1978.

Rosenberg, Bruce A. *The Art of the American Folk Preacher.* New York: Oxford University Press, 1970.

Spencer, Jon Michael. *Sacred Symphony: The Chanted Sermon of the Black Preacher.* New York: Greenwood Press, 1988.

Townes, Emilie M. *In a Blaze of Glory: Womanist Spirituality as Social Witness.* Nashville: Abingdon Press, 1965.

Washington, James M., ed. *A Testament of Hope: The Essential Writings and Speeches of Martin Luther King, Jr.* San Francisco: HarperCollins Publishers, 1991.

CIVIL RIGHTS

Belfrage, Sally. *Freedom Summer.* New York: Viking Press, 1965.

Branch, Taylor. *Parting the Waters: America in the King Years, 1954–63.* New York: Simon & Schuster, 1988.

Dittmer, John. *Local People: The Struggle for Civil Rights in Mississippi.* Urbana: University of Illinois Press, 1995.

Cagin, Seth, and Philip Dray. *We Are Not Afraid: The Story of Goodman, Schwerner, and Chaney, and the Civil Rights Campaign for Mississippi.* New York: Nation Books, 2006.

Carson, Clayborne, et al, eds. *The Eyes on the Prize: Civil Rights Reader.* New York: Penguin Books, 1991.

Farmer, James. *Lay Bare the Heart: An Autobiography of the Civil Rights Movement.* New York: New American Library, 1985.

Findlay, James F., Jr. *Church People in the Struggle: The National Council of Churches and the Black Freedom Movement, 1950–1970.* New York: Oxford University Press, 1993.

Katagiri, Yasuhiro. *The Mississippi State Sovereignty Commission: Civil Rights and States' Rights.* Jackson: University of Mississippi Press, 2001.

Levy, Peter B. *The Civil Rights Movement.* Westport, CT.: Greenwood Press, 1998.

Marsh, Charles. *God's Long Summer: Stories of Faith and Civil Rights.* Princeton, NJ: Princeton University Press, 1997.

McAdam, Doug. *Freedom Summer.* New York: Oxford University Press, 1988.

McCord, William. *Mississippi: The Long Hot Summer.* New York: W. W. Norton, 1965.

Olson, Lynn. *Freedom's Daughters: Unsung Heroines of the Civil Rights Movement from 1830 to 1970.* New York: Simon & Schuster, 2001.

Payne, Charles M. *I've Got the Light of Freedom: The Organizing Tradition and the Mississippi Freedom Struggle.* Berkeley: University of California Press, 1995.

Walter, Mildred Pitts. *Mississippi Challenge.* New York: Aladdin, 1996.

FOLK CULTURE AND THE VERNACULAR

Abrahams, Roger D. *Deep Down in the Jungle: Negro Narrative Folklore from the Streets of Philadelphia.* Chicago: Aldine Publishing Co., 1963.

Brewer, J. Mason. *American Negro Folklore.* Chicago: Quadrangle Books, 1968.

Bundles, A'Lelia. *On Her Own Ground: The Life and Times of Madam C. J. Walker.* New York: Scribner, 2001.

Cohn, Lawrence, ed. *Nothing But the Blues: The Music and the Musicians.* New York: Abbeville Press, 1993.

Courlander, Harold. *A Treasury of Afro-American Folklore.* New York: Smithmark Publishers, 1996.

Dance, Daryl Cumber. *From My People: Four Hundred Years of African American Folklore.* New York: W. W. Norton, 2002.

———. *Shuckin' and Jivin': Folklore From Contemporary Black Americans.* Bloomington: Indiana University Press, 1978.

Dundes, Alan. *Mother Wit from the Laughing Barrel: Readings in the Interpretation of American Folklore.* Englewood Cliffs: Prentice Hall, 1973.

Graves, Tom. *Crossroads: The Life and Afterlife of Blues Legend Robert Johnson.* Spokane: Demers Books, 2008.

Hughes, Langston, ed. *The Book of Negro Humor.* New York: Dodd, Mead, 1966.

Hurston, Zora Neale. *Every Tongue Got to Confess: Negro Folk Tales from the Gulf States.* Foreword by John Edgar Wideman. Edited by Carla Kaplan. New York: HarperCollins Publishers, 2001.

———. *Mules and Men.* 1935. Reprint, New York: Harper Perennial, 1990.

Oliver, Paul. *Blues Fell This Morning: Meaning in the Blues.* 2nd ed. Cambridge, UK: Cambridge University Press, 1990.

CLASS AND COLOR PREJUDICE

Birmingham, Stephen. *Certain People: America's Black Elite.* Boston: Little, Brown & Co., 1977.

Brown, William Wells. *Clotel or the President's Daughter.* New York: Carol Publishing Group, 1989.

Frazier, E. Franklin. *Black Bourgeoisie.* Glencoe, IL. Free Press, 1957.

Golden, Marita. *Don't Play in the Sun: One Woman's Journey Through the Color Complex.* New York: Doubleday, 2004.

Graham, Lawrence Otis. *Our Kind of People: Inside America's Black Upper Class.* New York: HarperCollins Publishers, 1999.

Kerr, Audrey Elisa. *The Paper Bag Principle: Class, Colorism, and Rumor and the Case of Black Washington, D.C.* Knoxville: University of Tennessee Press, 2006.

Morrison, Toni. *The Bluest Eye*. New York: Holt, Rinehart & Winston, 1970.

Scales-Trent, Judy. *Notes of a White Black Woman: Race, Color, and Community*. University Park: Pennsylvania State University Press, 1995.

Thurman, Wallace. *The Blacker the Berry: A Novel of Negro Life*. 1929. Reprint, New York: AMS Press, 1972

EMMETT TILL

Houck, Davis W., and Grindy, Matthew A. *Emmett Till and the Mississippi Press*. Jackson: University Press of Mississippi, 2008.

Huie, William Bradford. "Approved Killing in Mississippi." *Look*. January 24, 1956.

Metress, Christopher, ed. *The Lynching of Emmett Till: A Documentary Narrative*: Charlottesville: University of Virginia Press, 2002.

Pollack, Harriet, and Christopher Metress. *Emmett Till in Literary Memory and Imagination*. Baton Rouge: Louisiana State University Press, 2008.

Whitfield, Stephen J. *A Death in the Delta: The Story of Emmett Till*. New York: Free Press, 1988.

RACISM AND THE COLOR LINE

Anderson, Alan B., and George W. Pickering. *Confronting the Color Line: The Broken Promise of the Civil Rights Movement in Chicago*. Athens: University of Georgia Press, 1986.

Bell, Derrick A. *Faces at the Bottom of the Well: The Permanence of Racism*. New York: Basic Books, 1992.

Chesnutt, Charles W. *The Wife of His Youth, and Other Stories of The Color Line*. Boston: Houghton Mifflin, 1899.

Du Bois, W. E. B. *The Souls of Black Folk*. 1903. Reprint, Fawcett Publications, 1961.

Hendrickson, Paul. *Sons of Mississippi: A Story of Race and Its Legacy*. New York: Vintage Books, 2004.

Litwack, Leon F. *Trouble in Mind: Black Southerners in the Age of Jim Crow*. New York: Vintage Books, 1999.

Massengill, Reed. *Portrait of a Racist: The Man Who Killed Medgar Evers*. New York: St. Martin's Press, 1994.

Oshinsky, David M. *"Worse Than Slavery": Parchman Farm and the Ordeal of Jim Crow Justice*. New York: Free Press, 1997.

Vollers, Maryanne. *Ghosts of Mississippi: The Murder of Medgar Evers, The Trials of Byron De La Beckwith, and the Haunting of the New South*. Boston: Little, Brown & Co., 1995.

INDEX

Abrahams, Roger D., 98, 99
Aiken, Charles S., 141–44
Anderson, Frank, 106, 107
Angelou, Maya, 15, 26n1, 95, 143n1, 187, 188
Augusta Institute, 72
Augustine, Saint, 21
Austin, Sharon Wright, 150n3

Barfield (Baker), Minnie R., 67
Barksdale, Richard, 66
Barnes, Thomas "Quote," 67, 72
Barnett, Ross, 147
Bevel, James, 213, 214
Blanchard, Melissa, 11–12, 87
Bibb, Henry, 102–3
Bible belt, 89
Bilbo, Theodore, 147
Birmingham, AL, 157, 183–84
Black Church, 164, 165, 192, 219; positive impact of, 121–22; 123, 126
Black minister (preacher), 126, 133, 165; and civil rights, 169, 174n6; as preacher, 128, 131–36, 139; prestige of, 125, 126; in revivals, 106, 106
Black Muslims, 120
Bland, Bobby Blue, xvi
Bledsau plantation, 34
Block, Samuel, 169, 212, 213, 214
Blues, 79–84; artists influenced by, 84; Hughes's description of, 82; revival of interest in 81; themes in 79, 80
Bolivar County, 6n3, 211, 212, 215
Bolsterli, Margaret, xv, 218
Braden, Carl, 214
Bradley, Mamie Till, 156
Brazeal, Brailsford R., 73

Brothers, Earnest, 107n1
Brown, Amos, 72, 74
Broad Street High School, 62, 72, 173
Brown v. Board of Education, 149–51
Brown, Emma, 79, 113
Brown, Henry B., 150n2
Bryant, Carolyn, 155
Bryant, Roy, 154, 155
Buchannan, Leo, 62
Buckeye, xvi, 37, 42, 52–54, 88, 106
Buckner, Mary Alice, 59
Buckner, Willie, 68
Butler, Jerry, 200
Butler, Terry, Jr., 49
Butler, Terry, Sr., 49

Cain, Herman, 76n
canvassing, 173
Carroll County, 4, 5
casinos, 89, 90, 91, 206
Chandler, Arthur (Big Son), 16, 115
Chandler, Ella Mae, 30
Chandler, Willie, 16
Chandler, Jesse, 16
Chandler, Stone, 115
Chaney, James, 194
Choctaw Indians, 6, 217
Civil Rights Accommodations Act (1964), 170, 204
Civil Rights Movement, xvi, xvii, 60, 61, 64, 129, 164, 169, 174, 181, 184, 185, 187, 188, 192, 193, 220, 222
Clapton, Eric, 84
Clark, Kenneth and Mamie, 147
Cleveland, Mississippi, 82, 161, 162, 213
Coahoma County, 6, 211, 215

Index

Cobb, James, 2, 6, 204, 217
Coffee, John, 4
Cohn, David, xvi, 2, 5n2, 190n1, 208
Coleman, J. P., 177, 178
Coleman, Wisdom F., Jr., 62
color consciousness, 95, 96, 99
color line, 145–51, 160, 165, 170, 199
color prejudice, 221
colorism, 94
Cone, James, 120, 143n3
Cook, Michael, 66
Courts, Gus, 169
Craig's Store, 52
Crystal Grill, 170

Dancing Rabbit Creek, Treaty of 3–6
Daniels, Jonathan Myrick, 193
Davis, Abraham L., 151n6, 209n2
Delta, xiii, xv, xvi, xvii; description of, 1–6, 160, 161, 163, 197; hopeful change in, 163, 165, 204; poverty and suffering in, 140, 141, 150n3, 207, 211; problems facing, 145–48, 153–55, 169, 205, 206–9
De Rosier, Arthur H., Jr., 217
Dickerson, Solomon, 42, 43
Dixie Theater, xvi
Dillon, Seth, 195
Dittmer, John, 174n, 220
Dockery Church, 162
Dockery farm, 82
Dollard, John, 98–99, 217
Domino, Fats, xvi
Douglass, Frederick, 53, 128, 167
Du Bois, W. E. B., 99n7, 120, 126, 128, 131, 145, 146, 165
Duck Hill, 56
Dunbar, Paul Laurence, 23
Duncan, Charles, 66
Dylan, Bob, 84

Eastland, James O., 39, 160
Eaton, John, 4
Ebony Magazine, 126, 127, 176
Edwards, David Honeyboy, 82–84, 85, 87
Edwards, Ethel, 56
Elliott, Franklin (Yank), 55

Elliott, James O. (Joe), 55, 59, 112
Elliott, Minnie, 55, 58
Elliott, Roy C. (Teen), 55, 112
Emancipation Proclamation, 182

Farrakhan, Louis, 120
Florence, Enoch, 72
Flood. *See* Great Flood (1927)
Fifteenth Amendment, 182, 204
Fourteenth Amendment, 146, 150, 151, 182
Freeman, Morgan, 62, 68

G. P., 41, 43n4
G Street Boys, 55–60
Gambling, 9, 11, 12, 87–90; in family, 9–12; history of in Mississippi, 88; on plantation, 88; problems of, 90
Gaming Control Act, 89
Gaming Commission, 91
Gandhi, Mahatma, 189
"Gangsta rap," 200
Gant, Harvey, 71
Garner, Albert, 61, 161, 169, 175–76, 212–14
Garner, Annie, 62
Garner, Cora Markham, 115, 116
Garner, Jonas, 88
Garner, Richard, 107
Garner, Sonny, 106
Garner, Johnny, 12
Garner, Stonewall, 40
Garrison, William Lloyd, 191
Garvey, Marcus, 96, 99n7
Georgia Pacific Railway, 43n4
Glen Allan, xvi
God's Trombones, 132
Golden Graduates, 199
Good Hope M. B. Church, xvi, 52, 80, 105, 121
Goodman, Andrew M., 194
Graham, Barbara Luck, 151n6, 209n2
Great Flood of 1927, 147
Gregory, Dick, xv, 169, 174n6
Greene, Dewey, Sr., 172, 173
Greene, Dewey, Jr., 173, 214
Greene, Dorothy "Cookie," 64, 117, 173
Greene, Freddie (mother), 117, 173,
Greene, Freddie (daughter), 115, 117,

Greene, George, 115
Greenwood Commonwealth, 174n2
Greenwood LeFlore, 1, 3–5
Greenwood, Mississippi, xiii, xvi, 5, 11, 15–17, 42, 43n1, 81, 83, 119, 142, 170, 188, 198–99, 213–14
Greenwood Comprehensive Plan, 205, 207, 209n1
Griffin, Charles (Charles Lee), 58, 64, 82
Grill, 56, 81, 188
Gunn, Giles, 66

Hamer, Fannie Lou, 160, 163, 177, 187
Hampton, Robert, 64
Harlan, John Marshall, 150n2
Harper, Gary, 68
Hayes, Joe S., 70
Hazelhurst, Mississippi, 83
Henderson, Stephen E., 65, 75, 76, 81
Henry, Aaron, 31n
Higgins, Barbara, 66
Hodges, Daniel 18, 26, 76
Hodges, Ellen, 30
Hodges, Ethel Mae, 19n4
Hodges, John Oliver: early impact of Black Church on, 121, 122; on first meeting father, 15–16; intellectual pursuits in cotton field, 56–58; involvement in civil rights, 160–62; in Mississippi Sovereignty Commission files, 212, 213, 214; on relationship to Medgar Evers, 175–76
Hodges, Oliver, 16, 17
Hodges, Osby, 18
Hodges, Tommie James, 15, 17
Holland, Endesha (Ida Mae Holland), xvi, 62, 174n5, 187–90, 218
Holmes, Hamilton, 71
Hood, James, 71
Hooker, John Lee, 81, 82, 84
Hope, John, 72
Hoskins, Tommy, 67
Hotel Plaza, 28, 64, 175
House, Son, 82
Howard, Titus, 4
Hughes, Langston, 82, 97
Hughes, Susanne, 66

Huie, William Bradford, 222, 157–58n2
Hume, Jeanette, 66, 75, 76
Humphreys County, 6n3, 211
Hunter, Charlayne, 71
Hurston, Zora Neale, 93, 221

Ile Ife, Nigeria, 198
Influenza. *See* Spanish Flu Outbreak (1918)
Invisible Institution, 120, 123n
Isaquena County, 6n3, 211

Jackson, David, 88
Jackson, Ellen, 59
Jackson, Andrew, 3
Jackson, Jesse, 90
Jackson, MS, 74, 175, 178, 213, 214
Jackson, Roswell, Jr., 75
Jackson, Roswell, Sr., 75
Jackson State University, 150n4
Johnson, Aaron Rev., 172, 173
Johnson, James Weldon, 132, 133
Johnson, John H., 199
Johnson, Lyndon B., 170
Johnson, Nathaniel, 13
Johnson Street, 80, 88
Johnson, Robert, 82–85
Jones, Albert, 212, 213, 214
Jones, Edward A., 66
Jones, Mayrene Washington, 195
juke joints, 80

Kairos, 182
Kellum, J. W., 180n6
Kennedy, John F., 75, 178, 183, 184, 185
Keys (Chandler; Hodges) Edna, 15–17, 22, 23, 28–30, 56, 113
Keys, John Eddie, Sr. 28–30
Keys, John Eddie, Jr., 30
King, Martin Luther, 73, 74, 75, 140, 141, 143n3, 149, 176, 182, 183, 184
Kingston, Rev. W. H., 80, 106-7, 134
Knight, Gladys, 200
Ku Klux Klan, 143, 189, 194

Lacy, Rube, 83
Lanterns on the Levee (Percy), 218

Index

Laurent, Vicki Jo, 24, 149
LeFlore, Greenwood, 6, 11, 28
Leflore Theater, 170, 171
Lester, Julius, 133
Letter from a Birmingham Jail, 184
Lindsey, Michael, 58, 115
Leonard, Alice, 68
LeFlore County, 1, 5, 160, 167, 169, 207, 211, 212, 214, 215
Lewis, Bill, 88
Lewis, John, 187
literacy tests, 160, 167, 168, 177
Liuzzo, Viola Gregg, 193–94
Lockett, Julius, 73
Lofton, Joe Lee, 63, 64, 81, 102, 174n3
Lomax, Michael, 76
Long, Charles, 66
Look magazine, 153, 156
Louie, Lillian, 173

Mabus, Ray, 190
Malmaison, 5
Malcolm X, 87, 95, 96, 98, 99, 175, 188, 218
Marius, Richard, 159–60, 161, 162, 164, 166
Martin, A. O., 66
Martin Scorsese Presents the Blues, 85n3, 85n9
Massengill, Reed, 209, 222
Mays, Benjamin E., 71, 72, 74, 75, 120, 219
McDowell, Fred L., 62–63
McDowell, Todd, 88
McGhee, Anne, 64
McGhee, Ben, 170
McGhee, Clarence, 170
McGhee, Jake, 63, 64, 169–70
McGhee, Laura, 169–70, 172
McGhee, Silas, 169–72; beating of, 171; shooting of, 172
McLaurin (McLauren), Charles, 213, 214
McLaurin Street, 80, 188
McLaurin Street School, 53,
McNeal, Jeffie, 26, 55, 56, 60, 72, 81, 112, 115
McNeal, John, 26, 56, 60, 112
Mendelsohn, Jack, 176
Merrill Scholar, 75–76

Milam, J. W., 153–57
Miller, Bobby, 195
Miller, Lorrine, 70
Ministerial Improvement Association, 176
Mississippi Gaming Control Act, 89
Mississippi River, 1, 2, 4, 89
Money, Mississippi, 41, 154, 155
Monica, Saint (Augustine's mother), 21, 22
Montgomery Bus Boycott, 157
Montgomery Improvement Association, 193
Morehouse College, 17, 65, 72–76, 81, 96, 161, 181
Morgan, Emma Lou, 95
Morgan, Peggy, 179
Morrison, Toni, 95, 222
Moses, Robert "Bob," xv, 169, 212–14
Muddy Waters (McKinley Morganfield), 79, 82, 85
Muhammad, Elijah (Elijah Poole), 120
Mulira, Jessie, 101

NAACP, 61, 99, 129, 169, 172, 175–78
Native Son (Wright), 143
Neshoba County, 194, 209
Norman, Ralph, 160
Northwestern University, 76
Noxubee County, 3, 6n3, 8, 11
Nuwer, Deanne, 89, 91n

Oakland, California, 18
Once Upon A Time When We Were Colored (Taulbert), xvi
Outlaw, Solomon N., 67–69, 114

Parchman State Penitentiary, 82
Parker, Charlie, 40
Parker, Mack Charles, 25
Patton, Charley, 82–83
Payne, Charles, 174n5, 178, 188
Peacock, Willie, 169
Pearson, Pauline, 62, 199
Percy, William Alexander, xvi, 1, 2–3, 47–49
Percy, Leroy, 39
Phifer, Claudette, 72
Pink Service Station, xvi, 36, 41, 42
playing the dozens, 93, 97–99

Index

Plessy v. Ferguson, 145, 146,149, 150nn1–2, 157
Portland, Oregon, 15, 17, 18, 181
Poll tax, 160, 167, 168, 173
poverty in Delta, 90, 141, 142, 150n, 207, 209, 211
Powdermaker, Hortense, 48, 218
Presley, Elvis, 84
Price, Cecil, 149
Prince, Dan, 179

Quitman County, 6n3, 211, 215

Raboteau, Albert, 66, 103, 219
race relations, xvi, 161, 163, 204, 206, 208
Race Track, xvi, 36, 41, 42
Raitt, Bonnie, 84
Reconstruction, 47, 179
Reeb, James, 193
Richards, Keith, 84
Richmond, California, 15, 17, 18, 30
Robertson, Frances, 70
Robert, Joseph T., 72
Robinson, Theotis, 71
Ross, Ida, 34
Ruleville, MS, 108, 159–66, 177, 213, 214

Santana, Carlos, 84
Santelli, Robert, 85
Scarbrough, Tom, 212, 213, 214
Schwerner, Michael, 194
Scott, Nathan A., 66
segregation, 146–49, 178, 182, 184, 192, 207, 208; in public education, 147, 150–51n6, 157, 177
sermon, 105; art and technique of, 133–36; objective of, 129
Sharkey County, 211, 6n3
Shellmound, 34, 41, 42
Sharecropping System, 29, 48
Shuttlesworth, Fred, 183
Sims, Ollie B., 52, 66
Smith, Beverly, 195
Smith, Frank E., 3, 6, 218
Smith Houston, 75
Smith, Jonathan Z., 66
Sovereignty Commission, 212, 220, 150n5
Spanish Flu Outbreak, 16, 19n1

Splash Casino, 89
Spruell, Fred, 68
Stewart, Tonea (Tommie Harris), 62, 68
Stamps, Pauline Pearson, 62, 199
Sunflower County, 1, 39, 60, 211, 212, 213, 214
Surney, Lafayette, 212, 213, 214

Tallahatchie County, 211, 6n3
Taulbert, Clifton, xvi, 218
Taylor, Mary Lou, 62
The Temptations, 200
Thompson, A. G., 34
Thompson, Katie, 34
Thompson, Lee D. (Bully), 19n3, 33–35
Thompson, Pearlene, 34
Thompson, Willie Green, 34
Thoreau, Henry David, 184
Threadgill High School, 198
Threadgill, L. H., 59, 173
Threadgill, Mary, 62
Thurman, Howard, 126,
Thurman, Wallace, 95
Till, Emmett "Bobo," xv, 25, 102, 153–58, 179
Tillich, Paul, 66, 182
Tunica, 89, 90, 108
Tunica County, 6n3, 90, 141, 211
Turkey day classic, 125
Turner's Chapel A. M. E. Church, xvi
Tuskegee Institute, 60, 72
Twyner, George, 67
Twyner, Lynn, 201

University of Chicago Divinity School, 66, 74, 125, 148
University of Minnesota, xvii
University of Tennessee, 162, 168

Vardaman, James K., 147, 168
Vaughn, Stevie Ray, 84
Vollers, Maryanne, 179, 222
Voting Rights Act, 204, 208
Voting Rights Law of 1957

Wakefield, Dan, 179–80n6
Walker, Madame C. J., 97

Index

Walthall Theater, xvi, 41, 47, 64, 80
Ward, Benjamin, 76
Ware, William, 67, 116
Washington, Booker T., 61, 74, 119, 146
Washington County, 211, 39
Wesley, John Milton, 159, 163,
Where I Was Born and Raised (Cohn), xvi, 5–6n2, 218
The Blue and White Parties, 67
White, Bukka, 82, 84
White Citizens Council, 173, 193, 194, 195
White clergymen, 184
White, Jack, 84
White, Ruth, 34
White Stripes, 84
Whittington, Aven, 39
Charles Whittington Plantation, 42, 56, 57
Whittington, William, 39, 43n1
Whittington Plantation, 36, 37, 39, 40, 49, 53, 81
Wideman, John Edgar, 156, 221
Williams, Jasper W., 134–35
Williams, Leola, 67, 68, 72
Williams, John, 4
Williams Landing, 4

Wilson, Charles and Te'Andrea, 208
Wilson, Arybelle "Abelle," 8, 17
Wilson, Clara, 18, 19n2
Wilson, Ella (Aunt Nig), 18
Wilson, Ellen, 18, 19, 30
Wilson, Eli, 7–13, 71
Wilson, Fred, 8–13, 17, 103, 113
Wilson, John, 9, 13, 87
Wilson, Obe, 8, 9, 11–13, 59, 79, 87, 88
Wilson, Rosa, 9
Wilson (Hodges), Samantha, 8, 16–19, 21–23
Wilson, Scott, 8, 103, 106
Wilson, Susanna, 11
Wilson, Thorn, 8
Witten, John, 180
Wright, Mose "Preacher," 22, 25, 26, 154, 155
Wright, Richard: critique of religion, 140, 142–44; on living Jim Crow, 25, 154, 157n1, 189, 204
Yazoo-Mississippi Delta. *See* Delta
Yu, Anthony C., 66
Yazoo-Mississippi Delta, xiii, xiv, 1, 197
Yazoo River, 3, 106, 107

Zellner, Robert "Bob," 193

www.ingramcontent.com/pod-product-compliance
Lightning Source LLC
Chambersburg PA
CBHW022215090526
44584CB00012BB/563